A Journey for Three Seasons

A Journey for Three Seasons

A Personal Travel Journal Through Europe and Eastern Europe

Dolores De Mayo

Writers Club Press

San Jose New York Lincoln Shanghai

A Journey for Three Seasons
A Personal Travel Journal Through Europe and Eastern Europe

Writers Club Press
an imprint of iUniverse.com, Inc.

For information address:
iUniverse.com, Inc.
5220 S 16th, Ste. 200
Lincoln, NE 68512
www.iuniverse.com

EDITOR: Kathy Painter

ISBN: 0-595-13711-3

Printed in the United States of America

To Barbara and Frank De Mayo who made it all possible, and to my mother's good friend Ruth Swayne, who gave me my first travel journal.

CONTENTS

FOREWORD

Do you like to travel but think you can't afford to? Are you interested in searching for your roots in person? Do you enjoy diversity in your types of accommodations and spontaneity in your travel strategies? Even if you are just an armchair traveler, you may find this personal accounting of *A Journey for Three Seasons* to be entertaining as well as enlightening. This book is not a travel guide. There is very little about what a place looks like and what there is to do in the city. One can obtain that information from any good guidebook. This book is about people, happenings and personal experiences, the outrageous and the delightful.

INTRODUCTION

Three years before I took early retirement from teaching, I started planning this trip. I wanted to return to Italy and see all of it rather than just the highlights I had seen on my three previous visits, the last one nearly 30 years ago. I wanted to see my relatives in Italy again, and I wanted to find out if all four of my grandparents really were born on the Island of Ischia off the coast of Naples. If this turned out to be true, it would be quite possible that my two brothers were also my cousins. (Remember that old song, "I'm My Own Grandpa"?) Besides Italy, I also wanted to see Eastern Europe because I had never been there and I knew it was only a matter of time before it became westernized. But most of all, I wanted to spend an entire year living abroad.

I mentioned all this to my brother Frank and his wife Barbara. We had traveled many times together or with one other person. I thought they would say, "A year? That's crazy!" Instead they said, "How soon can we leave?" This caught me off guard. "Well, I'm not sure I want to go with you. My preference would be to invite a wealthy and handsome younger man. Let me think about it for the next three years until I retire."

Though Frank is eleven years older than I am, he was not due to retire until 1996 because he waited until he was 63. After retirement and before the trip, he and Barbara wanted to move back to California from Oregon, where they had spent the last 27 years. The timing was perfect. Barbara had one stipulation though. She wanted to look up the origins of her German grandparents in Hessen.

I really couldn't have chosen two more experienced people for traveling. Frank had been a salesman all his life. When I was in the Peace Corps in Honduras, he and Barbara had come to visit me. They fell in love with the whole idea of Peace Corps, helping people to help themselves without any religion being involved. They went home and signed up. They were sent to Fiji and loved every minute of it, just as I had. About a year after they came home, my other Brother Nick (known in the wasp world as Bob De Mayo) acquired a half interest in a bare root rose business called Week's Roses. They needed two salesmen to go across the country in huge campers. One would take the northern route and one the southern, selling roses to nurseries. Frank got the northern route. Barbara was his navigator and chef. They spent about six months of the year doing this for the next six years. Between them they had more road experience than the pioneers. I still would have preferred a handsome fifty year old with lots of money, but one can't have everything in life.

I love to travel. It's probably in my blood since my grandparents made that horrendous trip from Italy to Ellis Island in New York more than a century ago, and my parents moved us from Brooklyn to Pasadena, California, in 1948 when I was six. Having stayed single, and by nature being somewhat frugal (some might even say cheap) I've always had enough money to travel during my summer vacations. Most of the time I have traveled with friends or relatives, and was able to go economically all over the world without having to take tours. Once in a while, I resorted to tours and found myself saying, "Moo-oo-oo!" every time I was herded with the group. I really much prefer to travel on my own with just one to three other people. However, I do not like to travel alone. When you see something wonderful, as you inevitably do, there is no one with whom to share your delight.

After my decision to spend a year abroad, the very next winter was one of the worst in the history of Europe. I took one look at the icy pictures in the newspaper and immediately cut the trip down to three seasons.

Off and on during the next three years, Barbara, Frank and I discussed all the different ways we could possibly travel. We all agreed that we wanted to stay in each place for at least a week and maybe even two. More than likely our trip would begin in Holland or Germany because those were the best places to get a car. We were willing to do a marathon drive in the beginning of the trip in order to get quickly to Italy and sunshine. We wanted to see only places we had not seen before and to stay mainly in rural areas, with side trips into the big cities. We also wanted to stay mostly in apartments so we could cook for ourselves. Eating every meal out is not only expensive but can be very tiresome. Besides, Barbara is a wonderful cook!

One summer about 30 years ago, I bought a new VW camper in Germany. They cost $3,500 at that time. Now they are $35,000. But my cousin Patti and I lived and traveled in the camper for three months. Then we left it at the docks, and the VW company shipped it home to me. It was all prearranged by the Auto Club and I paid for it before we left. I remembered that camping was very cheap, and thought maybe we could do this again. My idea was that each time we had to do one or two night stands we could camp instead of staying in hotels, and the rest of the time we could use the camper as a car. I wrote to the VW company in Germany. They were very sorry, but they no longer had this service. I called the German and Dutch consulates in Los Angeles and got information on camper and car dealers in both countries. I wrote to all of them about renting or buying a used camper or car for a seven and a half month trip. A multitude of information came back and I compiled all that with information I had also received on train travel, local fares versus the Eurail Pass. I even checked into shipping a camper from the U.S. to Europe.

While Frank and Barbara were working in California, as they did part of every year, we put together all the information I had gathered. We eliminated train travel immediately. None of us wanted to shlep suitcases no matter how economical it was. Shipping their personal Tioga camper to Europe was out too. The cost was prohibitive for both the shipping and the cost of gas for such a big camper. (Had they had a VW, it probably would have been more economical to ship it there and back rather than buying and selling a camper.) I still thought that combining camping and apartment stays was a good idea. Frank crunched the numbers to see how much more expensive it would be to rent or buy a camper rather than a car. It was definitely more money, but when he added an estimated price for hotels and eating in restaurants, which was what we would have to do without a camper, it just about evened out the costs.

The most innovative reply to my inquiries about campers had come from a man named Rene at a place called Braiteman and Woudenberg in Amsterdam. Rene gave us all the prices for both renting and buying. He also sent pictures of the different kinds of campers he had in stock, what was included with them, and what features each one possessed. He pointed out to us that it was much more economical to buy a camper for such a long trip, and he would agree in advance to buy it back at 60% of the actual cost of the camper at the end of our trip. Once again Frank figured the arithmetic. It took a long time to go through all the information, but It turned out that Rene's plan was the best one for us.

The next problem we had to resolve was finances. What would be the estimated cost of the trip, and how could we possibly carry enough money for seven and one-half months? We first made up a budget including everything for which we would need money, based on 226 days of travel. This was a little longer than we wanted to stay, but because we were traveling on Frequent Flyer miles, the airlines gave us very little choice. We were scheduled to be there from April 4 to November 17. The following is the original sample budget:

ESTIMATED COSTS FOR EUROPE
(Based on 227 days)

CAR:
1. Camper	$18,000	(We wanted a newer model to

	avoid mechanical problems)
2. Gas and Oil	1,000
3. Insurance	2,500
4. Repairs and maintenance	500

FOOD:
1. Eat dinner out 2x each week ($60 per time)	3,840
2. Grocery stores ($100 per week)	3,200

ENTERTAINMENT:
1. $30 a day, ($10 each)	6,780

HOTELS:
1. 7 nights	400

APARTMENTS
(Just a guess)
	4,500

CAMPSITES:
(Another guess)
	2,400

TRANSPORTATION:
1. Taxis, subways, busses, and ferries	500
	$43,620.

We originally thought it would cost us about $15,000 each. With our estimated budget on paper, the final problem we had to overcome was how to get this money to Europe. First we thought of putting it into a European bank account. However, unless you have a permanent address, you can't do this. We did not want to carry the money in traveler's checks for many reasons: too bulky, no interest on thousands of dollars, and poor rates of exchange. We definitely wanted to get interest on the money as we went along. That was when we discovered Money Market Accounts. This can be done at any bank, but they pay very low interest. We decided to go with an investment company. The interest was more than double that of a bank. Any investment company or mutual fund that issues Visa or Master Cards, credit as well as debit, will do.

We chose an investment company in which Barbara and I already had accounts. We told the young man we wanted to put $20,000 each (a little extra just in case of trouble) into an account that could be accessed from anywhere in the world. He didn't even bat an eye. He set it up on his computer while telling us we could each have a debit card with the same number and pin number. This card could be used at any ATM that took Visa worldwide and it could also be used as a credit card. By having three the same, we would still have two if one got eaten by a machine. We told him we would need about $18,000 in cash as soon as we got to Amsterdam in order to buy a car. He assured us there would be no problem. We just had to go into any bank and ask for a cash advance. He also gave us toll free numbers to call from all over Europe in case we had any difficulties, or if we just wanted to know how much money was left in the account. As it turned out, everything he said was true. But at the time, we all looked at him skeptically, and later decided to carry a thousand dollars each in travelers checks, just in case!

The actual packing for the trip was problematic. We needed clothes for three seasons, but we also needed to bring nine novels that none of us had read, five very heavy travel books, one camping book, and many maps as well as various informational packets we had received from foreign tourists offices, not to mention three sleeping bags, sheets and towels. We purchased the camping book, *Europa Camping and Caravanning 1998* from REI, sporting goods store. I was sure it weighed at least one hundred pounds. I hurt myself each time I lifted it, but it was definitely the most important book we brought.

I personally had to bring enough contact lens solutions for seven and a half months, these various bottles alone weighed in at twenty pounds. However, as I suspected, I was unable to find contact lens solutions anywhere we traveled except for one store in Germany. We allowed ourselves only one large suitcase each, but I brought two cloth bags that folded into their own pockets for my extra bottles. I opened one inside the other for extra strength while on the airplane. Frank brought his army duffel bag for the sleeping bags, sheets and towels, so he and I had two bags each.

I wrote an extensive itinerary for our trip. We were going to spend the two months of spring in Italy, the summer in Eastern Europe, two weeks of the fall in Germany, and the last month back in sunny Italy, saving the last week for the drive back to Amsterdam. With this schedule, we would not be in any Western European countries during the summer or high season.

By April we had most of the bugs worked out of our European plan. I retired in June of 1997, sold my house and put all my furniture in storage in Lakeport, California, where I eventually planned to settle. Barbara and Frank had already bought a house in Lakeport, which is on Clear Lake, and I lived with them off and on until we were ready to leave in April of 1998. Frank and Barbara's son Gary, graciously agreed to stay at their new home while we were away. Since he was there, he paid the bills, rather than having a banking service pay them. He also took us to the San Francisco Airport and picked us up on our return.

At this time, I must explain a few incidentals that will help the reader to better understand my journal. On the first week of the trip, we changed the whole itinerary. Europe looked so small on a map. Doing one night stands for the first week of the trip, while we drove to Italy, was not one of my better ideas. We decided that returning there after Eastern Europe would just require too much driving time. So we spent two and a half months in Italy the first time, and did not return.

At the end of many of my daily recordings, there are references to hotels or campgrounds. These are the places where we stayed. The directions and addresses are either from the camping book or from the place itself. Many of the directions are decidedly nebulous, but we were almost always able to find them. The places that do not have these directions were the ones that we found just by following posted signs, of which there were many for both camps and hotels.

Along with my journal, I kept a daily written budget where I itemized everything we spent each day. For example, we bought fruit to eat about 10 A.M. every morning, and had an ice cream almost every day. However, a daily budget is very repetitious, so I categorized everything into a weekly budget, listing any food not purchased in a restaurant as groceries. The following is a sample of our daily budget for one of our most inexpensive days in Poland:

TUES. JULY 21 KRAKOW
(Drove to Auschwitz, museum free)

Camping	$13.00
Parking	1.50
Coffee	3.00
Groceries	1.00
Beer and ice cream	4.00
2 Booklets	
(About Auschwitz)	2.00
	$24.50

Remember this was for three people, but also remember we undoubtedly had groceries from a previous shopping trip already in the car. This would have been recorded in the budget at another time. We spent the whole day of July 21 at the museum and had lunch in the camper. We were also camping, so there were no restaurant or hotel bills.

There are a few items in the weekly budgets that I must explain. One of them is "spending money." Personal gifts and souvenirs that each of us bought were not included in this budget, unless we bought them together. We each brought traveler's checks and credit cards from a personal bank account for this purpose. However, we frequently just needed a few dollars for purchases and didn't want to bother using an ATM. When this happened, we each took equal amounts from the "kitty" a purse I carried that contained a small amount of cash. This money was listed under "Entertainment" as "spending money", so some of our personal items were included in the budgets. Once in a while we were forced to get a larger amount of kitty money than I wanted to carry. When this happened, we divided it between the three of us and each carried it in his or her money belt until it was needed in the kitty. But that was kitty money not spending money.

The second item I must explain is "money exchange." Only one ATM ever charged us a fee. Our investment company only charged us $1 after the first five transactions in one month, but the banks sometimes had fees too. All but one time we were able to avoid getting nailed by those banks. However, whenever we exchanged cash from one country to the next, there was always a hefty fee, no matter if it was done at a bank or at the border. Even exchanging American dollars or travelers checks was very costly. Credit and debit cards were absolutely the most economical way to get money.

Toilet fees also appear randomly in the budget. Almost everywhere in Europe, if you use a public toilet, you pay. However gas stations and restaurants are sometimes free, so the fees show up in the budget very infrequently. Also there are McDonald's everywhere, and they are always free.

The last unexplained item in the Budget is "camper payment." The camper was much cheaper than anticipated because we bought a 1981 VW, instead of the newer larger one we had intended to get. It cost only $4,658.50 including the insurance and taxes, and after we got 60% of the cost back at the end of the trip. I averaged it out on a daily basis for 194 days because the first week we didn't have the camper and, as you will see, we came home 26 days early. It came to $24 a day or $168 a week.

Now I must tell you about division of duties. Frank did almost all of the driving. I relieved him on long drives for about an hour after lunch, but after the car started making weird noises, somewhere in Italy, I stopped driving altogether. Barbara did all the navigating, all the cooking and everything else. She tried to keep up the family tradition of pasta three times a week: meat sauce on Sundays, clam sauce on Thursdays, and spinach, broccoli, lentils or escarole with macaroni on Tuesdays, with no red sauce. The other four nights she made delicious meals out of whatever we could find in the markets. Only ten of her recipes are included throughout the journal. These were recipes that she knew by heart, as she carried none with her. She did variations on most of the same recipes each week, and many of the meals we had were improvised as she went along. I did almost nothing. I did do the dishes and carry the money, but aside from that, I was pretty useless. However I'm cute and funny so they put up with me. Besides, I planned the whole trip!

Now many people may think that a Kitty is not always an even distribution of money. Frank and Barbara both drink more than I do. Beer and wine was included in a lot of the grocery money and all of the restaurant meals. One drink and I am under the table, so even when we went out on the town, I would only have a half bottle of beer. However, most of the time when we stayed in hotels, I had my own room. So we figured it all evened out in the end.

For three weeks of our time in Eastern Europe, Marsha Keen, a teacher friend of mine joined us. She paid one fourth of the daily budget not including the car. This was all accounted for in the weekly budgets during the time we were in East Germany and parts of Poland. We did not camp while Marsha was with us because it would have been too cramped in the camper. Instead, we stayed in apartments and hotels and use the camper as a car only.

Week Number One April 3 Through April 9, 1998

FRI. APRIL 3 LAKEPORT TO SAN FRANCISCO, CALIFORNIA

This was the first day of our trip of a lifetime. I had been planning and organizing it for three years, and now the time had arrived. My nephew Gary drove us from Lakeport over the mountain to Highway 101, and down through Santa Rosa. Went over the Golden Gate Bridge and into Golden Gate Park to see the tulip garden. Gary wanted us to have a sampling of what we would see in Holland. The tulips were all in bloom and it was lovely. Took a hotel in Burlingame near the airport. Gary drove back home to be in charge of all bills and correspondence for the next seven and a half months. Slept until 5 A.M.

SAT. APRIL 4 IN FLIGHT TO AMSTERDAM, HOLLAND

Took shuttle to San Francisco Airport at 6 A.M. Had coffee to wake us up and fortify us for the horrendous flight ahead. Barbara and Frank went business class. Said it was much roomier and the food and booze were great. I went economy. Slept and read most of the way, so it was fine.

SUN. APRIL 5 AMSTERDAM, HOLLAND

Arrived early in the morning. Called a camp near the airport to see if they had cabins to rent. Cabins were all full. Shades of things to come?

After getting Dutch money with one of our new ATM cards, we took a cab to a hotel on Haarlemer Street, in the area near Braiteman and Woudenberg, where we planned to buy our camper.

Got our first shock. The hotel cost more than the hotel at the San Francisco Airport, and the room was much smaller and very basic. Breakfast was included, but there were absolutely no services with the room. Not only did they not clean the bathroom, but we had to make our own beds! It was a good thing we were planning to camp and stay in apartments. There were lots of young kids staying here, and the smell of pot permeated everything. Took a long nap and went out to explore the city. Turned out that Braiteman and Woudenberg was only a block away from the hotel.

MON. APRIL 6 AMSTERDAM, HOLLAND

Breakfast was a slice of thin sandwich bread, Barbara calls it "crappy kid bread", with baloney and Velveeta cheese. Hoped we could leave soon. Went to Braiteman and Woudenberg first thing after breakfast. First thing was about 10 A.M. for us. Met Rene, the guy with whom I had been corresponding for the past three years. He was every bit as sassy and impertinent in person as he was in his letters. Enjoyed him immensely. We checked out the campers he had. There wasn't much choice. Had we followed Rene's advice, he would have had one waiting for us. However, we didn't want to reserve one sight unseen, and we weren't at all sure with what size vehicle we really wanted to deal. Narrowed it down to an 1981 VW with a pop top but no toilet, and an old French Puegeot with a chemical toilet. Evidently much of Europe and all of Eastern Europe has no sewer hookups, so most of the campers have chemical toilets.

Frank and I nearly flipped when we realized the full toilet had to be hand carried to the dump every day. Much as we wanted more room, we didn't have any desire to deal with sewage. An advantage to the VW was its small size going down Europe's impossibly skinny streets. The size of the streets in Amsterdam alone was gut wrenching. On the other hand, the Puegeot was very roomy with lots of storage space. Being cramped for seven and a half months, was not something any of us wanted either. Another concern was being robbed and we decided that no one would bother with either one of these old heaps. Hopefully!

Went to a nearby cafe for coffee and to crunch all the numbers as well as to debate all the pros and cons for each vehicle. The VW won. We really wanted to stay in apartments more than we wanted to camp. With the VW we would be forced to do so.

TUES. APRIL 7 AMSTERDAM, HOLLAND

Took the trolly to the Van Gogh Museum. What we saw was excellent, but most of the paintings were out on loan to the United States, the story of my life. The trolly ride was fun and thanks to our Let's Go book, we knew how to buy tickets and get them stamped. We were still paying one hundred dollars a night for a room that was an exact replica of the tiny room I'd had for five dollars a night thirty years ago. It had a bathroom now, but that was the only difference.

Went for a boat ride up and down the canals. Then walked all over town again looking for a good Indonesian restaurant. We were getting high just breathing. Marijuana wafted through every open window and doorway. It was just as I remembered from my last time here. Found an Indian restaurant that turned out to be quite good, and the incense helped bring us down. The restaurant also had the extra added bonus of a laundromat next door. The same guy ran both places, so when you finished eating, your clean clothes awaited you. Very enterprising!

WED. APRIL 8 AMSTERDAM, HOLLAND

Went to the information booth on the second floor of the train station this morning. They sold us train tickets to Keukenhof Gardens and we got there without a hitch. Had to walk about a mile from the station to the gardens. Unbelievably beautiful. I think every kind of bulb flower known to man was represented in the flower bed arrangements. Sent some bulbs to ourselves and relatives. Since we took it out of the "kitty," I included it in the budget. Carried leftovers with us from the Indian dinner last night and ate them in the gardens. Delicious! Took the train back in the afternoon and had bad Dutch pizza for dinner. The camper will be ready in the morning.

THURS. APRIL 9 AMSTERDAM, HOLLAND

Rene had the VW camper fully outfitted with pots, pans, dishes, etc. and it was ready and waiting for us this morning. Had to fill out insurance papers and make a trip to the bank to get money. Rene wanted cash so we used our joint ATM card. We were amazed how easy It was to get money in this new age of plastic. The camper cost us $8191.20, about $3250 of which was insurance and taxes. Rene assured us that when we returned the car, we would get back about $3400, 60% of the cost, excluding the VAT (Value Added Tax) and the insurance.

Took off in the afternoon. Headed to the original camp that we had called the first day from the airport. Wanted to check out the cabins and didn't want to go too far in case there were problems with the camper. Good move. Nothing worked! We could get no water in the sink and the electric line, the one Rene had given us to plug into each campsite's electric units, didn't fit. We had no choice but to spend the night with no water and no electricity. Checked out the cabins. Thought maybe we could spend the night there, but the cabins had nothing inside them but two beds and a table and chairs. There was no kitchen, no bathroom and no running water. So much for staying in bungalows.

Encountered our first unisex bathrooms in the campground. Somewhat disconcerting to see a strange male face peering back at you in the mirror. Slept in our sleeping bags in the camper. I almost froze to death. I'd never been good in cold weather, even under the best of circumstances. This was ridiculous! All I could think of was returning to my nice warm bed in California. By morning I was almost in tears. Called Rene and told him we would be there in an hour.

*Camping Het Amsterdamse Bos A9 exit Aalsmeer, signposted.

ITEMIZED WEEKLY BUDGET # 1
LODGING
Hotels (6)	$490.00
Camps (1)	16.00

FOOD
Restaurant:
Dinners (5)	216.00
Lunches (4)	74.00
Groceries (12 meals)	71.00

ENTERTAINMENT
Bars & Cafes	47.50
Museum	21.00
Boat Ride	22.50

CAMPER
No Camper Payment
Start-up Costs	6.00
Gas	15.00

TRANSPORTATION
Shuttle	4.00
Taxi	30.00
Trollies	6.00
Trains	52.50

INCIDENTALS
Laundry	5.00
Money Exchange	3.50
Account Book	1.00
Postage	4.00
Gifts	49.00
Phone Calls	1.00
	$1134.00

WEEKLY BUDGET #1

Fri.	$241.50
Sat.	8.50
Sun.	160.50
Mon.	161.50
Tues.	237.50
Wed.	237.50
Thurs.	87.00
	$1134.00

$1134 divided by 7 days = $162 per day. $162 divided by 3 people = $54 per person, per day.

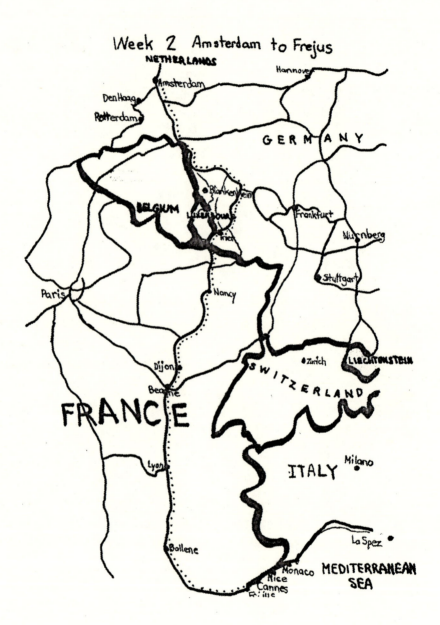

Week 2 Amsterdam to Frejus

WEEK NUMBER TWO APRIL 10 THROUGH APRIL 16, 1998

FRI. APRIL 10 HERTOGENBOSCH, NETHERLANDS

Drove back to Braitman & Woudenberg to get the camper fixed. The traffic in Amsterdam was scary. Bicycles, cars, pedestrians and assorted four legged creatures all came at us at once and from every direction. It was horrifying! On the way back, the stick shift started grinding whenever Frank shifted. The mechanic got right to work on the car and had everything working within an hour. He oiled the shift box too and it didn't make anymore noise—for an hour or two. I talked to Rene about almost freezing to death and he gave me an extra sleeping bag to use. Bless him!

We drove to Hertogenbosch, on our way to Germany. The camp was very nice. It even had a bowling alley. Went out to the camp bar for a little excitement after dinner. There were nothing but teeny boppers in the bar. Almost all were between the ages of twelve and fifteen and all were smoking and drinking beer. Barbara and I tried a new kind of beer. Turned out it was very low in alcohol. Evidently the kids like it better when they first start drinking. This must have been for the eight to ten year olds, because we were the only ones in the room drinking the stuff. The extra sleeping bag kept me warm and comfortable all night.

*Vinkel: Feriendorf Camping Vinkeloord, Directions: Vinkeloord 1

SAT. APRIL 11 BLANKENHEIM, GERMANY

Now that we were in Germany, I could see that things had changed in thirty years. Unfortunately their graffiti and litter problems were almost as bad as ours. (Not quite, but almost!) The roadside rest was a complete mess. It was sad to see. It had all been so spotlessly clean thirty years ago. It was really cold. This was not my idea of spring, but then I only knew spring in California and Honduras. The showers in the camps were heated, but the wash rooms were not, so camping was a chilly experience.

Got a hotel tonight so we could be warm. For $90 we got two rooms with a private toilet we alone shared across the hall, no shower. The hotel was pretty elegant, but the bathroom situation was only slightly better than our five dollar a night rooms from thirty years ago.

SUN. APRIL 12 THE MOSEL RIVER AND INTO FRANCE

Today was Easter Sunday. Breakfast was included with our hotel last night. Along with an excellent meal, we had colored Easter eggs and lots of chocolate. I was going to like Germany.

We were moving right along every day in order to get to Italy and some sunshine. Drove through the Mosel Valley following the river. The road zig zaged continually. Very beautiful but also very touristy. Barbara and Frank made this drive in 1969. They said it was much less crowded then. Stopped at a flea market in the rain. Bought hot peppers for the pasta sauce. The Mexican influence, on the west coast of the United States, had made us like our food a little spicier than Europeans seemed to like it. There were no longer any border crossings in Western Europe. It was very nice not having to waste time checking in and out. The car was acting up. It was very sluggish going uphill.

Stayed in a camp on the river. The owner's son-in-law was an American G.I., and he translated for us. We had to use our own toilet paper. Naturally, I forgot and had to go all the way back to the camper. I hoped this was not the way it was going to be in every campground.

MON. APRIL 13 BEAUNE, FRANCE

Drove through part of Luxembourg, Nancy and Dijon. Stayed in a really nice camp with private dressing rooms, each containing a sink, and the toilets had toilet paper. When we drove into Beaune (pronounced Bone), it looked like Las Vegas, cheap hotels and casinos. The campground was right in town just outside the walled inner city, but away from the casinos. The town inside the walls was delightful, old and interesting.

*Beaune: Camping Municipal les Cent Vignes. Directions: Left of RN 74 to Dijon

TUES. APRIL 14 BEAUNE, FRANCE

Enjoyed a two and a half hour walk around this little medieval city and had a wonderful time oohing and ahhing over everything. Unfortunately, the car wouldn't start when we got back to the camp. Had to be towed about a mile away to a little garage. Two Frenchmen with really cute little tushes worked on it, bent over the engine, for three hours. The good part was that there was a laundromat right across the street, so we got the wash done while we waited. The bad part was that the car wasn't getting any gas. Cost $126 to get a new hose for the gas line. However, it did solve the "sluggish" problem we were having. The car was still making grinding noises every time we shifted, but we were getting used to it. Didn't seem to make any difference in the way it ran. As anyone who has ever driven an older VW van knows, it's a screaming muscle car!

WED. APRIL 15 BOLLENE, FRANCE

Writing the date in this journal reminded me that today was tax day. Hoped I had paid my taxes correctly. I hate it when Uncle Sam wants me. Drove through Lyon, which along with Dijon had grown to be a megalopolis since I had last seen it. Traveled partly on the freeway and partly through the towns. I liked the freeway better because I was just getting use to a stick shift again. Also the freeway was elevated and we could see everything. Barbara liked the highway through the towns better. Frank, who did most of the driving, didn't seem to care as long as we fed him regularly, especially macaroni.

We were now in a campground in the hills and woods above Bollene. It was pouring. Camping was not fun in the rain. There was no place to go. This camp was run by an Irishman from Australia and his French wife. They had stables and horses to ride. Everyone was very friendly.

* Bollene: Camping La Simioune. Directions: Highway exit Bollene, east of village.

THURS. APRIL 16 FRIEJUS, FRANCE

The rain stopped and we hiked through the pine woods for about two hours this morning. It was lovely. Drove to Friejus in the south of France and camped. Uneventful.

* Frejus: Holiday Green. Directions: Motorway exit Frejus, direction Bagnois.

ITEMIZED WEEKLY BUDGET # 2
LODGING

Hotels (1)	$105.00
Camps (6)	109.50

FOOD
Restaurants:

Dinners (1)	38.00
Groceries (20 meals)	107.00

CAMPER

Camper payment	168.00
Start-up costs	22.50
Gas	189.50
Oil	7.00
Repairs	126.00
Road tolls	52.50

ENTERTAINMENT

Cafes & Bars	31.00

INCIDENTALS

Laundry	14.00
Postage	8.00
Gifts	6.50
Phone calls	5.00
Toilet fees	.50
	$990.50

WEEKLY BUDGET #2

Fri.	$ 96.50
Sat.	214.00
Sun.	84.00
Mon.	109.00
Tues.	228.00
Wed.	140.50
Thurs.	118.00
	$990.00

$990 divided by 7 days = $141.42 per day. $141.42 divided by 3 people = $47.14 per person, per day.

SPICY ITALIAN MEAT SAUCE

BROWN IN SMALL POT
1/4 cup olive oil
3 cloves chopped garlic
1/2 chopped medium onion (optional, makes sauce a little sweeter)

BROWN IN SMALL FRYING PAN
2 Italian sausages or
1/2 lb meat balls

ADD
browned meat
1 large can tomato sauce or chopped tomatoes
1/2 cup water or wine
1 teaspoon sweet basil
1/2 teaspoon oregano
1/2 teaspoon hot red pepper flakes
1/2 teaspoon salt
Cook at a simmer for one hour. Turn gas off and:

ADD
1/2 cup finely chopped fresh parsley

SERVE
over one pound of pasta, any shape. Serves three.

ITALIAN MEAT BALLS

MIX TOGETHER IN BOWL:
1 lb ground round
3 slices stale bread or bread crumbs
1/2 teaspoon basil

1/4 teaspoon oregano
1/2 cup fresh parsley
2 Tablespoons fresh Parmesan cheese
1 egg
ROLL INTO BALLS AND BROWN

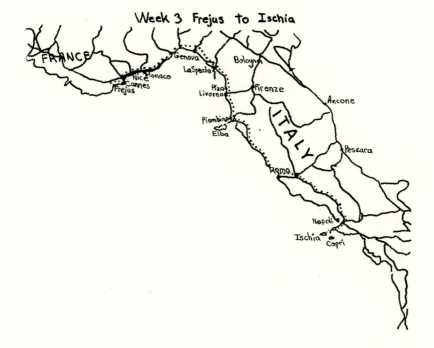

WEEK NUMBER THREE APRIL 17 THROUGH APRIL 23, 1998

FRI. APRIL 17 BAGLIASCO (GENOA), ITALY

Drove to Cannes on the Mediterranean this morning. Beautiful but heavily populated. Stopped at a sidewalk cafe for coffee and croissants. It blew our budget but the ambiance was worth it.

When we drove across the Italian border all hell broke loose. These are my people, but I must tell it like it is, has been and probably always will be. Italians have absolutely no concept of driving regulations. They seem to be the only people in Europe with this problem. They drive in any and every direction, regardless of which way the traffic is going. We entered Italy through Ventimiglia, and within three seconds each of us had a panic attack. The traffic was mind boggling. Frank drove out the nearest exit.

Twenty minutes later, we were in the heart of downtown Genoa. It was surrealistic. I had never seen so many people and cars all trying to occupy the same speck of turf at the same time. Somewhere within the space of the first three minutes, Frank became an Italian maniac. He hollered "Yahoo!" and we wove in and out of spaces not big enough for a bicycle let alone a car. He was laughing maniacally and shouting, "Now I get it. I'm Mario Andretti!" By the time we got out of Genoa, Barbara and I were paralyzed with fear. Eventually, by getting back on the freeway, the traffic lessened, and the two of us started breathing again.

Found a camp on the top of a mountain overlooking the Mediterranean in Bagliasco. Had to walk down five thousand steps to the town. Then we had to come back up, but at least we were safe from traffic for most of this journey. Tried to get dinner in town, but nothing opened until eight P.M. So we just had a sandwich.

Back at the camp, we found they had a full restaurant with wonderful aromas, but no one was hungry, so we just had a drink. The restaurant was run by a guy from Chile. Had a nice conversation on the state of world affairs in Spanish. The weather was still very cold.

*Bogliasco: Camping Genova Est di Bogliasco. Directions :Hy. exit Genova-Nervi, SS 1 Direct. La Spezia

SAT. APRIL 18 PIOMBINO, ITALY

There were plastic greenhouses all over the countryside. Evidently this was how they grew their produce here. The freeways in Italy were navigable if you stayed very alert. I had been driving after lunch so Frank could take a nap. It was scary, but I managed.

Found a nice camp with private bathrooms. Each camping place had a room attached with a toilet, shower, and sink inside and a place to wash dishes outside. It really made camping quite posh. We were heading for the island of Ischia, where we intended to spend a week.

*Riotorto-Perelli (Livorno) Camping Orizzonte. Directions: Turn off road SS 1 direction Piombino, 4km

SUN. APRIL 19 ROME, ITALY

Drove down the coast of Italy to Rome, avoiding any and all moderate to large sized cities. We came to Rome just to visit our relatives. We had all been here before and really had no desire to see it again. Not that it wasn't a wonderful interesting city, it was just too congested and none of us had recovered from our traffic experience in Genoa.

Found a campground just on the outskirts of Rome on the ring road. No private bath, but lots of trees and a nice setting. Called our cousin's cousins, who lived in the heart of the city. Antonette is an Italian American who married Paulo, an Italian citizen, and went to live in Italy without speaking a word of the language. In large Italian American families, all your cousins' cousins are your cousins too. Probably not unlike what Southerners call "Kissing Cousins." We were invited to lunch (the main meal) tomorrow. This camp was right on a bus line to the city. It also had a huge market across the street.

*Roma: Roma Camping, Motorway exit no. 1. Direction: to center.

MON. APRIL 20 ROME, ITALY

Left the camper at the camp and took the city bus to Rome, an eye popping experience. I was so happy we weren't driving. Disembarked at the Via Venito and walked three miles, according to Barbara's pedometer, through the heart of Rome to Antonette and Paulo's apartment. Antonette introduced us to her young student, who was about to depart. She had been giving him English lessons and she encouraged him to speak to us. He was about fifteen. He said," Hello", and bolted out the door as quickly as he could.

Lunch was really fun and delicious. They were unbelievably hospitable and welcoming. We hadn't seen each other for almost thirty years, but it seemed like it was yesterday. I had sent a letter saying we were coming, but I'd mailed it to the wrong address, so they had no clue until we called. No matter! They had a fabulous four course meal ready and waiting. Antonette said there was no macaroni at lunch because she didn't want us to be too full for sight seeing. Frank lived for macaroni and I thought he would choke, but he held it together until we were on our own after lunch. Then he lamented loudly. In spite of the lack of pasta, we enjoyed ourselves immensely and scarfed up the antipasti, chicken cutlets, and tiny artichokes, cooked in garlic and olive oil, that could be eaten in their entirety. It was a memorable meal.

Paulo and Antonette's oldest son Stefano, a university professor, also had lunch with us. Their other son Sandro, was a recently graduated lawyer and could not be home for lunch. Both young men lived with their parents and would probably do so until they married. All of them spoke English fluently. Stefano said his mother didn't speak Italian when he was little and that he helped to teach her. After a delicious desert of Italian ice cream cake, Sandro the second son came in just to meet us and say hello. He was due in court and could not stay long.

Stefano, had been to the United States many times on business for his university. Because he was fluent in both languages and had talents that American businesses coveted, he could easily have secured a high paying job in the States. He also had lots of relatives in the States and dual citizenship. He chose, however, to remain at what he said was a low paying job in order to stay in the heart of his family and his country. Paulo and Antonette wanted us to stay another day. They had tickets to a symphony they wanted us to give us. They were so amenable, but we really didn't want to stay any longer than one day in the big city.

After lunch Stefano took Frank, Barbara and me to the church of San Pietro in Vincoli where Michelangelo's statue of Moses is located, right next to Stefano's university. Before he dropped us off, he gave us a quick tour of the City, around the Coliseum, et al. He, like all Italians, drove with one hand on the wheel and the other waving in wild animation, frequently leaning back to the rear seat for eye contact with Frank and Barbara. He told us his parents didn't drive any more because his mother had been in a terrible accident. This information surprised no one.

After letting us off at the Moses statue, he insisted on picking us up at 5:P.M. and driving us back to the camp. Moses was the only thing we really wanted to see again in Rome, so afterward we wandered around the

Coliseum area, stopped for drinks and enjoyed people watching for about two hours. There is no better occupation than people watching in Italy.

At five, Stefano came to take us home. That twenty minute ride took us over an hour in intense, hair raising traffic, but it had been a wonderful day.

TUES. APRIL 21 LAGO DI PATRIA (NAPLES), ITALY

Spent the morning at the supermercato across the street from the camp. Aside from a whole lot of groceries, we bought a plastic folding table and three cloth and metal folding chairs. Now we could sit outside the camper to eat and play cards. Rene gave us a new deck of cards with the camper and Frank had been playing Solitaire whenever he had the chance. I had never played before, but he and Barbara were going to teach me.

Couldn't find an opened camp in the Naples area. There were camps everywhere, but it was not the season yet. Got a hotel in Lago di Patria, a suburb of Naples. This area was less than desirable, but the Hotel Emilia was not too bad. Had a great dinner there. Frank had antipasto di mare. He loves fish of every kind, and doesn't even mind tentacles and suction cups. Everything had been marinated in garlic and olive oil. He said it was the best he'd ever eaten. Barbara and I had pizza, and we instantly knew why people always rave about Neapolitan pizza. It was truly another memorable meal.

Hotel Emilia catered to Russians, we knew not why, but every man in the place looked like a cross between Mafiosi and KGB. They had many meetings in a big open room off the lobby, and the hotel staff was very preoccupied with their Russian guests. Almost all of these people dressed in double-breasted suits. The whole scene looked like it was taken right out of a Damon Runyon movie.

*Hotel Emilia: Via Domitiana Km. 43,3000, Uscita Tangenziale Lago di Patria Phone (081) 5091441 Fax (081) 5091181

WED. APRIL 22 ISCHIA PORTO, (ISLAND OF ISCHIA), ITALY

Drove to the ferry in the Port of Naples. Got there with three minutes to spare and sailed with the camper to the Port of Ischia. The isle of Ischia is where all four of our grandparents where born. At least that was what we had always been told. Frank and I decided that, if it was true, we were probably cousins as well as brother and sister. The island after all is very small and rumor had it that the four grandparents came from the same tiny town of Forio.

We drove off the boat and up to an official to ask where the Tourist Information was located. The man spoke English and one thing led to another. Naturally he had a friend who had an apartment for rent. The friend came running over and said to follow him on his motorcycle. He brought us to a nice little apartment with a kitchen, two bathrooms and three bedrooms. He made us understand that only two bedrooms and one bath were to be used. We haggled very little and got it for $50 a day. It included a large gated area for the camper. We took it for a week.

Later we went walking and stopped at a sidewalk cafe where we met some very exuberant teenagers. They thought we were German because almost all the tourist here were from Germany. When they found out we were American, they all wanted to come and live with us. Then when they heard we were from California, they were sure we could introduce them to Leonardo Di Capprio. It seemed the movie Titantic was as big a hit with Italian teenagers as with American. Only two of them could speak a little English, but they translated for everyone. The kids invited us to come and see their school play on Friday. They will be doing Sophocles. We, the English speakers, agreed to go and see their Greek play presented in Italian.

Back at the apartment, we found that our host, Mario, had rented the other room and bath to a French couple. We now had to share our cozy little apartment. The French couple spoke English quite fluently and were very nice. I invited them to have tea with us. I said, "Would you guys like some tea?" Phrasing typically used in California. The man looked at me and said, "You guaais? I am afraid I don't understand this word, guaais." I quickly rephrased my question. Now we know why Mario gave each of us a key to our own rooms.

*Mario Jovene: Via Acquedotto, 188, 8007 Ischia Tele: 081/901212

THURS. APRIL 23 ISCHIA, ITALY

Walked downtown with sacks of dirty clothes this morning. The laundry wanted $45 to do the wash, and we figured they would probably dry clean it, so we lugged it back home. The day was overcast and cold. I talked to Mario's wife to see if she had a machine we could use. She didn't speak English, so she made scrubbing motions with her hands. I got the point! We did our laundry by hand and hung it outside. Later we walked to Castello Aragonese, the famous castle in the sea. We thought my maternal Grandfather might have been born here. My Aunt Tosca told us he was born in Castello Mare, but the only place we could find with that name was in Naples. Since Castello Mare just means sea castle, it was possible that this may have been what he meant.

WEEKLY BUDGET #4   APRIL 17—APRIL 23
LODGING
Hotels (1) $61.00
Camps (4)   97.50
Apartment (3)   101.00
FOOD
Restaurants:
Dinners (2)   57.00
Groceries (19 meals)   85.50
ENTERTAINMENT
Cafes & Bars   76.00
Ischia Castle   17.00
Spending Money   84.50
(50,000 Lira each)
CAR
Camper Payment   168.00
Gas   147.50
Road Tolls   39.50
Parking   1.00
TRANSPORTATION
Bus (& map)   7.00
Ferry to Ischia   29.00
INCIDENTALS
Telephone Card   5.50
Table and 3 Chairs   51.50
Newspaper   1.50
                        $1029.00

WEEKLY BUDGET #4

Fri.	$174.00
Sat.	$117.00
Sun.	114.00
Mon.	101.00
Tues.	219.00
Wed.	201.00
Thurs.	103.00
	$1029.0

divided by 7 days = $147 per week. $147 divided by 3 people = $49 per person, per day.

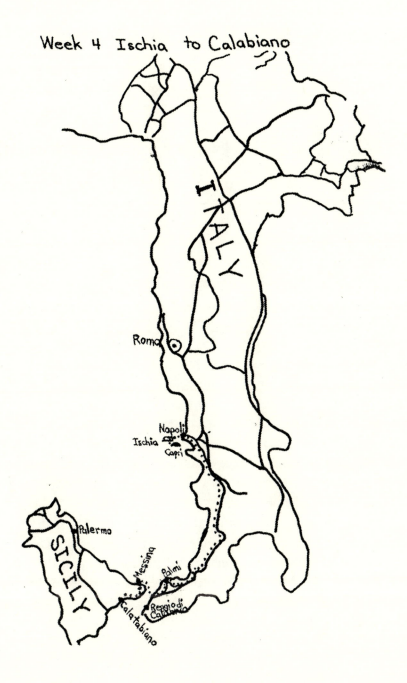

Week 4 Ischia to Calabiano

ITALY

Roma

Napoli
Ischia
Capri

SICILY

Palermo

Messina
Palmi
Calatabiano
Reggio di
Calabria

WEEK NUMBER FOUR APRIL 24 THROUGH APRIL 30, 1998

FRI. APRIL 24 ISCHIA, ITALY

Today was the first warm and beautiful day we'd had since getting to Europe. I actually went without a coat until evening. Took a drive around this delightful island. We figured the best place to find records of our grandparents would be in Forio at the church, since this was where they were all supposed to have been born. The church was closed, so we asked a shopkeeper where we could find the priest. She told us the priest only came once a week. For a few months before I left California, I had listened to a number of Italian language tapes. With this and my Honduran Spanish, I found that I was able to communicate a little, very little. Kept wandering around the town and came to a large Basilica. This priest was inside working with huge books that looked like records (of our ancestors?). The door was made of glass and I made a lot of noise trying to open it. He saw me, but ignored me.

We walked through the town and up a steep hill. On a cliff, overlooking the sea on three sides, was a quaint little white church The one depicted on all the post cards and called the Sanctuary of the Soccorso. The view was breathtaking. We wandered around absorbing it all for a good half hour, wondering what possessed our grandparents to leave. I guess eating regularly was a big factor .

Down the street from the church was the municipal office building. Everything was closed for lunch, but Barbara and I found an open door with three women inside eating their lunches. I told them that I couldn't speak Italian, but with hand gestures and Spanish, I got them to understand that I wanted to see the records of my ancestors. They wanted to know my name. Barbara wrote it down with the American spelling and the Italian spelling, De Mayo and Di Maio. One of the three women was also a Di Maio. I opened my arms and said, "Cugina!" This made them all laugh. My new "cousin", Teresa Di Maio, told me to come back at 5 P.M. on Monday afternoon and she would help us.

Frank had been outside the building all this time examining the town memorials. On them he found the last names of nearly everyone in our family. Only the name of my maternal grandfather, who was reportedly born in Castello Mare, was missing. The names Di Maio, D'Ambra, Morgera, Migliaccio, and Castaldi were all in evidence. These were the last names of most of our aunts, uncles and cousins.

We drove around the rest of the island and were very sorry that our apartment was not either in Forio or San Angelo. Each of these locations was a beautiful little seaside village just made for walking and browsing. There was much less traffic than in Ischia Porta, and the whole island experience would have been even more enjoyable. Hindsight!

In the evening, we went to the Greek play the local high school was performing. We weren't sure at which school it was being performed, as there were two schools together. Naturally we went to the wrong one first. By the time we found it and got inside, we were about a half hour late. We couldn't understand anything, but it was evident that the kids had worked very hard. At the end, the performers gave thanks to all the people who had helped and almost all of them had our family names. When they called up Franka Di Maio, Frank started to go up on the stage. Barbara and I restrained him, pointing out that Franka was a woman, and that he, Frank, really hadn't done anything to help.

SAT. APRIL 25 ISCHIA, ITALY

Went on a hike today up to the top of Mt. Epomeo. The travel book we were using, said it was an easy 30 minute hike. Of course it forgot to mention that you should start from the restaurant three quarters of the way up. We started from half way up the mountain. Two hours later, we got to the top. There were many older people climbing up. Most of them were German. I think there were more Germans in Ischia than Italians. Everybody said Guten tag as they passed. We said this to an elderly couple as they came down the mountain, and the man gave us an earful in Italian. We really didn't blame him. It was his country after all. So we started saying Buon giorno to everyone.

The last half mile or so was very rugged, and we had to pull ourselves up while we crawled. As we were doing this, a very fit looking older woman in a sporty hiking outfit, passed us by and said, Ist Gut! From that moment on, anytime we did anything difficult, but good for our health, this was our battle cry! *Ist gut!*

SUN. APRIL 26 ISCHIA, ITALY

This morning we took the hydrofoil from Ischia to the Isle of Capri, without the car. None of us had ever been to CaprI. The island was as beautiful as it had been reported to be, approached from the sea. We disembarked and went right to the Blue Grotto boats where we bought tickets for a small motor boat that held about twenty people. There were many of these small boats. We motored for about twenty minutes, viewing some unusual stone walls along the side of the island, and sheer rock that went up about a thousand feet. There were houses cut right out of the rock. It was quite dramatic.

When we arrived at the cave, there were about twenty-five small boats hovering around the mouth of it. Some were like the larger motor boats that we were in, and the rest were very small row boats. Each rowboat could take a maximum of four people, including the oarsman While we waited for a rowboat, the oarsman and the motorboat drivers yelled back and forth to each other. When Italians talk, it always sounds like they are about to resort to fisticuffs. It was just like being back in Brooklyn. We felt very much at home.

The sequence of events went like this. Two or three people would climb from the big boat to a rowboat and the gondolier would row them to the cash register on yet another boat. Each person was charged 700 Lira more than the price quoted at the start of the trip. This was evidently a tip. It would have been infinitely more expedient to collect all of the money, including the tip, at the ticket booth on shore, but clearly this had never occurred to them. A woman from England was sitting next to me. She leaned over and said, "It's all vedy inefficient, isn't it?" We just roared! It was like a scene from a bad Fellini movie.

When it was our turn, we were told to sit in the bottom of the rowboat, not on the seats. I bitched about it until I saw how small the mouth of the cave was. The surly rower laid down the oars and pulled on a chain attached to the walls of the cave. As he did so, he had to lie straight back with his head practically in my lap. Had he been a little more congenial, I might have enjoyed it. Once inside, he absolutely demanded that we look at the blue water and enjoy its color. He might as well have said, "Zig Heil!" His attitude was so contemptuous that it was comical.

All the gondoliers sang Santa Lucia. We joined in the singing, trying to get into the spirit of the occasion, but it was difficult because they were so outrageously obnoxious. The blue water, which seemed to be a great source of pride to these men, wasn't any bluer than water anywhere in the world where light can come into a dark space. Nevertheless, it was worth every penny for the buffoonery alone. The whole experience was absurd.

After the boat trip, we explored the island mostly looking for a place to have lunch. We found a street named after our grandparents and, out of sentiment, followed it up to the top of the mountain. It was quite a climb. Later we discovered that the end of this street was just about where the funicular ends. We could have ridden up on the funicular in less than five minutes. The masses of humanity, largely American, made the rest of the time on the island quite tiresome. We were all happy to get back to Ischia.

MON. APRIL 27 ISCHIA, ITALY

Went back to Forio to see my "cousin" Teresa at 5 P.M. She took down from a high shelf some very large books with records of the town's people. Frank had to help her as, like the rest of the Italians from this area, she is not very big. She couldn't find any of my grandparent's names. Her boss came in and got a little angry at her for wasting time. She explained that we all had the same last name. This piqued his interest, as it was evidently an unusual occurrence. However, he lost interest very quickly and said Teresa would have to look on her own time. Teresa told us to come back tomorrow.

TUES. APRIL 28 ISCHIA, ITALY

Enjoyed this wonderful picturesque island all morning. Went back to the municipality in Forio for the third time in the afternoon. This time we were prepared. We figured it would take Teresa a great deal of time to look through the records. So we put 50,000 lira in an envelope with our address and gave it to her. Her two co-workers were standing next to her as she extracted the money. The two of them got hysterical, one of them hit her head with the heel of her hand and said, "Crazy Americans! They don't understand the value of money!" I understood enough Italian to get that loud and clear. 50,000 Lira was about thirty dollars. We figured it would take her about three hours at ten dollars an hour. Sounded reasonable to us. She insisted we give her enough for the stamps only. She also said that there was another small part of Forio that had another records office and maybe our grandparents came from there. This was quite possible, but if all four of them came from this very small section of Forio, then Frank and I really would be cousins, maybe even first cousins. Evidently, it was not only royalty that was inbred!

Frank was not feeling well this afternoon, so Barbara and I went down to one of the thermal baths for which Ischia is famous. I had a massage. It seems that Americans in general are more modest about nudity than Europeans. Europeans seem to strip anywhere and everywhere without thinking anything about it. I, on the other hand, had a great deal of trouble disrobing in front of a perfect stranger. She didn't even give me a towel. Then the woman, who did not comprehend my anguish in the least, kept opening the door so that all the men and women outside could observe my embarrassment. I decided I didn't need anymore massages on this trip.

WED. APRIL 29 PALMI, ITALY

Sadly said good-by to Ischia this morning. We had originally planned to spend a month here and, as we headed back to Naples on the ferry, I felt a little disheartened that we had changed our plans.

On the ride down the autostrada towards Sicily, the scenery was unexpectedly beautiful. The road runs through a valley with unbelievable mountains on either side. I had no idea Italy was so incredible magnificent. Before this trip, I had only seen the enormous cities overburdened with teaming humanity.

About four in the afternoon, we left the autostrada and headed for the sea. There were innumerable olive groves in this area, and we found it much to our liking. We found a camp across the street from the ocean in Eden Park. The camp was not really opened. There were many people working at getting it ready. The proprietor said we were welcome to camp. Went for a walk on the beach and found huge chunks of marble washed up on the sand, pieces bigger than I was. I like to collect souvenir rocks, and I added to my Italian collection here. The boulders wouldn't fit in my suitcase and regrettably, I had to leave them behind.

* Palmi: Eden Park: Found by signposts, not in our book

THURS. APRIL 30 CALATABIANO, SICILY

The camp owner never asked me for any money last night, so I went in search of him this morning. We paid 20,000 Lira, about $17. If I hadn't asked, I don't think he would have cared. He really wasn't opened.

We drove the rest of the way to Villa San Giovanni, just above Reggio di Calabria, where we took the ferry across to Sicily. As in Ischia, we got to the ferry with only seconds to spare and went right across. The ferry cost $34.50 for us and the car, round trip. We landed in Messina, an incredibly huge metropolis, totally devoid of driving regulations. Sped through it as quickly as possible, but it took forever in the traffic. Once free, we headed south.

Found a camp with a small castle on the property called Castello di San Marco. They had bungalows with two bedrooms, a kitchen and a bathroom. Not at all bad for $40. The camping bungalows here came fully equipped with cooking utensils, including everything one would need for making spaghetti. This of course was very important to us. They also came with bedding. There were no towels however, so I went down and asked the woman in charge. Thankfully, she spoke Spanish, but she didn't understand the word for towel in Spanish. I didn't know how to say it in Italian, so I demonstrated for her by putting an imaginary towel behind my back and doing the Twist. She imitated my motions, laughing uproariously. By this time we had gathered quite an audience. Everyone was laughing and making suggestions as to the meaning of this word. Finally someone said, "Asciugamani" and we got our towels.

*Calatabiano, Camping Castello di San Marco. Directions: SS114, turn direction sea 8 km south Taormina.

ITIMIZED WEEKLY BUDGET #4

LODGING
Apartment (5)	$255.00
Camp (1)	17.00
Camp Apartment (1)	39.50

FOOD
Restaurants:
Dinners (2)	70.00
Lunches (2)	58.00
Groceries (17 meals)	105.00

ENTERTAINMENT
Cafes & Bars	16.00
Blue Grotto Tour	42.00
Spending Money	84.50

CAR
Car payment	168.00
Gas	106.00
Road tolls	3.50
Parking	3.00

TRANSPORTATION
Ferries	66.00
Boat to Capri	68.00

INCIDENTALS
Postage	18.00
Cousin Teresa	11.50
	$1131.00

WEEKLY BUDGET #4

Fri.	$120.00
Sat.	209.00
Sun.	228.00
Mon.	181.00
Tues.	113.50
Wed.	128.50
Thurs.	151.00
	$1131.00

$1131 divided by 7 days = $161.57 per day. $167.57 divided by 3 people = $53.85 per person, per day.

Week 5 Calabiano to Mazara Del Vallo

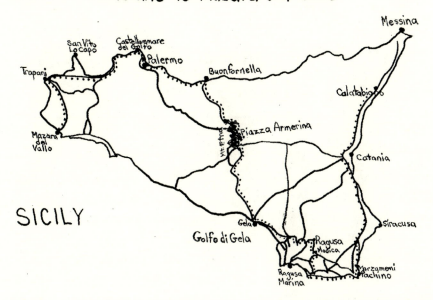

SICILY

Week Number Five May 1 Through May 7, 1998

FRI. MAY 1 MARZAMEMI, SICILY

It was cold again! May first is a big holiday in Italy and we got stuck in traffic on the way to Siracusa. Kept driving looking for a camp that wasn't there. The scenery was very nice with many citrus orchards.

Finally found a nice camp with bungalows. Took one for three nights. It cost $47, but it was even nicer than the one we'd had last night. It seems that bungalows in Italian campgrounds are quite common. For this we were very thankful. We thought it would take us forever to find apartments to stay in, and then we realized we needed only look as far as the nearest campground. The town we were in, Marzamemi, was a very quaint little seaside village.

*Marzameni: IL Forte, Capo Passero, Siracusa, Direction: Between Siracusa and Pachino, at the coast.

SAT. MAY 2 MARZAMEMI, SICILY

Frank was just beginning to feel a little better, though he still sounded like he had a cold. But May second is his birthday, and to celebrate, we went to the Vendicari Bird Sanctuary. There were Greek ruins of an ancient tuna fish smoking factory. It was right on the Adriatic Sea and quite beautiful, with thousands of spring wild flowers. Met two English women who were our neighbors at the camp, a mother and daughter. The daughter was married to an Italian and the mother was visiting from England. Since the daughter lived here, she knew all about the ruins and gave us a guided tour. She also told us not to go to Gela, a city along the south coast of Sicily. She said it was a big Mafia city and it wasn't safe.

On the way out of the Sanctuary, an incredible thing happened. We said, "Buon giorno," to an Italian family going in. The man said, "You speak English?" The conversation went like this:

Barbara: "We're from the San Francisco area."

Man: "Really, I have an aunt in Burlingame."

Me: "That's where the airport is! We flew out of there."

Man: "Well, I didn't stay in Burlingame. My aunt has a place further North."

Frank: "Really? We live further north, about three hours above San Francisco.

Man: "No kidding? My aunt lives about that far above San Francisco too. She lives on a big lake.

Me: "So do we!"

Man: "I don't remember the name of the town, but the lake is called Clear Lake. She lives in the north part."

Barbara: "Lakeport?"

Man: "Yes, that's it. How did you know?"

Me: "Because that's where we live!"

Everyone: "Wow!" We exchanged addresses. He will call when he comes next year.

Set out to see Eloro, more Greek ruins, but stopped for lunch and a nap in the camper first. The runes at Eloro were all fenced off, so we couldn't get too close. However the view of the ocean and the wild flowers were worth the trip. We drove through the town of Noto, but none of us thought it was as picturesque as our book depicted.

In the evening, we walked into Marzamemi to celebrate Frank's birthday in a local restaurant. This town has only about three streets, but it is on the water and is quite lovely. Dinner was good but Barbara's pasta sauce is spicier and more delicious. I treated for Franks big day, so the price of this dinner is not listed in the budget. It was $37. We also found a packing plant that sold all kinds of exotic Italian delicacies in jars. We bought a few to try. Walking home was a cold and windy experience.

SUN. MAY 3 MARZAMEMI, SICILY

Took a long ride along the south coast of Sicily this morning and up into the hills. Our destination was an archaeological dig in the Cava D'Ispica. It took us about two hours to get there, and naturally it was closed for lunch. In Italy this can mean anywhere between two and four hours. We set up our patio furniture, took a nap and read. Eventually it opened. It was quite nice and we climbed around looking at all the historical landmarks for about an hour and a half. On the way out, who should we meet but the Italian family with the aunt in Lakeport. Talk about a small world.

MON. MAY 4 PIAZZA ARMERINA, SICILY

The first thing we did this morning was go back to the packing plant that sold all the exotic delicacies in small jars. Couldn't believe how delicious they were. The best ones were the artichoke and eggplant spreads that we have been putting on all our sandwiches. Stocked up, knowing that it was doubtful we would ever find them again. They shipped all over Italy but alas, would not ship to the States.

Next, we set out to find an ATM machine. Marzamemi was too small, so we drove into Pachino, a slightly larger town almost at the very southeastern tip of Sicily. There were three machines in town, but it was Monday, and they were all out of money. We tried the next big town, Modica, and the next, Ragusa, on our way West and then North through the very middle of the island. All to no avail. The machines were new here, and the people used them a lot on the weekends. So if you want money in Sicily, don't try to get it on a Monday!

I was sick. The wind was blowing constantly in southern Sicily and my sinuses were going crazy. Either that, or Frank very generously gave me his disease. I slept through most of the morning journey. Went as far west as Gela, the Mafia town the English woman had told us about, and then went north through the mountains to Piazza Armerina. It was very cold and we wanted to stay in a hotel. Unfortunately, there were very few hotels. Went to a rather fancy one, Hotel Paradicio, but it was full. Asked the desk clerk about camping places and she said there were none. She felt badly that she didn't have a room for us and said we could camp in the parking lot. We told her we had no toilet. She discussed it with her boss, who was standing next to her, and they decided we could use the hotel bathroom. We were totally amazed that they would be so accommodating. However, we've experienced this attitude often in Italy. They may be lousy drivers, but they are really warm hospitable people.

Nevertheless, I was too sick to camp in the cold, so we pushed on. Drove to a little town called Aidone further up in the mountains. This was where one of our cousins' mother came from, and we had planned to see it anyway. The hotel was way above our budget. We drove back through Piazza Armerina to Romana D'Casale and finely found a hotel. It was one big room with a bath for $59, and we took it for two nights. Barbara cooked dinner in the camper in the parking lot because we had food that couldn't be wasted.

TUES. MAY 5 ROMANA D'CASALE (PIAZZA ARMERINA), SICILY

Four of our cousins had made a trip to Sicily last fall. My cousin, Marcia, sent us all the maps and books that they had used. She also told us that they were sorry to have missed the famous mosaics at Piazza Armerina. We were determined not to make the same mistake, so we went. The mosaics were fascinating! They had been buried underground for centuries, but were now beautifully displayed. We passed the whole morning enjoying the beauty of this ancient art form.

I wanted to visit Aidone again in the afternoon, but I was too sick to go anywhere. We all just hung out, rested and read.

WED. MAY 6 BUONFORNELLO, SICILY

Drove past Mount Etna and the middle of Sicily. What a beautiful island! Arrived at the North coast and got a camp on the beach at Buonfornello. Out of the mountains, the weather was much warmer. This was another camp with a private toilet and cold shower. Quite nice. The hot showers were in another part of the camp. The proprietor gave us tokens for them, but we couldn't find them and there was no one to ask. We were the only people in the campground. Went walking on the beach where I added to my collection of shells and rocks.

*Buonfornello: (East of Palermo) Camping Himera. Directions: A 19, exit Buonfornello, signposted.

THURS. MAY 7 MAZARA DEL VALLO, SICILY

Drove along the North coast, which in my opinion, is far more beautiful than the South coast. But the island really isn't very big, and we soon found ourselves back on the south coast again. Had enjoyed the day stopping to see cute little towns and just dinging around. Now it was getting late and the sky was clouding up. Decided to spend the night, then head back to the North coast in the morning. Found a rather deteriorating camp with no working hot water. It cost $3 more than last night, with no private bathroom and no beach. There seemed to be little rhyme or reason for prices in campgrounds. We were the only campers once again. There were many camping vehicles scattered throughout the campground with no one in them. People evidently left them here all year. We had seen this in almost every camp.

*Mazara del Vallo: Sporting Camping Club. Directions: Road 73, southeast of Marsala.

ITEMIZED WEEKLY BUDGET #5 MAY 1—MAY 7

LODGING

Hotels (2)	$118.00
Camp Apartments (3)	141.00
Camps (2)	37.00

FOOD

Restaurants:

Dinners (1)	39.00
Breakfast (1)	12.00
Groceries (19 meals)	84.00

ENTERTAINMENT

Cafes & Bars	2.00
Ispica Caves	7.00
Mosaic Museum	7.00

CAMPER

Camper payment	168.00
Gas	130.00
Road tolls	1.00
Parking	1.00

INCIDENTALS

Postage	2.00
	$751.00

WEEKLY BUDGET #5

Fri.	$115.50
Sat.	100.00
Sun.	78.00
Mon.	146.00
Tues.	169.50
Wed.	51.50
Thurs.	90.50
	$751.00

$750 divided by 7 days = $107.14 per day. $107.14 divided by 3 people =$35.71 per person, per day.

CHICKEN PICCATTA

FLOUR::
4 chicken breasts, boned and pounded

BROWN:
chicken in olive oil and black or white pepper

REMOVE:
chicken and deglace pan with white wine—save the wine

ADD:
1 small onion
3 cloves garlic and brown lightly

ADD:
chicken breasts
wine broth
1 Tablespoons lemon juice

SIMMER:
1/2 hour

SERVE:
over rice or noodles

Week 6   Mazara Del Vallo to Sferracavallo

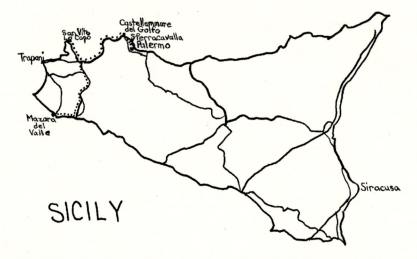

SICILY

Week Number Six May 8 Through May 14, 1998

FRI. MAY 8 CASTELLAMMARE, SICILY

Drove back to the North coast to the town of Castellammare del Golfo, not to be confused with Castellammare off the coast of Naples. It took about an hour and a half to get there from the South coast. We took a nice apartment in a campground for $40 a night with all the amenities. It was on the beach and only about a mile from town. We done good!. We decided to stay for three nights. Once again, we were the only ones in the camp. Today was the third warm day since we started. The seashore was quite beautiful, though the beach could have been a lot cleaner.

I was still not feeling very well, so I took a nap while Barbara and Frank walked to town for groceries. It was very difficult to shop for anything in Italy. The stores didn't open until 10 A.M. Then they closed again at 12 noon. Sometimes they opened again at 5 P.M. and sometimes they didn't. We had decided that if we wanted groceries, we would have to get them between 10 A.M. and noon. This was not always convenient, but it was necessary!

The camper was acting up again. We couldn't always shift, and when we did, it made an awful grinding noise.

*Castellammare: Directions: Signposted, at the beach.

SAT. MAY 9 CASTELLAMMARE, SICILY

Today I was feeling better, but Barbara was sick. It must have been a virus since we all got it. We just hung around the apartment the whole day. Each of us needed to do laundry, and there was a big wash tub with a scrubbing board outside in which to do it. We walked on the beach and rested, read and played cards. In the evening, we walked into town for dinner.

SUN. MAY 10 CASTELLAMMARE, SICILY

Went for what our book, Let's Go, described as a two hour hike along the coast in Zingaro National Preserve. Five and one half hours later, we came back, nearly dead! I didn't think my legs would ever work again. We never did get to the end, the town of San Vito lo Cabo. The trail is on a cliff overlooking the Gulf of Castellammare, in the Mediterranean Sea. The views are dramatic and almost worth all the pain. It was an extremely hot day, over 100 degrees. Whenever we were too hot and exhausted to go any further, we would climb down a very steep path to the ocean. This took at least half an hour. Then, after resting and cooling off in the water, we had to climb back up. This took at least 45 minutes. We did this twice before we figured out that it expended more energy than anyone had left.

We went as far as the Grotto Grande, a large cool cave where we sat and ate the picnic lunch from our back packs. Long before we got back, we finished all the water we had been carrying. When we arrived back at the park entrance, I staggered up to a ranger saying "Aqua, aqua!" He pointed to a large water trough and all of us plunged our upper torsos into the water and drank insatiably from the faucet. Nix Gut!!

The *Let's Go* travel book we were using was written for very fit twenty year olds. I am in my fifties and Barbara and Frank are in their sixties. Like most senior people these days, we figured we could still do anything and everything. Nevertheless, we will take the times allotted in the book for hiking with a large grain of salt from now on.

MON. MAY 11 CASTELLAMMARE, SICILY

Spent the morning buying a few supplies we needed. We had to go to at least five stores for every three items. Drove to San Vito lo Cabo, the furthest Northwestern point of Sicily.

This was the place we tried to walk to yesterday. It took two hours in the car. Of course, we had to go in a circuitous route as there were no direct roads, but still I wouldn't have, under any circumstances, called it within walking distance. The scenery in this part of Sicily is sensational. The high rugged mountain peaks tumbling down to the sea, really are awesome. On the way we saw marble being mined. It looked like cities cut into the hills because they take it out in huge rectangular shapes that look just like buildings. The rocky mountains are full of iron and rust, making them exceedingly colorful. On the whole, the drive was pretty spectacular. I never dreamed that Sicily would be so beautiful.

The town of San Vito lo Cabo gave me a feeling of spaciousness and light. It is a small town with fairly wide streets and lots of white sandy beaches. This was not the tourist season but this is a tourist town, so we actually found a restaurant that was opened. Most of the restaurants we've encountered in the small towns of Italy have been closed at the time of day that we perceive to be lunch time, about one P.M.. However, they don't seem to open later in the afternoon either.

After lunch, we drove to the San Vito side of the Zingaro National Park. We decided, from looking at the map and the terrain, that yesterday we had been only a kilometer or two from this end. I was thankful we hadn't tried to make it. This side of the trail is far from the actual town of San Vito, and even further from drinkable water.

TUE.. MAY 12 SFERRACAVALLA, SICILY

We wanted to see the capital city of Palermo, but none of us wanted to stay there, so we set out for a campground in Sferracavalla. This is another beautiful little seaside village about a half hour by bus from the capital. Of the two camps in this town, one had no bungalows and the other had very inferior ones. However, the proprietor of the second camp was a very accommodating old guy, that reminded me of my grandfather. The bungalow was one room with a bath and a front porch. It was far from elegant. In fact, it was far from pleasant. All the dishes had been left unwashed, but Grandpa gave us clean sheets and towels, and we were able to make it semi comfortable. We took it for four nights.

After settling in, we went for a walk around the town. It was really a lovely little village, but utterly filthy. There was trash and grime everywhere. People unwrapped whatever they were eating and just let go of the wrappers. No one even thought about the litter or considered using a pooper-scooper, and there was dog shit everywhere. The animals here were very sad too, as they were every place we had been in Italy. People fed them, but they were very damaged and in need of tender loving care. More important, they were in need of veterinary services. However, I hadn't seen any untended children. Thirty years ago in Italy, many children were as bad off as the animals. Progress was definitely being made.

*Palermo-Sferracavallo: Camping Internazionale Trinacria. Directions: Via Barcarello, SS 113, km 273/1. Tele: 0 91/53 05 90

WED. MAY 13 SFERRACAVALLA, SICILY

Set off to see Palermo this morning. I had my binoculars on the side of my backpack, in the net that holds a water bottle. Grandpa came up to me chattering in Italian and trying to pick my pocket. He got the binoculars out and handed them to me, while shaking his index finger at me knowingly. He was obviously trying to tell me that I was a prime target for the infamous pickpockets of Palermo. I took heed and put them inside. This garrulous old man, directed us on how to take two busses into the city and where to catch each. It was amazing how much we could understand without really speaking the language.

Once in the city, we headed to the American Express office to pick up our mail. Rene had sent us an important paper for the car, and two relatives in the states sent news and good wishes.

We wanted to take a guided bus tour of the city, but there were very few and none that day. Barbara, who was a whiz with a map, gave us a guided walking tour. Everything in Palermo was in such disrepair that the whole city was kind of sad. We walked through the enormous market place, which was always interesting, and had fun bargaining for a few needed items. Palermo's famous Fountain of Shame, which must have been something to see in its day, epitomized the deterioration of the entire city. The statues were cracked and broken beyond repair. In fact, it looked like Mrs. Bobbit had passed each one with her trusty knife and hacked off any penis that was even slightly erect. After a long search, we found a little restaurant that was opened. Even in the capital city this was a problem. Then we walked back to where the first bus had left us, about three and a half miles, and saw the ordinary part of the city on foot.

Back in our little village of Sferracavalla, we looked for an open grocery store. It was about four in the afternoon. A number of little groceries were still closed. We found a tiny one where two young men were waiting on customers. One of them had "Rosario Di Mayo" on his apron. As we were leaving the shop, I asked if that was his name. He nodded in the affirmative. I told him in Italian that it was my name too, and he asked me to tell him my first name. I said,"Dolores." He got all excited and dragged me back into the shop where he showed me a picture of an enormous nun in a white habit. The printing underneath said, "Dolores Di Majo, 1888-1967" He said, "Mi zia!" (My aunt) Then he grabbed his co-worker and said, "Franko Di Mayo, mi fratello." (My brother) I grabbed Frank and said, "Frank De Mayo, mi fratello!" We all started laughing and all the other customers, who had been watching with rapt attention, started laughing and talking at once. I put my hand out to shake his and said, "Cugino" (cousin). That brought the house down. I tried to find out why he had a "y" in his name when it is not an Italian letter, and why his aunt's name was spelled with a "j." He indicated that "y" and "j" were interchangeable, but I couldn't understand the rest of his explanation. He did say, however, that his family was originally from Naples, so we actually could have been cousins from a few generations ago.

My father told me a story when I was a kid about the spelling change in our name. He said that his father worked on the docks in New York as a longshoreman when he first came to America. The Irish were in power then, and Italian laborers were not looked upon with particular favor. In fact, he was frequently beaten up. So his father, my grandfather, changed the spelling so it was like County Mayo in Ireland. How a dark wiry little Italian, who spoke no English, thought he could pass himself off as an

Irishman, I couldn't say. We moved to California when I was six, and from then on De Mayo was Mexican. So I guess it's an international name. I thought I might change my name back to Di Maio. I was feeling very Italian!

THURS. MAY 14 SFERRACAVALLO, SICILY

Spent the morning on the beach. Frank actually went in the water, but it was still too cold for Barbara and me. The weather was lovely and warm though, and we all enjoyed the sunshine. In the afternoon, we went back to what we now called "The Cousins' Shop." This time the father of the two young men was there. He is Rosario Di Mayo Sr. They were very excited about seeing us again and people started coming out of the wood-work to watch us. Evidently the story of the distant, possible relatives from America had been spread all over town. This time they had presents for us. They gave us cloth and plastic shopping bags with the name of the store, Rosario Di Mayo, on them. And they gave me a prized picture of their aunt, Dolores De Majo. I didn't want to take it because each of them carried a picture in his wallet and it was obviously very important to them. Nevertheless they insisted, so I took it. Frank actually remembered to bring his camera, something we all constantly forgot that we had, and we took pictures of all of us together. We promised to send copies when we returned home in November.

ITEMIZED WEEKLY BUDGET # 6 MAY 8—MAY 14

LODGING

Camp Apartments (7)	$276.50

FOOD

Restaurants:

Dinner (1)	41.00
Lunches (2)	58.00
Groceries (18 meals)	110.50

ENTERTAINMENT

Cafes & Bars	17.50

CAMPER

Camper Payment	168.00
Gas	47.00

TRANSPORTATION

Bus	9.00

INCIDENTALS

Map	1.50
Postage	1.00
Medicine	5.50
Mosquito net	2.00
	$737.50

WEEKLY BUDGET #6

Fri.	$108.50
Sat.	106.50
Sun.	66.00
Mon.	166.00
Tues.	77.00
Wed.	120.50
Thurs.	93.00
	$737.50

$737.50 divided by 7 days = $105.35 per day. $105.35 divided by 3 people =$35.11 per person, per day.

Week 7 Sferracavallo to Santa Cesarea Terme

ITALY

SICILY

Brindisi

Lecce

Otranto

Santa
Cesarea
Terme

Castro

Taranto

Rossano

Crotone

Messina

Sferracavallo

Palmi

Reggio
di Calabria

WEEK NUMBER SEVEN MAY 15 THROUGH MAY 21, 1998

FRI. MAY 15 SFERRACAVALLA, SICILY

In the morning, we stopped by the "Cousins Store" to give them some presents we had brought from America for our relatives in Lavorno. We had T-shirts and key rings (easy to pack and carry), and we had a couple of extra ones just in case. We gave them two California T-shirts for the young men and a key ring for the father.

Afterwards we took the bus back to Palermo to finish our walking tour. Six busses passed us by before one stopped. None of the other people at the bus stop seemed to know why, but they all had definite opinions about what the bus drivers could do with themselves. Even little old ladies dressed in black, shook their fists and cried out in disgust. Eventually a bus stopped, and we got to town. We had to go to American Express again. Since we changed our itinerary, none of the dates matched our travels any longer and we needed to leave a forwarding address. They really do not have this service, but the woman in the office was very understanding. I gave her a self addressed envelope with money for a stamp and she said she would forward it to Florence. (That was the last time an American Express office was accommodating. We eventually wrote home and told people not to write, and we stopped going to the offices. Instead we used our pre-paid phone cards. It was much easier to call.)

Back in the village, we stopped for groceries for the last time at the "Cousins' Store." Franko was in a very bad mood and wouldn't talk to us. We weren't sure if his girlfriend jilted him or if Popa took the T-shirt meant for him. Rosario tried to explain but we understood nothing. However the customers and the two Rosarios, father and son, were genuinely sorry to see us go. Outside the shop an old man came up to us and started speaking in very rusty Spanish. He had evidently heard on the local grapevine about the Spanish speaking Americans in town, and he had come to get in on the act. He told me he had fought in the Spanish Civil War. He wanted to tell me about it, but he had forgotten most of his Spanish and kept reverting to Italian. Consequently, I could understand very little.

Everywhere we went in this village, people seemed to know us. Americani, they would say with a smile. Little kids would yell out, "You speaka English?" but that was all they could say. It was kind of fun being so suddenly famous.

SAT. MAY 16 PALMI, ITALY

Our two weeks in Sicily were over. Again, I was very reluctant to leave. I hadn't expected to like Sicily so much. Drove along the North coast of the island to the ferry. We already had return trip tickets, and had very little trouble finding the correct ferry. Sailed across to the Calabria area and drove about an hour to a lovely campsite in Palmi. It was on a cliff overlooking the Tyrrhenian Sea, a beautiful setting with many trees. The old man who owned the place spoke English and had sailed all over the world, including America.

After we set up camp, a wedding party came, including a bride, a groom, various relatives and a couple of photographers. It seemed this was the in place for wedding pictures. There were five or six other campers and they all came out to watch. We were having wine and toasted the newlyweds. This was one of the few camps where there were other campers.

Most were German, but one was English and we exchanged advice on what to see and do, as we were traveling in opposite directions.

*Palmi: Camping San Fantino. Directions: Via San Fantino, Taureana Palmi. Tele: 09 66/47 94 30

SUN. MAY 17 ROSSANO, ITALY

Today was another driving day across the instep of the boot and up the coast, on the Golfo di Taranto, to Rossano. All the scenery was beautiful and mountainous. On the road up the coast, we only saw the water every now and then, but it was still very alluring. We found a camp with a really nice little two bedroom bungalow, a short walk from the beach for only $38. We were the only ones in camp except for the workers who were trying to get everything ready for the crowds next month. We decided to stay for three nights.

Phoned my nephew Gary at home with our prepaid telephone cards. It was so much easier than trying to find American Express offices. All was well at home.

*Rossano Scalo: Marina di Rossano Village Camping. Direction: SS106, uscita Rossano. Tele: 09 83/51 20 69

MON. MAY 18 ROSSANO, ITALY

It poured all day and it was cold again. Went grocery shopping in the rain this morning. The weather cleared up somewhat in the afternoon and we went for a quick walk on the beach between the raindrops. The camp was very nice. The cabins were separated from each other by trees and grass. There were ruins to explore, and it was only a short walk to the beach.

TUES. MAY 19 ROSSANO, ITILY

The morning was free of rain. Went for a four mile walk along the beach. The Bay of Toranto is beautiful but, as usual, the trash here was overwhelming.

Barbara likes to draw, so after lunch she went out to make a sketch of an eighth century chapel that just happened to be inside the campground. There was a very loud "Crack!" and suddenly the electricity all over the camp, and as we soon found out all over town, went off. A tree branch had fallen on the electric wires very near where Barbara was working. She came back to the bungalow to get Frank and me so we could see what had happened. While we were looking up at the damage, an old battered white truck, with a very old wooden ladder, pulled under the wires where the tree branch was caught. Two men jumped down from the cab of the truck and proceeded to horrify us with their antics. The three of us stood and watched the spectacle with our mouths opened. We hadn't seen anything like this since they stopped showing Laurel and Hardy movies on television.

First one of the two men got up on the bed of the truck with a rope in his hand and tried to lasso the branch that was caught between the wires. When his John Wayne act didn't work, he extended the very rickety old ladder high up into the air and leaned it on the bare electric wire. It seemed not to occur to either of them that they could lean the ladder against the cab of the truck. At this point, the man with the lasso started to climb the ladder. I couldn't help myself. I let out a scream yelling something about how he was going to kill himself. They didn't understand my words, but they definitely got the meaning of my scream. The climbing man said to us,"No?" and climbed back down where the two of them could discuss the merits of what they were about to do.

They evidently decided that their idiotic scheme wouldn't work, so they carried the ladder to the twenty foot cement pole on which the wires were attached. The pole was notably lose and quite unstable. However, that was not the worst part. It was also a half of football field away from the branch. They extended the ladder as far as it would go, which was three quarters the way up the pole. The lasso man climbed it and attached himself to the wobbly pole with the belt off his pants. My guess was that he wore a large one just for this type of emergency. Then he took his lasso and threw it about ten more times. Each time we were convinced that his death was immanent. I mumbled something about a Polish joke to Frank and Barbara. (They are never Italian jokes to Italians, even those born in America!) Finally, the man hooked a wire.

Unfortunately, it was not the wire on which the branch was hanging. He tied a loop in the rope, let out a lot of slack, and tried to shoot the rope down to the other end of the wire. Surprise, there was a catch of some kind in the middle, and the rope got stuck. Unstrapping himself and climbing down the ladder, he started snapping the rope to get it over the bump. Meanwhile, the other guy was just standing there watching him do everything. He finally got the rope down to the end where the branch was hanging. Then he pulled tight on the rope, which pulled the wire back, so it was taut like a cross bow, and he let it go. This caused the wire to snap against the branch. Eventually, by repeating this method again and again, the branch fell. The three of us applauded and yelled, "Bravo!" The amazing part of all this was that these two guys were from the Electric Utility Company. This was an official Electric Utility Company truck and ladder. There was no "cherry picker" basket and the ladder should have been burned as fire wood twenty years before. We Americans are very spoiled.

After having lunch in our little home, we drove to the city of Rossano. This city has two parts. One is the port by the beach where we were staying, and the other is up on top of a medium high mountain. We went up the mountain. Rossano is an old and crumbling medieval village and we really enjoyed walking around looking at everything.

Found another town memorial from the second world war, the third or fourth we had encountered, very much like the one in Ischia. As usual not one family name did we find. It was obvious that our family really was from Ischia. Wanted to see a fresco in one of the churches. A shopkeeper told us we must wait until five o'clock for the church to open. We have heard this, "It will open at five o'clock" story many times. The shopkeeper also said that no one painted the fresco. It came by a miracle. Waited until five thirty. None of the churches opened, so we went home. Decided that an open church in Italy would be the real miracle.

WED. MAY 20 SANTA CESAREA TERMI, ITALY

This morning I went to the office of the campground to pay for the three nights in our bungalow. Our book and the man that registered us, both said that they took Visa. When I handed the Visa card to the young woman in the office, she looked at me panic stricken and said in English, "Money, check?" It was almost a plea. We got a much better rate when we used a credit card, so I said very firmly, "No, Visa!" Her smile drooped and she went into the back room. She returned with a box so large, she was staggering under its weight. From it, she unpacked four different parts to her Visa machine and attempted to set it up, all the while reading the directions for each different procedure. It took her a good twenty minutes before she got it working and inserted my card. I had to admit though, I was beginning to enjoy their inefficiency. It was very comical. We waited a full ten minutes longer before the machine printed out that the line was busy. There must have been only one line in all of Calabria because no one used Visa, except at the ATMs, and I believe that that is a different department because it is debit not credit. She tried again. We waited another ten minutes and again it printed out that the line was busy. I told her I'd come back later.

Every place we have tried to use a credit card, there has been an interminable wait. It usually had nothing to do with the machine or the line. The problem was that almost no one in the country knew how to do it. However, I feel quite certain that by the time I visit Italy again, they will have learned. Like us, once they catch on to the convenience, there will be no stopping them. When I returned, she had reread all the directions and this time it worked.

Drove for most of the day. Went to three camps before we found one that we liked. It took over an hour to find one of them, and it was closed. The book said it was closed, but I read the Roman numerals wrong. Frank wanted to clobber me, and I couldn't say that I blamed him, but he just drove on mumbling under his breath.

In the evening, we drove to the nearby town of Castro for dinner. Again the town is very picturesque, high on a cliff overlooking the sea. We enjoyed dinner because the woman and her son who waited on us reminded us of all our relatives. They laughed a lot because they couldn't understand anything we said, and they tried very hard to be accommodating. The son even ran out to the store to get a bottle of wine for us. When we said good-by, we realized it was dark outside. I don't drive in the dark at all in strange places, and Frank doesn't really like to either. This was a mountainous road, and he had had quite a bit of wine. Dumb! We managed to get back to the camp, but I mentioned that I didn't ever want to do that again. Frank of course denied that there was anything to worry about. Such a typically male attitude. (Barbara and I made sure that we stayed in camps that were on bus lines from that time to the end of the trip. Frank, being oblivious to everything but food and wine, never even noticed.)

*Santa Cesarea Terme: Camping La Scogliera. Direction: At the SS 173, turn off 2 km south of village. Tele: 08 36/94 98 02

THURS. MAY 21 SANTA CESAREA TERME, ITALY

We were now back on the Adriatic Sea, on the Eastern side of the heel of the boot. We had been on this sea before on the Eastern side of Sicily. Set out this morning to explore the towns of Otronto and Santa Cesarea Terme. Both were fascinating. I really loved this part of Italy. Very few tourists ever come here, except on cruise ships. It was a shame that only the infrequent traveler got to see it, but it was wonderful for the few who did venture this far. The tourists were few and far between, and the sights were incredible.

Otronto is a city within and without the walls of a castle. The castle is built out of and onto the local sandstone rocks. Most of the town is built in the same manner as the castle. In the Duomo, or Cathedral, are beautifully finished mosaics based on the tree of life. But the art museum was my personal favorite. The paintings in the museum were being restored. There were no guards, very unusual, and we were able to get up very close to the paintings. Barbara, our traveling artist, pointed out that they stretched the old canvas over a new canvas. This gave a firm backing in the places that were beginning to disintegrate and enabled the artists to repair the damage. Frank and I of course didn't believe her until we got up close enough to touch the paintings with our noses. She was right.

The second town, Santa Cesarea, was where we were camping. It must have been an ancient Greek and later Roman bathing place right on the sea. There are ruins of swimming pools and bath houses all along the shore. We spent a couple of hours climbing over and exploring everything, accompanied by a local dog who kept jumping into the water and amazing all the bathers with his swimming stunts. The weather was warm, and it was a glorious day.

Back at the camp, after our usual Thursday night linguini with clam sauce, Frank stepped out into the dark to go to the bathroom. He started bitching about needing a flashlight because all the lights had been turned off. Barbara was scrambling to find one in a hurry just to shut him up. Suddenly the tirade stopped, and a sheepish Frank stuck his head back inside the camper. He admitted that he had been facing the wrong way. The lights were not out at all. When we had come back from the day's excursions, he had parked the camper in the opposite direction. Of course, he blamed it all on me!

WEEKLY BUDGET #7
  LODGING
Camp Apartment (4) $143.00
Camps (3)   58.00

FOOD
Restaurants
Lunches (1)   11.50
Dinners (1)   35.00
Snacks & drinks   6.50
Groceries (19 meals)   64.00

ENTERTAINMENT
Otranto museum   3.50

  CAR
Camper payment   168.00
Gas   124.00
Road tolls   7.00

TRANSPORTATION
Bus to Palermo & back   9.00

INCIDENTALS
Postage   10.00
                           $639.50

WEEKLY BUDGET #7

FRI.	$ 92.00
Sat.	111.00
Sun.	78.00
Mon.	97.50
Tues.	75.50
Wed.	129.50
Thurs.	56.00
	$ 639.50

$639.50 divided by 7 days = $91.35 per day. $91.35 divided by 3 people = $30.45 per person, per day.

SPICY ITALIAN TOMATO CLAM SAUCE

BROWN IN SMALL POT:
1/4 cup olive oil
3 cloves chopped garlic

ADD:
1 large can tomato sauce or chopped canned tomatoes (28 oz.)
1/2 cup water or wine
1 teaspoon sweet basil
1/2 teaspoon oregano
1/2 teaspoon hot red pepper
1/2 teaspoon salt

Cook at simmer for 1/2 hour. Turn gas off and

ADD:
1 can whole or chopped clams with juice
1/2 cup finely chopped fresh parsley

STIR UNTIL HEATED AND SERVE:
over one pound of cooked linguini. Serves three or four.

Week 8 Santa Cesarea Terme
to
Lake Trasimeno

Venice

Lake
Trasimeno

Ancona
Civitanova
San Elpidio
San Benedetto

Roma

Bari

Monopoli
Brindisi
Lucca
Gallipoli   Santa Cesarea
San   Terme
Giovanni
Leuca

Week Number Eight May 22 Through May 28, 1998

FRI. MAY 22 MARINA SAN GIOVANNI, ITALY

This morning we drove along the east coast of the heel of the boot of Italy to Cabo Santa Maria di Leuca. This is the most southern point of the heel. From the shore, if you look to the northeast, you will see the Adriatic Sea. If you look to the north west, you will see the Golfo di Taranto. In either direction, the view will be more than magnificent.

Stopped in the town of Leuca to walk around and see all the different architectural styles of the homes. The local gentry are evidently famous for building unusual architectural designs. This was quite a feat because it is not a very big town. Nevertheless, some of the houses are very unique. While there, we went to a nearby grocery store and asked the owner if he had any local wine. Our book said that the wine was quite good in this region. He had homemade wine and olive oil. When I asked him if it was any good, he put his index finger to his cheek and twisted it back and forth, saying Buono. We have seen this expression often in Italy and, since he thought his wine was so good, we decided to give it a try. Bad move! The olive oil was good but the wine made Frank sick with a case of the runs. Barbara and I wouldn't even try it, but Frank will drink anything.

From Leuca we drove up the west side of the heel to Gallipoli. It was so immense and intimidating that we drove right through it. Couldn't find a camp, so we went to the Hotel Torre di San Giovanni. After some dickering, we got two rooms with baths and breakfast for about $90. Not within our budget, but we were satisfied. Looking at the pictures on the walls of the reception room a while later, I realized this place was some kind of sanatorium with thermal baths, frequented by many movie stars. Liz Taylor and Sofia Loren were represented as well as others I can't remember. Again, it was not the season yet, and there were only a few other guests. We did not run into any famous notables.

*San Giovanni: Hotel Torre or possible Hotel Marina San Giovanni. (Sometimes my notes are not too good) Direction: On the Gulf, between Leuca and Gallipoli.

SAT. MAY 23 MONOPOLI, ITALY

Yesterday I had to bargain with the manager quite a bit to get breakfast thrown in with the price of the hotel. Today he got even. Breakfast was melba toast and coffee, not even a pad of butter! We drove across the heel of the boot from Gallipoli to Lecce, and then on past Brindisi part way to Bari. The scenery was not very interesting until we got back to the east coast. Once again we were on the Adriatic Sea.

It was still morning and we found a camp right away. This one had its bathrooms underground. Each camping plot was assigned a private bathroom, and we were given our own key. It was actually very nice but completely unnecessary, as we were the only campers. We put up our patio furniture, to insure our location from the multitudes, and set off to see an archaeological dig and the famous conical homes of the area.

The Roman ruins at Egnazia were not nearly as interesting as the ones we had seen in Sicily, but the museum was nice The senior citizens, Barbara and Frank, got in free. Afterwards, we set out for Fasano: the Selva, on top of a hair raising mountain. It was evident that there was a Grand Prix planned for the next day. I couldn't even imagine navigating that winding, tenuous road any faster than our old VW would go. It was scary doing 20 and 30 miles per hour. The view from the mountain top was breathtaking, literally. The conical houses, called "trulli", were quite interesting, and since we had everything we owned with us, including the camera, we were able to get some pictures. Frank still wasn't feeling great after indulging in bad wine, so we came back to camp took naps, read and played Solitaire. I was getting better, once in a while I could even win without cheating!

   *Monopoli (Bari): Camping San Stefano. Direction: 3 km. south of village. Tele: 0 80/77 70 65

SUN. MAY 24 CIVITANOVA, ITALY

Did another marathon drive today. It took us nine hours to get from Monopoli to Civitanova. We wanted to stay four nights in one place, so instead of wasting one on the way, we drove like maniacs. Every time we do this, we kick ourselves and say never again! We stopped to see San Benedetto del Tronto on the way. The family of our neighbor in Lakeport came from this city on the sea, and we wanted to check it our for her. It was very nice. Had coffee, took pictures and went on.

In the camping book, we found a camp in Civitanova that claimed to have cabins and to take Visa, a very desirable combination. We had a great deal of trouble finding it. Stopped for directions at a local bar and a helpful young man tried to explain the location to us in Italian. When that didn't work, he grabbed Barbara's hand and led her outside to his motorcycle.

He hopped on and indicated that we should follow him with the car. We did, and taking our lives in our hands, zipped through the city behind him. He got us there in about ten minutes through a very circuitous route. We thanked him profusely. We would never have found it without his help.

Upon arrival, we inspected the bungalows and decided that the area inside our VW camper was considerably larger. It was far too late to look for anything else, so we camped. It poured! It got cold again! We were tired and grouchy! We promised each other once more that we would never drive more than 200 km in a day. Barbara made our Sunday pasta with meat sauce, and we were consoled. In spite of what the camping book said, they wouldn't take Visa!

*Civitanova Marche: Camping le nuove Giare. Direction: SS16 exit Civitanova, 200 m from the sea. (Lies, all lies) Tele: 07 33/7 04 40.

MON. MAY 25 SAN ELPIDIO, ITALY

In the morning, we set out for another camp just south of Civitanova. The book said this one had cabins, too. We had passed close to it yesterday, but since they didn't take Visa, we had gone on. We never seem to learn. The railroad tracks go along the beach here. In order to get to the campground, you must drive through a tunnel that goes under the railroad tracks. There were tunnels every mile or so, but each one was smaller than the next. There was only one large enough to accommodate our VW. None were large enough for a real camper. In my opinion, this was not a very logical place to put a campground. We had very little hope for San Elpidio as we pulled up. Surprisingly enough, they had very nice little two bedroom bungalows, and miracle of miracles, they had washing machines. We took it for three nights instead of the four we had previously planned.

This was the first place in Italy that we had found working washing machines Dryers were still unknown, futuristic devices that were nonexistent in Italy. It rained the entire day. We settled in and started doing laundry. Frank rigged up a clothes line that was mostly underneath the porch. One of the washing machines kept going for more than two hours. Finally it stopped. I opened the door and was instantly drenched. The water had never gone out. I put the rest of the clothes in the other washer, and it was still going when I was ready for bed. Decided to just let it go. In the morning, when I came to retrieve the clothes, it was still going. This time, I opened the door with great caution, and jumped quickly out of the way when it flooded. There didn't seem to be soap left in the clothes, so I just squeezed out as much water as possible and hung them on the line back at the house. It would take all three days for these clothes to dry.

*Porto Sant' Elpidio: Camping La Risacca. Direction: at the beach.

TUES. MAY 26 SAN ELPIDIO, ITALY

Walked to town for groceries this morning. It was cold and overcast, but at least it wasn't raining. Went to the ATM to get money, and decided not to fret anymore about campgrounds that take Visa. It was much easier to get the money from the ATM and it really didn't cost any more.

In the afternoon we walked a couple of miles down the beach looking for sea shells and rocks. Came to what looked like an abandoned house where we saw five rather unkempt looking men lurking about. Decided this must be where the homeless stay. This was purely conjecture on our parts because we hadn't seen homeless people anywhere else in Italy. They didn't seem to have the problem we have.

WED. MAY 27 SAN ELPIDIO, ITALY

I had a kid in my class a few years ago named Elpidio. I was very fond of him and his sister Diana, who was in my class just recently. But I was not enamored with the town of San Elpidio. The area is rather flat and uninteresting for a sea shore.

Went in the car to a little town on top of a mountain, Torre di Palme. Great view of the ocean and surrounding hills. The town was very nicely restored. Spent the day wandering around enjoying the views and the town itself. Very few of the restorations we had seen were this well done. We took a picnic lunch with us and enjoyed the day very much.

Later, we met an old man cleaning up outside a church in Torre di Palme and chatted with him for a while. He spoke no English, so it was a challenging conversation. When he found out we were from California, he wanted to know if we had a Mexican coin that he could give to his grandson. We had none, but offered him American coins. He insisted we only give him one of little value because he didn't want us to waste our money. We left him with his treasure, grinning from ear to ear.

Had dinner at the camp restaurant. The manager's wife cooked. It was one of the best meals we had had in Italy, not counting Barbara's or our cousins'. That woman could really cook. Even Barbara liked it!

THURS. MAY 28 LAKE TRANSIMENO, ITALY

Drove through a lovely area of Umbria this morning to the Frasassi Caves. The caves, set inside a beautiful mountain, were the best I have ever seen, and I've seen caves all over the world. These were bigger and more impressive than Carlsbad Caverns or the Oregon Caves. There was a guided tour in Italian and we kept lagging behind because the three of us hate crowds. The guide asked us to keep up and I told her we couldn't understand what she was saying. She made one of the Italian tourists get behind us to make sure we stayed with her. This pissed off Barbara and Frank. They particularly resent being told what to do because they are old and ornery. I chatted with the man so he wouldn't get any madder than he already was at the imposition put upon him, as well as at the stupid Americans. Chatting, however, is difficult when you don't know the language. When we finally got to the end, I heard him tell the guide that we were crazy Americans. Putting her hands up, shrugging her shoulders and muttering "Uha!", she accepted this as if it accounted for everything.

After lunch in the camper, we drove on to Lake Transimeno. One of the books we brought with us was Frances Mays' *Under the Tuscan Sun*, and this is the lake near her home in Tuscany. The camp was nice, and we felt very much at home being on a lake again.

*Passignano sul Trasimeno (Perugia): Camping Europa. Directions: Directly at the lake. Tele: 0 75/82 83 05

ITIMIZED WEEKLY BUDGET #8

LODGING

Hotels (1)	$ 93.00
Camp apartments (3)	174.00
Camps (3)	57.50

FOOD

Restaurants	
Dinners (2)	74.00
Groceries (19 meals)	128.00

ENTERTAINMENT

Cafes & Bars	23.00
Museum	2.50
Cave Entrances	25.50

CAMPER

Camper payment	168.00
Gas	146.00
Road Tolls	17.00

INCIDENTALS

Tips for Bags	4.00
Newspaper	1.50
	$914.00

WEEKLY BUDGET #8

Fri.	$229.00
Sat.	81.00
Sun.	163.00
Mon.	96.00
Tues.	101.00
Wed.	171.00
Thurs.	73.00
	$914.00

$914 divided by 7 days = $130.57. $130.57 divided by 3 people = $43.52 per person, per day.

Week 9   Lake Trasimeno to Florence

Week Number Nine May 29 Through June 4, 1998

FRI. MAY 29: FLORENCE, ITALY

On the way to Florence, we drove to Cortona, where Frances Mays the author of *Under The Tuscan Sun* has her house. She lives on a mountain overlooking the whole valley and part of Lake Transimeno. There is a switchback road going up and the view would have been quite spectacular had it not been for the smog.

Drove on to Florence, and after looking at three camps in the surrounding areas, we came to Certosa. Here there were a number of brand new bungalows, newly made in Holland. This was amazing. When we were in Holland, we found only one room bungalows with no amenities. The ones they exported to Italy were by far superior. Certosa has the same prices year round. There is no off season in Florence. The bungalow, which had two bedrooms, a bathroom and a very nice kitchen, cost $64 a night. The camp was on a bus line directly to downtown, about two blocks from the Duomo. We had to walk about a half mile to the bus, but it was less than a half hour ride.

To stay in a hotel in downtown Florence would cost anywhere from $200 to $300 a night, for not much more than a "Comfort Inn" type of accommodation. A pension would cost about $150. These Italian bungalows are the best kept secret in Italy. Eating out is fun, and I love to do it, but three meals a day, seven days a week can get old very fast, not to mention expensive. Of course, if you are only staying a short time or you are on a tour it's probably preferable, but for the people doing it on their own for a longer period of time, bungalows are absolutely the best deal in Italy.

The Certosa campground had washing machines, a bar and restaurant and a big, above ground, large, plastic type swimming pool. It had warmed up considerably and we all took a dip in the afternoon. We could visit our relatives from here, so we decided to stay nine nights. We had all been to Florence before, but we agreed before starting the trip that we would like to see the city again. Unlike Rome, Florence is a small town inside of a big city. It is also a city that one can visit again and again, and it is always a moving experience.

In the evening we called our cousins. The manager in the camp spoke English fluently, as did almost everyone in Florence, and he spoke to our cousin, Nicola, in Italian for us. We'll go for the big family dinner on Sunday.

*Firenze-Certosa (Florence): Camping Internazionale Firenze. Direction: Exit Florence-Certosa, direction Florence 1 km, signposted. Tele: 0 55/2 37 47 04

SAT. MAY 30 FLORENCE, ITALY

Took the bus to the city this morning. Heard nothing but English on the streets. With very few exceptions, like in Capri, this was the first time we had heard English from any other people besides ourselves since we got to Italy. It was very disconcerting to walk down the street and understand other people's conversations.

After twenty eight years, Florence was still beautiful, though a little worn around the edges. The Duomo was being cleaned and it was truly glorious under all that black grime. Decided they should allow nothing but bicycles, horses and walkers inside the old city. The pollution from the cars was horrible. We saw all the usual tourist attractions and went home on the bus exhausted but exhilarated. Took another swim. It stayed light until after ten P.M.

SUN. MAY 31 FLORENCE, ITALY

We drove to Livorno (Leghorn to the English speaking) to visit our relations. After the Second World War, my parents and other assorted New York relatives used to send care packages to these people. Life was very hard in Italy after World War II.

It is said that everyone has a twin somewhere in the world. I was in my twenties when I visited Italy the first time, with my cousin Patti. When my mother's cousin, Felicia, opened the door, Patti and I just stood there with our mouths opened. She looked so much like my mother that we felt like we were seeing a ghost. My mother had passed away when I was seventeen. Felicia not only looked like my mother, she had all her mannerisms and a very similar personality. She didn't know we were coming and we hadn't phoned because we couldn't speak Italian. Nevertheless, she welcomed us with opened arms. She fed us, pampered us and made us feel like we were newly found daughters. She even had baby pictures of my brothers and myself. Her husband Vladamiro, who sang like Mario Lanza, entertained us with familiar arias from all the operas. He did this on the road while taking us sight seeing in his little VW bug. It was so beat up, like most Italian cars, that he had to tie the doors shut with a rope. Like my mother, Felicia died all too young, in her early fifties, and Vladamiro followed soon after with a broken heart.

On this visit, we were going to see Felicia's brother, Nicola, and sister, Maria. We would also see Felicia's son Roberto, who is now a lawyer, and assorted young adult cousins, who had all been children when we last saw them. These people were related to us on both sides of the family, their father, on my mother's side, and their mother on my father's side. So we were double cousins. From the way we were greeted, you would never have known so many years had elapsed since we had last seen each other. Our cousin Nicola (Lino) and his wife Rosseta hosted the dinner with their daughter Lucia, her husband and two children. Lucia spoke quite a bit of English, as it is taught in the schools here now. At first, she was very hesitant, but as the day wore on, she became quite fluent.

Near the end of the unbelievably delicious six course six hour meal, Roberto, Felicia and Vladamiro's son, came for coffee with his wife and two children. He had been about sixteen when we had last seen him. We were told that Roberto was now an avocado. With the green fruit in mind, it took us a while to realize that it was avocato or advocate which means lawyer.

When we were here before, Roberto had been recovering from a medical problem that left him with a withered arm and leg on one side of his body. We could not understand what had happened to him, at that time. Now he could tell us himself, in English. He was one of the one in a million children that got polio from the polio vaccine. It was such a tragedy. However, he overcame both the adversity of infantile paralysis and being orphaned as a teenager to go on and make a good life for himself. The rest of the family, his aunts, uncles and cousins, were visibly proud of him, and didn't hesitate to tell us how smart he was. Roberto promised that when his two little boys were older, he would come and visit us in America.

About this time, Julio the son of the house came home. He had been a rather homely child, but he was now a tall, good looking young stud of about thirty four. He was single and he liked to travel, unlike his parents Lino and Rosseta, who thought a two hour drive was the end of the world. Julio also said he would come to visit us.

Next to show up was Maria, Lino's sister and her husband Cesarea (Chez-a-ray). None of these people came until after dinner as Lino and Rosseta's apartment was not very big. Maria, who is my age, was quite subdued as a middle aged woman. The last time I had seen her, she had held her hands far apart and asked me, "El senori di America?" Evidently American men had a reputation in Italy regarding their genitalia. She was quite a character in her youth. She insisted that we come to her house for dinner next. We promised to come back the next Sunday, on our way to visit Lino and Maria's older brother Ciro (Cheer-o), who lived on the nearby island of Elba.

While speaking to all of our cousins of the past and our mutual relatives, we discovered that this family, as well as my maternal grandfather, was not originally from Ischia. They did indeed come from Castello Mare, but in Naples, not Ischia. They had moved to Ischia, my grandfather included, when Nicola and Maria were toddlers. This revelation was recorded into the genealogy chart I had brought with me from California. Frank and I were delighted that we weren't really cousins after all. The confusion came from the fact that one of my father's aunts had married one of my mother's uncles, and one of my mother's aunts had married one of my father's uncles. Hence, there are Di Maio's and De Mayo's on both sides of the family. It was no wonder that we were all slightly crazy!

MON. JUNE 1 FLORENCE, ITALY

While we were in Tuscany, we wanted to see some of the interesting little towns that all the books spoke of so lovingly. Arezzo was today's destination. All of us were disappointed. It wasn't nearly as nice as the little towns on the heel of the boot. It was a walled city, but it was like a hundred other little walled cities in Italy.

TUES. JUNE 2 FLORENCE, ITALY

Took the bus back into Florence this morning. Spent most of the day in the Pitti Palace. We all like art museums, but Frank got tired of all the religious art. He spent a good portion of his time watching the police chase off the venders in the courtyard. The vendors were from all over the world and sold their wares without a license. They would spread a cloth on the ground, set out their goods, and they were in business. Each time they were run off, they had to return and set up the whole store again. For this reason they couldn't display more than they could run with and carry. While Frank was looking out the windows from above in the Palace, he saw this happen at least four times. These people got a lot of exercise.

We all wanted to see Michelangelo's David again, so after a leisurely lunch, we walked to the Galleria dell' Accademia, which houses David and a number of Michelangelo's unfinished works. The line went around the block and it was all in the sun. Decided that nothing was worth standing in the sweltering sun for two hours, and found a little sidewalk cafe. After a cool drink, Barbara and I did a little shopping while Frank sipped his beer and people watched. About 5 o'clock we started back to the bus. Had to pass the line for David on the way. It was much shorter and the sun was much less intense, so we got in line. We still had to wait for almost an hour. The line was made up almost exclusively of English speaking people, so we chatted about world news and things to do in Florence. None of these people had ever heard of bungalows in campgrounds. David, as always, was magnificent and well worth the wait.

When we got off the bus and started walking to the campground, a guy from New Zealand, whom we had met in the David line, passed us in his car, honking and waving. He had been staying in the Certosa area too. He parked his car and ran back a half a kilometer to catch up with us. He wanted to know how to find bungalows in Sicily. We told him we had an international camping book that listed which campgrounds had bungalows, and since he didn't have the book he should go to any Tourist Information office and ask for a list of campgrounds in Sicily. If that didn't work, he should just ask for bungalows in each campground. Many of them had cabins. He thanked us profusely and ran back to his car.

WED. JUNE 3 FLORENCE, ITALY

This morning we drove off to see the Chianti area. This was the area, according to Frank, from which the only good Italian wine came. He didn't like most of the wine in Italy. Both he and Barbara found French wine far superior. I know nothing about wine. I'd much rather have ice cream. Drove first to the small town of Greve where we intended to do a 2 kilometer hike to the castle in the next town. It was hotter than hell and all uphill on a mountain road, so we scratched that idea. We were learning from our mistakes. Went to the triangular piazza for which Greve is famous, shopped and leisurely meandered around. Back in the camper, we found a shady place for lunch and a nap. Unfortunately, every trucker in Italy thought it was nice too. It was far from restful.

In the afternoon, we drove through the beautiful Chianti countryside to San Gimignano. This is a famous 13th century city within the walls of a medieval castle. It was never bombed in the war and due to its location was not weathered by sea air, so it is extremely well preserved. In fact it is remarkably beautiful. However, the masses of humanity, in the form of tourists, made all of us feel like we were spending a day in the castle at Disneyland.

All through the Chianti area the smog was oppressive. Chianti reminded me very much of the Napa Valley, near Clear Lake in California. The evenly spaced grapevines, nestled in the rolling hills, were very much like Napa. It seemed larger and more serpentine than Napa and it probably was even more beautiful, but in Napa, when you look up, the sky is almost always amazingly blue, just like in Clear Lake, which claims to have the cleanest air in America. In Chianti, when you look up, you see nothing but smog. It is worse than Los Angeles. If they could clean up the smog in Chianti, it would far surpass Napa and Clear Lake, it is that magnificent! What a tragedy!

THURS. JUNE 4 FLORENCE, ITALY

Still in the bungalow in the campground. There were about 12 or 15 bungalows and they were all empty save ours, but the city was packed with people. I would guess that they were all paying $200 a night or more. What a shame that no one knew.

Went back to Florence today and saw the Galleria degli Uffizi, more religious paintings. Nevertheless, some of them are truly fabulous. I couldn't help thinking of Mark Twain and his belittlement of famous works of art in his book *Innocents Abroad*:

"We wandered through the endless collections of paintings and statues of the Pitti and Uffizi galleries, of course. I make that statement in self-defense; there let it stop. I could not rest under the imputation that I visited Florence and did not traverse its weary miles of picture-galleries."

I think Frank and Twain had a lot in common, and after a few hours, I could understand how they felt.

Had lunch out, window shopped on the Ponte Vecchio where only the very affluent can afford to buy, and generally enjoyed the rest of the day. Returned to camp in late afternoon and went swimming.

ITIMIZED WEEKLY BUDGET # 9 MAY 29—JUNE 4

LODGING

Camp apartments (7)	$448.00

FOOD

Restaurants:

Lunches (2)	51.50
Groceries (18 meals)	99.00
(one meal at relative's)	

ENTERTAINMENT

Cafes & Bars	51.00
Museums	80.50

CAMPER

Camper Payment	168.00
Gas	139.50
Parking	1.00
Road Tolls	22.50

TRANSPORTATION

Busses	14.50

INCIDENTALS

Phone Card	3.00
Gifts Candy & Wine	
(for Relatives)	28.00
Gifts for visits to Come	39.00
Laundry	21.00
USA Today (Newspaper)	2.00
	$1168.50

WEEKLY BUDGET #9
Fri.	$159.50
Sat.	174.50
Sun.	139.00
Mon.	162.50
Tues.	179.00
Wed.	165.00
Thurs.	189.00
	$1168.50

$1168.50 divided by 7 days = $166.92. $166.92 divided by 3 people = $55.64 per day, per person.

Week 10   Florence and Surrounding Areas

Livorno
Vada
Piombino
Elba
Florence
Sienna
Ancona
Roma
Napoli

WEEK NUMBER TEN JUNE 5 THROUGH JUNE 11, 1998

FRI. JUNE 5 FLORENCE, ITALY

Drove to Sienna this morning. The drives in this area are lovely but again, very smoggy. I loved the main square in Sienna. It is shaped like a scallop shell. The old city is well preserved and a pleasant place to stroll around. Enjoyed the day immensely.

SAT. JUNE 6 FLORENCE, ITALY

Took the day off today to catch up with cleaning the car, laundry, and reading. We also wanted to go swimming and just lounge around. In the evening, we walked into town for a delicious Tuscan dinner. Northern Italian food is very different from the Southern Italian that we were used to. Tomorrow we will go to Cousin Maria's for another all day meal. We still haven't found out much about our family history because Lino and Maria know very little, other than where they were born. They both said Ciro would know because he is the oldest. We will find out if this is true on Tuesday when we see him.

SUN. JUNE 7 VADA, ITALY

Drove back to Livorno and immediately got lost. We were supposed to go to the same Shell station from where we called Lino last week, but we couldn't find it. Tried to call Maria but no one answered. I called Lino, hoping he could help us, but Rossetta answered and started yelling at me in order to help me understand Italian. I understood nothing. I waited while she went to get a slightly English speaking neighbor to talk to me. Meanwhile, Lino got on the phone. I interpreted what he said to be something like, Maria is in the hospital. The neighbor woman arrived and told me that Lino would come to pick us up. I asked about Maria being in the hospital, but neither of us understood the other.

Lino arrived and I rode with him while Barbara and Frank followed in the camper. As we were passing the hospital, he said, "Maria." I was getting very upset because I pictured her as having been in a terrible accident or needing emergency surgery. It turned out that, as we were passing the hospital, we were also passing the Shell station from where we were supposed to have called Maria. Maria, who was very excited about us coming to see her, didn't wait for the phone call. Instead, she went to the Shell station to wait. In Italian, the word for wait and the word for hospital sound almost identical to the untrained ear. Back at the house, when Maria and Ceasera's daughter Anna explained all this to us in English, we all had a good laugh.

Anna took us on a tour of the house her father's family had lived in for well over a hundred years. The upstairs apartment was occupied by Anna, her husband and their little boy, who was about three or four and hell on wheels. They were in the process of remodeling the whole floor. The downstairs apartment was occupied by Maria and Ceasera. It was a nice comfortable home for all of them. Evidently people in Italy buy their homes or apartments and live in them for generations without thought of change. Roberto was still living in the apartment his parents had occupied when I had visited them thirty years before. The only ones who had moved were Lino and Rossetta. They had downsized when the kids left home.

The six hour dinner Maria made for us was all fish, starting with antipasti di mare, spaghetti di mare, pan fried pesci di mare, insalat di mare, etc. The fish consisted of every eatable sea animal known to mankind, and many that I would never have considered to be eatable. I am not a big fish eater, but I did my best. The suction cups on the octopus nearly did me in. I just closed my eyes and swallowed. Things that I absolutely couldn't deal with, I surreptitiously slipped onto Frank's plate when no one was looking. Frank will eat anything that comes out of the sea and bless him, he cleaned his plate. After dinner, the whole extended family showed up again for dessert and coffee. No, it wasn't fish, just fish shaped cake. They had all come to say good-by. We didn't find out any more about the family heritage. We had brought our genealogy papers with us, but no one wanted to look at them. They just told us to ask Ciro. We figured out afterwards that none of older people could see the papers. No one seemed to wear glasses, and by the time you hit fifty, you really need them to read.

We took our leave about six P.M. and started driving down the coast. We had driven along this coast two months ago when we first got to Italy. We hadn't stop to see the relatives at that time because we had been in such a hurry to get to Ischia and warm weather. Since it was so late, we decided to go to the nearest camp on the sea. We wound up in Vada just south of Livorno at a place very aptly called Three Fishes. Our camping plot was right on the ocean. The camp was quite respectable and clean. Took a nice long walk on the beach. I contemplated letting all the fish inside me visit the waters of their birth, but kept telling myself that fish was brain food and I needed to keep it in me.

*Vada (Livorno): Camping Tripesce (Three Fishes). Directions: At the sea bank. Tele: 05 86/78 80 17.

MON. JUNE 8 ELBA (ISLAND), ITALY

Drove from Vada to Piombino and took the ferry to Elba. Once again we didn't have to wait at all. On the island, we drove to four different camps looking for bungalows. We were going to be here for four nights and didn't really want to camp, but summer had arrived and Elba is always very popular. By the time we got to the forth place, which the book said had no bungalows, we had decided we would have to camp. The woman in charge spoke fluent English, as well as a few other languages. We told her we really wanted an apartment, but since she didn't have any, we would take a campsite. She looked at us with a puzzled expression and said, "But we have apartments." The book did not say there were bungalows because there weren't any bungalows. What they had was a large duplex and one side was available for the next four nights. It was an old Mediterranean style building with great tiles and lots of ambiance. There was one bedroom a kitchen and a bath. The kitchen had a bed in it for me. It was just a short walk to the beach. There were cute little donkeys on the property as well as cats and a multitude of birds. It was also only a few miles from Cousin Ciro's place in Portoferraio. What more could we ask?

Called Ciro from the camp phone. He had spent quite a bit of time in the states when he was young because he had been a sailor on the merchant ships. He never came to California, but he visited our New York relatives quite often and he spoke a lot of English. We had never met him before because none of us ever had time to go to Elba on our previous trips to Italy, though we were always invited and encouraged to do so. We were excited about meeting each other. We all felt like we'd known each other for years. He told me his daughter Gina would take a day off of work the next day to show us around. I protested, saying we would be fine on our own. He agreed to this reluctantly, and said he would pick us up for dinner the next evening when Gina got off of work.

*Portoferraio-Acquaviva (Livorno). Camping Acquaviva. Direction: From Portoferraio 3 km direction Enfola, signposted. Tele: 05 65/93 06 74.

TUES. JUNE 9 ELBA, ITALY

Awakened this morning by the glorious sound of singing birds, followed by an incredibly noisy garbage truck. Went on a hike because it suddenly got too cold to swim. This island was even more beautiful than Ischia and I didn't think that was possible. The vegetation was very lush and almost tropical. Elba is the island where Napoleon was exiled. He actually didn't spend much time here though, foolish man. Like us, he probably had a lot to do and many more places to see.

At five o'clock, Gina pulled up in her car with her father sitting next to her. Ciro had had a stroke two years before and his arm and leg on one side were very weak. He moved very much like his nephew Roberto, who had been stricken with polio. We decided to follow them in the camper so they wouldn't have to come back in the dark.

The first thing I did when we got in the house was to give Ciro a kiss on both cheeks from his brother Lino. They live only about two hours from each other, but in Italy that seems to be a long journey. Ciro and his wife Adua had a beautiful apartment. His life work was making riggings on the old fashioned ships. Even as a seaman, this had been part of his job. It was all done by hand. The man was a true artist. Ciro had a framed macrame on the wall that had samples of all the different kinds of riggings he had made. Their home too was decorated with beautifully crafted furnishings of unusual types of wood. The sliding glass doors between the living room and dining room had beveled glass in each pane, surrounded by heavy wooden lattices. The effect was elegant.

Ciro may have been an artist of ropes and woods, but Adua was an artist in the kitchen. The dinner she made will live in my memory forever. That woman could really cook. It was night time so we only ate for about four hours, but every mouthful was unforgettable. We had the usual six courses with pasta, vegetables and meats, all cooked with succulent and unusual flavors. It wasn't what was made that was so unusual. It was how it had been prepared. Adua served a chicken dish after the pasta and gave me a huge helping. I put half of it back because I knew I wouldn't be able to eat it all. As I did so, Ciro looked at me and said, "You'll be sorry!" When the first bite hit my tongue, I knew instantly what he had meant. It just melted in my mouth. If there hadn't been so much other food, I definitely would have had seconds. We ate until we were ready to burst.

Gina and her husband Piero, who arrived just before dinner, both spoke fluent English, as did Gina's brother, Stefano. Stefano came home just long enough to meet us and have a little dinner. He was a young man with a date.

He was very personable and said he would like to come to visit us in California. He also said he had a small business on the other side of the island. He rented out jet skis and boats to tourists. Through the course of the evening, we found out that Gina and Piero used to manage the camp at Aquaviva where we were staying.

One thing that was very evident in Italian families was their affection for one another. They kissed on both cheeks, hugged and touched without the slightest provocation, and were genuinely delighted with each other's company. The children and parents were this way with each other even when the children were grown up. In this family it was even more conspicuous than with their cousins. I had never really been into touchy relationships with my relatives. A kiss hello and good-by had been about the extent of my sensitivities, but while watching Gina and Stefano interact with everyone else, including us, I had the sudden feeling of missing out on something very important in life.

When the family found out we would still be here tomorrow, they insisted we come back for dinner the following evening. We all inwardly groaned thinking of the twenty pounds we were sure to put on our already overstuffed bodies, but none of us was strong enough to say no to all this ambiance, culinary ecstasy and genuine affection. Ciro promised he would help me with the genealogy papers if we came about an hour early. We had done nothing that night except get to know each other and have a wonderful time.

WED. JUNE 10 ELBA, ITALY

Today we went to Marina di Campo on the other side of the island. This was where Stefano worked, but we couldn't find him. Marina di Campo is a quaint little town with an open air market that sells anything any tourist anywhere might need. The day was lovely and warm. We rented an umbrella, swam in the water and read on the beach for about three hours. The water was very shallow for a long way out. It was also so clear that I could see the bottom at all times.

Went again to Ciro and Adua's for dinner. We sat with Ciro in the kitchen while Adua cooked. We drank aperitifs and spoke of family. He knew many of our cousins in New York, but had lost track of them through the years. I wrote down the names and addresses of three different cousins in three states and left them with him. I told him I would send the rest when I got home. I didn't want to leave him with out any contacts. We still had a long trip ahead of us, and who knew if we would ever get home again.

Ciro really didn't know much more than his brother and sister about past family life. He agreed they had moved to Ischia from Castella Mare in Naples. He seemed to be pretty sure that my Grandfather Vito, who was Ciro's uncle, had moved with them. Vito had lived on Ischia until he was in his middle twenties. At that time he got a job on a ship that was going to America. When he arrived in New York, he jumped ship. I already knew the part about him jumping ship from my Aunt Tosca, who was Vito's youngest child and the same age as my brother Frank. What I didn't know for sure was where he was born. This information confirmed that he was not born on Ischia.

We filled out all the genealogy papers together, with the names of all the parents, grandparents and children in his family. Since we are related on both sides of the family, Ciro's mother being a Di Maio, I thought we could get information on both sides of my family. Unfortunately, Ciro only slightly remembered any of his grandparents. Even the present generation was confusing because all the kids have the same first names as their parents and grandparents. Each generation has a Ciro, Felicia, Anna, Maria and Nicola (Lino). Ciro did tell us though that his older sister Anna had been killed as a child during the second world war when the Americans bombed Naples.

When we were ready to go, Ciro gave us the framed macrame from the wall in his house as a momento. We were all very touched. We bid farewell to these wonderful people. Gena and Piero promised to come and visit us in the near future, so we did expect to see them again. We drove back to our camping apartment with each of us feeling the same warm glow of contentment and well being inside.

THURS. JUNE 11 FLORENCE, ITALY

Had to wait two hours for the ferry back to the mainland this morning. This was the first time we had ever waited for a ferry. We checked out the town of Portoferraio and did a little shopping. The summer had really arrived. The prices were up and it was crowded everywhere.

I was feeling very melancholy about leaving Elba. I would feel even worse when we left Italy for good in a few more days. Barbara and Frank seemed to feel the same way. We had so enjoyed Italy and the Italian people, from the border of France to the tip of Sicily and back up to the border of Austria where we would be soon. The first three times I was in Italy, I really didn't like it. The traffic was horrendous, this is still true, the crowds were suffocating, and the men were obnoxious. I think the main problem was that I only visited the touristy parts and I always went in the summer. The best parts of Italy are the out of the way places where most tourists don't go. The best time to go there is spring or fall. The men in Italy seem to have advanced a lot too. Before, they went after any woman not accompanied by a man. It didn't seem to matter if she was sixteen or sixty. They grabbed! They pinched! And they rubbed! I was literally forced to belt a few of them while screaming the few choice Italian swear words I knew, and even that was not enough of a deterrent. This time I didn't even see them bothering the single young women. I did see a number of buff young men with "STUD" written across their hairy chests, but even they seemed to keep their hands to themselves. Of course I only saw them for a few moments in time!

We drove again to the camp at Certosa in Florence. This time we didn't take a bungalow because it was only for one night. We camped and of course it rained, but we were still feeling pretty mellow.

ITEMIZED WEEKLY BUDGET #10
LODGING

Camp Apartments (5)	$320.00
Camps (2)	59.00

FOOD
Restaurants

Dinners (1)	40.50
3 at Relatives	
Groceries (17 meals)	98.50

ENTERTAINMENT

Cafes & Bars	16.50
Umbrella on Beach	4.00

CAMPER

Camper Payment	168.00
Camper Needs	6.00
Gas	93.50
Road Tolls	1.00
Parking	1.50

TRANSPORTATION

Ferry to Elba	42.00
Ferry Back	42.00

INCIDENTALS

Stove Lighter (didn't work)	5.00
Map of Elba	1.00
Postage	1.50
Newspaper	1.50
	$901.50

WEEKLY BUDGET #10

Fri.	$98.50
Sat.	132.50
Sun.	51.00
Mon.	243.50
Tues.	95.00
Wed.	131.00
Thurs.	150.00
	$901.50

$901.50 divided by 7 days = $128.78 per day. $128.78 divided by 3 people = $42.92 per person, per day.

PORK CHOPS A LA BARBARA

BROWN IN FRYING PAN
3 pork chops
1 onion, chopped
3 cloves of garlic, chopped

ADD
1/2 cup white wine
1/2 teaspoon paprika

SIMMER FOR 1/2 HOUR. TAKE OUT 1/4 CUP OF LIQUID AND ADD IT TO 1/4 CUP
YOGURT. MIX (Add a little water if too thick). POUR BACK INTO PAN AND MIX AGAIN.

ADD
1/2 cup of chopped parsley or cilantro, mix and serve over rice.

Week Number Eleven June 12 Through June 18, 1998

FRI. JUNE 12 LAKE GUARDA, ITALY

Drove from Florence to Lake Guarda at the foot of the Italian Alps. Got another pre-fab, two bedroom bungalow in a campground, but this one was Italian made and had air conditioning. The bungalow sat on cement blocks, so it bounced a little, but it was new and clean. It was a little smaller than the others though, and cost more than any we had had so far, $73 a night. The campground was in a very nice location on the lake. It was just a short walk along the shore to the cute little tourist town of Lazise, which was full of shops and restaurants. However, there were about two hundred camps in this area and they were all nicely located. This lake is even more beautiful than Clear Lake, the lake I intended to live on when I returned to the States. Unlike Clear Lake, it was way too cold to swim in Lake Guarda.

*Camping Lazise (Verona) This camp was not in our book. There were so many camps. We just chose randomly.

SAT. JUNE 13 LAKE GUARDA, ITALY

This morning we walked into town to shop for fly swatters, a necessity now that it was getting warm, and to find out about a ferry ride to the other end of the lake for tomorrow. We were successful in both endeavors.

The little town of Lazise is very quaint and it was fun to walk around it. The walk to the town from the camp was also very pleasant. We were still walking about four or five miles a day, and this was good because we were eating a lot without gaining weight.

In the afternoon, we took a bus tour into Verona. The bus came right to the camp to pick us up. Verona is about 45 minutes away from Lake Guarda. The Danish guide, who told about the city in English and German, was quite good and very entertaining. We saw all the highlights and then they left us in the city center for two hours on our own. We didn't have to deal with traffic or parking, something we liked doing less and less. It was definitely worth $19 apiece for door to door service. As far as I was concerned this was the only way to see a big city. However, Frank left his $60 prescription sunglasses on the bus, so for him the visit to Verona was a little more expensive. The camp people called the bus company about the sunglasses, but it was Saturday night and everyone was gone.

I was so glad we had decided to see Verona. Surprisingly, I still think it is the most beautiful big city in Italy. It is well laid out with rivers and bridges like Florence, but unlike Florence, there is a feeling of spaciousness in every direction. When we looked down on Verona from a nearby hill, it looked like a storybook village. The weather had been glorious for a few days, making everything perfect.

SUN. JUNE 14 LAKE GUARDA, ITALY

The ferry ride to Riva at the top of the lake and back again to Lazise was a nine hour trip, six hours on the ferry and three hours in town. We argued about spending a whole day on a ferry. Finally, we decided to take the ferry to Riva and take the bus back. We actually cut off about three hours by doing this. The scenery from the ferry is fantastically beautiful. The lake is surrounded by mountain peaks, much taller than the mountains surrounding Clear Lake. Some of them even had snow on top. We were in the Alps after all.

We had a nice lunch in Riva and walked all over the town, browsing in stores and seeing the sights. We had picked up a bus schedule before we left the camp, but had some trouble finding the bus station. Riva is a small town, and the bus station is definitely not in the center. We eventually found it and boarded the bus. The ride back was also very beautiful, but it was warm and I fell sound asleep. It only took an hour and fifteen minutes. All told, it was a six hour day.

In the evening, we walked back to Lazise for dinner on the lake. Barbara and Frank's dinners were pretty good, but mine was the worst meal ever eaten in Italy. I had cannelloni made with wall paper paste.

MON. JUNE 15 BOLZANO, ITALY

Spent the whole morning trying to track down Frank's sunglasses. No luck. The campground people were very helpful and made a number of phone calls on our behalf, but all to no avail. Finally gave up and drove on into the Italian Alps. Italy is easily one of the most beautiful countries in the world. The terrain is so diverse. The Italian Alps look just like Austria and even Switzerland, but those two countries don't also have warm beautiful beaches on the sea. The people close to the border seemed to speak both Italian and German with equal ease.

Stayed in a small camp that had music piped into the bathrooms and dish washing room. None of us had realized how much we had missed hearing music. The camper had no radio. I sang "Hello Dolly" with a full orchestra while I did the dishes. Unfortunately there was no one around to appreciate my talent. Later I found an Italian sticker for the car. I had looked all over Italy for this big black "I" on an oval white sticker, but until this last day in the country, I was unable to find one. We wanted the sticker displayed prominently on the front of the camper because we wanted to annoy Rene when we got back to Amsterdam. Rene, who is very funny, had indicated that once we entered into Italy, we would be leaving the civilized part of Europe. We had sent him a postcard from

Sicily telling him that the campgrounds in Italy were by far superior to any in Holland or Germany. Frank was convinced that Rene would deduct $500 off the price he would pay to buy back the camper as soon as he saw the sticker. But he thought it would be worth it just to get his goat.

This was our last night in Italy. I didn't want to leave, but I kept telling myself that I would definitely come back.

*Klausen'Chiusa-Gasteig (Bolzano). Camping Gamp. Direction: Near the Gamp inn. Tele: 04 72/84 74 25.

TUES. JUNE 16 FUSCHINA (INNSBRUCK), AUSTRIA

Drove high up into the Austrian Alps this morning to a little town called Fushina. Frank and Barbara have a good friend in Oregon named Fred Ziegler. His cousin Doris has a luxury hotel here in the mountains. The hotel is now run by her children since Doris' husband was seriously injured in a skiing accident. The whole family was very accommodating and they all spoke English. We enjoyed our two night stay immensely. This was a four star hotel and a real luxury for us. I had my own room and Barbara and Frank had an extra sitting room in their suite. Instead of $50 for the three of us, it cost $53 each, but all meals were included, so by western standards, it was not really that expensive. Of course it was off season for a ski resort. Our first meal was a hot lunch and our second was a buffet at dinner. Both were excellent. There was a German tour staying at the hotel, so the dining room was very busy. There was also an indoor swimming pool and a sauna. Two days ago they had had over a foot of snow. Needless to say it was freezing, even though the snow was mostly gone.

*Hotel Walserhof, A-6733 Faschina-Vorarlberg, Austria. Tele: 0 55 10/217.

WED. JUNE 17 FUSCHINA, AUSTRIA

This morning I had to go out to the camper to get some things I needed. While I was gathering my junk, a little boy about four years old came riding up on his tricycle. He chatted away to me, I think asking questions about the camper. Since I couldn't understand him, I just smiled and went on getting things out of the closet with my back to the child. When I turned around he was in the driver's seat turning the wheel this way and that and talking a mile a minute. I stood there watching him for a while. He was really enjoying himself. After a few minutes, he climbed out of the seat, jumped down from the camper, and hopped back on his tricycle. He then gave me the European hand motion that to us means "come," and to them means, "by-by." He said, Ciao and rode away.

When I saw Doris' daughter, I asked if the boy was her son. At first she thought it was because she had a seven year old, but when she realized who I was talking about, she started laughing. She said he was the son of one of the Yugoslavian workers who was doing some carpentry at the hotel. She said he talked to everyone all the time, but that no one could understand him because he didn't speak German. I, of course, thought he was speaking German. I ran into the little boy from time to time throughout the day. He always spoke as if we were old friends.

Went for a three mile hike in the Alps this morning after a delicious breakfast. Walked from Fuschina to Damuls, the next town up the mountain. We went to the post office, which was closed, naturally! It seemed that everything was closed from noon until two. The tourist office said that the post office was opened 24 hours, but no one was there. We decided we never really left Italy. Though we were unsuccessful in our post office venture, the journey was not wasted. We met some very classy cows, and walked along paths of glorious green hills while looking up at snow covered peaks. The sun was out, though it was bitterly cold. To California people, fifty degrees is bitterly cold. We had coffee in Damuls and hiked back to the hotel for a delightful hot lunch.

We all decided that a luxury hotel was really a nice break once in a while, and that we should do it more often. Barbara was happy not to cook for a couple of days, but only because the food was good. When the food was bad, she bitched about not getting to eat her own cooking. Went swimming in the heated indoor pool in the afternoon. There were only about six or seven people staying at the hotel today. The tour group had left this morning. We had the pool completely to ourselves. It was a little colder than I would prefer, but I sure liked the idea of an indoor pool. There were glass walls surrounding it, the kind that you could see out but no one could see in, and the view of the high snow covered Alps was spectacular. After our swim, we had drinks in the bar with Doris and her family.

This was the first time we had met her husband. He evidently had had a head injury because he not only moved slowly, but he didn't seem to be all there. It was very sad. The skiing accident had happened many years before when he was in the prime of life. We took lots of pictures of the family and ourselves outside, with the Alps for a backdrop.

The young ladies that worked at the hotel were delightful. They all spoke a little English, but not very well. When they made mistakes, they would giggle and cover their mouths. It was very cute. They had asked at breakfast what we wanted for dinner. Because there were so few people in the hotel, there was no buffet. We could choose from four entrees. Everything was delicious as usual.

THURS. JUNE 18 STUTTGART, GERMANY

The Austrian part of the drive to Stuttgart was very beautiful, if twisty, but this part of Germany was kind of flat and uninteresting. There were patches of bright yellow mustard every now and then, but that was its only claim to fame. Had to go through an eight and a half mile tunnel. On the other side we stopped for lunch in the camper and met an American military family that was doing the same. The young man had been stationed in Germany for a few years and was taking a vacation with his family and his mother-in-law who was visiting. We all agreed that we thought the tunnel would never end, and was kind of spooky. It cost $11 to go through it.

Stuttgart was another nightmare of tangled traffic and unbelievable chaos. We quickly looked in the book for a camp outside the city. The directions to the camps from our camping book were ridiculous. It was incredible that we had found so many of them.

None of the camps around here had bungalows, but the weather was still pretty nice, so camping was not too bad. We set up our table and chairs outside. This was like having an extra room. The bathrooms here were clean and nicely arranged. The people that work here were very helpful. The owner spoke English and was good looking. What more could I ask? The bartender was a woman from Yugoslavia. There were a lot of Yugoslavian refugees working in Germany. She was very friendly and had a daughter in the States. There was also an older German American couple that lived at this camp in the summer. They had a permanent mobile home and were very helpful to us. We needed to get the car looked at here and they called around for an appointment for us for tomorrow morning.

We came to Stuttgart to meet another one of Fred Ziegler's cousins. This one Frank had met when he visited in Oregon. His name was Wolfgang and Frank called him from the camp phone. He said he would pick us up at the camp the following evening with his wife and son and we would go out for dinner, his treat. Fred had written to let him know we were coming, but Wolfgang hadn't known when we would arrive. German hospitality seemed to be a lot like Italian. The people we met were all very gracious.

*Calw-Altburg (Stuttgart). Holiday Camp Altburg. Directions: B 296 direction to Altburg. Tele: 0 70 51/5 07 88.

ITEMIZED WEEKLY BUDGET #11 June 12—June 18
LODGING
Camp Apt. (3)	219.00
Lux. Hotel (2)	
(All meals inc.)	$318.00
Camps (2)	43.00

FOOD
Restaurants
Dinner (1)	42.50
Lunch (1)	30.00
Groceries (13 meals)	72.50

ENTERTAINMENT
Cafes & Bars	19.00
Bus Tour to Verona	57.50

CAMPER
Camper payment	168.00
Gas	133.00
Road Tolls	45.00

TRANSPORTATION
Ferry to Riva	22.50
Bus Back to Lazise	13.00

INCIDENTALS
Fly Swatters	2.00
Newspaper	1.50
Postage	7.50
Sent Package Home	38.50
Italy Sign for Car	1.50
Laundry	7.00
Tip for Frank's Glasses	6.00
	$1,247.50

WEEKLY BUDGET # 11

Fri.	$118.00
Sat.	173.50
Sun.	215.50
Mon.	137.00
Tues.	254.00
Wed.	197.00
Thurs.	152.00
	$1,247.00

$1,247.00 divided by 7 days = $178.14. $178.14 divided by 3 people = $59.38 per day, per person.

Week 12 Calw (Stuttgart) to Wehrda

Week Number Twelve June 19 Through June 25, 1998

FRI. JUNE 19 CALW (STUTTGART), GERMANY

Today we worked on getting the camper fixed. We had an appointment at the VW place that the American couple in our camp had set up for us. The gears had been making a horrible grinding noise every time Frank shifted. I wouldn't drive anymore until it was fixed. Frank thought it was fine the way it was, as it had been making the same noise everyday since we left Amsterdam. I was leery of driving in Eastern Europe without it being repaired. So we were compromising and having it checked out.

The VW mechanic in Calw took Frank and the car for a spin. Barbara and I waited in the waiting room where we were given coffee and cookies. It was really quite nice. After the man test drove the car and heard the noise, he put oil in the gearshift box. It didn't help. They didn't charge us for anything, which was very decent of them, but they also didn't fix it. The mechanic said it would cost $882 for the parts and labor to install a new gear box, or we could do nothing and wait until it really broke. Frank, of course, opted to do nothing. I hoped it would last!

In the evening, Wolfgang, his wife Lianna and son Fridrich, who was about twelve years old, picked us up and took us out to a very good German dinner at the Old Mill Hotel. Wolfgang and Lianna spoke English very well and Fridrick promised to learn so he could come to Oregon and California for a visit. What audacity we Americans have expecting everyone to learn our language. We came to their country and got by on a German vocabulary of not more than 50 words, and only Barbara could speak those.

While Fredrich entertained some young children whose parents were also eating at the hotel, the rest of us spoke of politics and life in Germany today. Wolfgang said that Germany will be the economic leader of the new Euro Union and France will be the political leader. He didn't seem to be totally comfortable with this, but he said that Germany continued to be punished for their part in the Second World War. He did say that he thought it was fair enough. I think it is very hard for Germans who weren't even born during the second world war to have the world still look on them as monsters. They will be paying for the sins of their parents and grandparents well into the next century. However, the world is very reluctant to give them power again.

I met a young German woman who was about twenty years old in a Spanish Class I was taking in Spain a few years ago. She was very bitter about taking the blame for something that happened before she was born. Wolfgang seemed to be much more accepting of his fate. He also seemed to be very realistic about where Germany was going in the future. He said they intend to be world leaders, actually they are already.

We had had our meal on an outside patio of the hotel and by ten o'clock, we were all freezing. They took us back to the camp and we told them we'd take them to dinner on our return from Eastern Europe.

Back at the camp, we decided to go into the bar for a nightcap. Some people were singing and harmonizing at another table. They were pretty good, so we applauded. The owner of the camp, the cute German guy, was with them. He came over and asked us to join them. We did, and we sang English and German songs until two in the morning. People kept buying us drinks. I had to keep refusing. Frank bought them a round, and I was getting crocked just on the fumes. The lead singer was an old man who owned the horse stable next door. The cute younger guy was the harmonizer. He spoke English and knew a lot of English songs. We had a great time because we all love to sing. In Italy, the land of opera, no one would sing with us. Even our relatives didn't want to sing. At home there has never been a party that didn't end up with everyone singing. We had to come to Germany for this to happen.

The good looking owner of the camp told me he had a woman, but he didn't say she was his wife. However she had gone home early and was in his bed, and since the camper was out, I had to be content with fantasies. We said good-by to everyone and promised to stop there again when we returned from Eastern Europe. We had told Wolfgang and Lianna that we wanted to come back and take them to dinner. We definitely planned on returning.

SAT. JUNE 20 MORFELDEN (FRANKFORT), GERMANY

We drove from Calw to a camp near Morfelden, close to the Frankfort Airport. We wanted to know how to find the airport when we picked up my friend Marsha in another week. She was planning on spending three weeks with us in Eastern Germany and Poland. About three years ago, Marsha and I had flown to Frankfort to do an Eastern Europe trip. As we got off the plane, they called out her name and told her to see the stewardess. Her father had had a heart attack and died. We got on the next plane back and never did see anything. Now she wanted to try again.

Very few camps in Germany have cabins. We were only staying one night in this place so we didn't mind. We set up camp and went for a walk along the winding local country roads to the town of Morfelden, about two and a half miles. We had a drink in a nice little outdoor cafe and returned along the highway, about three quarters of a mile. We did everything the hard way.

When we got back, I used my pre-paid phone card to call Marsha. It is definitely a must to bring three or four phone cards on a trip like this. It had been almost three months since we left home and I wanted to make sure Marsha was still coming. She said she was. I also called my 83 year old

Aunt Sabina, who still worked as a volunteer at Willard, my old school in Pasadena. She was fine and all was well at home.

* Morfelden-Walldorf (Hessen). Camping Unger. Direction: A 5, highway exit Langen-Morfelden, signed. Tele: 01 61 05/2 22 89.

SUN. JUNE 21 WEHRDA, GERMANY

For the next week, while we waited for Marsha to arrive, we planned to go the the Hessen area to look for evidence of Barbara's German grandparents. Barbara's maiden name is Euler, pronounced Oiler. There is a very tiny town in Hessen called Eulersdorf. That was where we planned to start, but first we had to find an apartment in the area. Using the camping book, we looked for a camp with bungalows. We found our first in Germany in a place called Kirchheim. Unfortunately, it was about $110 a night, so we kept looking. On days that we needed to find bungalows or apartments it usually took us an entire day. This was when we got bitchy and barked at each other the most. The rest of the time we got along pretty well.

Next we drove to a tiny town called Wehrda. It was out in the middle of nowhere, but the scenery was really beautiful and it wasn't too far to Eulersdorf. In this camp, we found the absolute best bungalow yet. It actually was a well insulated little two bedroom stucco house. There were five of these in the camp. It had a big kitchen, a good sized bathroom and a real living room. This was the first time we had a living room. In the living room there were comfortable couches, chairs, a coffee table, lamps and a television with cable. Of course we could understand nothing, but it had been a long time since we'd had a television. To top off all this good luck was the fact that it only cost $53 a night.

There were quite a few American military families staying here, some in bungalows and some camping, but the camp was far from crowded. After we settled in, Barbara and I walked up to an old cemetery above the camp, but we found no Eulers.

*Haunetal-Wehrda (Hessen). Camping Feriensiedlung Wehrda. Directions: B 27, exit Haunetall, signposted. Tele: 0 66 73/91 93 10.

MON. JUNE 22 WEHRDA, GERMANY

This morning we set out to find Barbara's roots. We found the little town of Eulersdorf and went to the cemetery. While we were reading all the names on the gravestones, a woman came from a house across the street and wanted to know what we were doing. There was almost no way to communicate, but when she found out we were Americans, she became very excited and insisted we accompany her across the street. On the other side, an old man of no less than 100 years, was sitting in the shade. The woman hollered something to him and he hobbled over to us to get involved. Evidently not much happened in this dorf. The woman took Barbara into the house and her husband came out and got Frank and me. He was so excited and happy to be helping us that he literally pulled us into the house. He had obviously just come in from working on the farm out back, and they were right in the middle of lunch when they spotted us across the street.

When they found out Barbara's name, the man grabbed the telephone book and started calling every Euler in it. I don't think he knew any of them, but it was plain to see that he was telling them about the American who was looking for her grandparents. Finally he called someone who evidently thought they could help. The couple gave us a map and told us where to go to talk to one of these Eulers. Our destination was a church two or three small dorfs away. At first we thought the couple was going with us. It was very hard to understand anything. However they just walked outside with us. The 100 year old man was waiting patiently in the shade for us to find out what had happened. The woman yelled some sort of explanation over to him and she and her husband went in to finish their half eaten lunch. The old man cornered Barbara as we were leaving, and she had no choice but to listen. When she got back to the camper, Frank asked what the old guy had to say. "I have no idea." said Barbara "He was obviously bored and just needed someone to listen. So I listened!"

After lunch in the camper along the way, we headed for the church in Lingelback. Frank took a nap in the camper, while Barbara and I went in search of Eulers. We knocked on the door of the minister's house repeatedly but no one answered. Evidently, he was napping too. We went to the grave yard next door and found a woman tidying up the graves. She knew a Euler, but didn't know how to tell us where to go. She indicated that we should follow her in her car. We woke up Frank and set off behind her. It was hard to believe how these people were going out of their way for us.

The woman took us to another farmhouse on the edge of town. She told us to wait, and she went in to talk to the people. Very soon another woman came out with her to talk to us. She said her name was Euler and that was the last thing we understood. They both wanted us to come back in the morning at ten. We agreed to do this, though we had no idea why we were doing it.

TUES. JUNE 23 WEHRDA, GERMANY

At ten o'clock in the morning we arrived in Lingelbach at the Euler farmhouse. We were greeted at the door by the same Euler woman we had met yesterday. She took us into her dining room where we met her husband Karl Euler. On the table he had two huge butcher paper sheets with Eulers dating back to the thirteen hundreds. We searched for close to an hour, but Barbara's grandfather Johannes was not there. There were a number of Johannes, but none had the right date of birth. It seemed Euler was as popular as Smith. Karl and his wife served refreshments. They were as pleasant and helpful as anyone could be, but we really couldn't understand much of what they said. We enjoyed the whole experience, but were no closer to finding out about Johannes Euler than we were before.

On the way back to Wehrda, we stopped for lunch in Alsfeld. This town dated back to the thirteenth century. The whole downtown area was made up of crooked streets and crooked Tudor houses. It was wonderful.

WED. JUNE 24 WEHRDA, GERMANY

Today was a day of rest. We rested in our lovely little home while doing the laundry. There were machines that worked in this camp, washers and dryers. The Germans are definitely more mechanically inclined that the Italians. Went for a long walk around the tiny town of Wehrda and out into the countryside. This was really a beautiful area. The young lady who ran the camp spoke English. She had been very pleasant and helpful. This morning she told us of a woman nearby that was very interested in genealogy and asked if we would like to meet her. We said we would and she set up a meeting at the woman's house for six thirty tonight. The woman said she would have someone there who spoke English.

At six thirty, we arrived at the woman's home, which was also a riding academy and had lots of horses and people about. She had evidently bribed two little neighbor girls of about 12 and 15 years of age to translate for us. They spoke very little English and they wanted nothing more than to escape. The woman was of no help, but she was old and cute and tried very hard. She showed us a book that she had made of all her relatives with their names and addresses. There were many living in my home town of Pasadena. A couple were actually in my neighborhood, but I knew none of them. After about fifteen minutes, a little boy came in and yelled to his sisters that dinner was ready. At least that was what we thought he said because the two little girls couldn't get out of there fast enough. We started laughing knowing exactly how they felt. We wanted to leave too. The old woman just wanted company and started to show us around her very old farm house. We were getting to see inside a lot of old homes and it was actually very interesting. After about an hour we were able to escape. We had learned nothing about Johannes Euler, but we did learn that old people were the same the world over. They just wanted someone to pay attention to them.

THURS. JUNE 25 WEHRDA, GERMANY

Before we left for the town of Fulda this morning, we had a little accident. The car was parked on an incline. Frank released the brake and stepped on the gas by mistake. We crashed into a little house, not our own, and put a good size hole in the stucco. Part of the bumper on the car broke off too. No one was around, so we decided to tell them we had done the dastardly deed when we returned.

Fulda was not as nice as Alsfeld, with its shopping street of crooked Tudor houses, but still it was a nice mixture of old and new with lots of parks. We walked through the gardens to "old town" and visited the church. Barbara had pretty much decided she was not going to find any actual records of her grandfather, so we just spent the day sightseeing.

Back in Wehrda, I mailed home a package of all the junk I had been buying. The post office was in someone's house and was only opened for two hours a day. The woman did not know how to send a package to the States as it was only the second package she had ever sent. She was very friendly, and seemed to know all about us. These were very small towns we were visiting and, just like in Italy, word had spread quickly. Americans looking for their roots were evidently not an everyday occurrence. The woman called her daughter to help because she spoke English, and the package went off without a hitch. The younger woman questioned us more about our search for Johannes Euler, so we figured it would probably be all over Hessen by the time we returned from Eastern Europe.

When we got back to the camp, we told the young manager that we were responsible for the hole in the wall and would pay to have it fixed. She was very pleasant, and told us not to worry about it.

WEEKLY BUDGET # 12 JUNE 19—JUNE 25
    LODGING

Camp Apts. (5)	$265.00
Camps (2)	38.50

    FOOD

Restaurants

Lunch (1)	15.50
Groceries (19 meals)	137.00

(One meal with Wolfgang)
ENTERTAINMENT

Cafes & Bars	25.00

    CAMPER

Camper payment	168.00
Gas	79.00
Oil & Lead Additive	9.50

(No Unleaded Gas)

Parking	2.50

INCIDENTALS

Local phone calls	7.50
Drugstore	3.00
Laundry	14.00
Postage	5.00
	$769.50

WEEKLY BUDGET # 12

Fri.	$94.50
Sat.	49.50
Sun.	115.00
Mon.	132.50
Tues.	153.50
Wed.	97.50
Thurs.	127.00
	$769.50

$769.50 divided by 7 days = $109.92. $109.92 per day divided by 3 people = $36.69 per person, per day.

Week 13 Wehrda to Michendorf (Berlin)

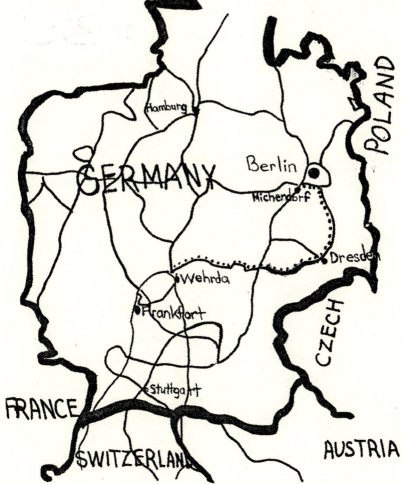

Week Number Thirteen June 26 Through July 2, 1998

FRI. JUNE 26 WEHRDA, GERMANY

Decided to keep our lovely home for an extra night and just drive to Frankfort and back to pick up Marsha. It was about a two hour drive each way. This was the direction we would be heading in tomorrow anyway. None of us wanted to face the ordeal of finding a hotel in Frankfort. This would be our eighth night here.

I had arranged with Marsha that she would get her luggage and meet us outside the airport. However, upon arrival, we saw that there was no choice but to park. So we parked and met her inside. She was as dazed as most people are when they come off a more or less thirteen hour plane ride, but we told her she had to stay awake for a while because we had plans. We drove back to Alsfeld so she could see this cute and crooked little town. We also needed to shop for dinner. Then we took her to our apartment. I told her this was the finest apartment we had had so far, and she better be ready for the fact that they would not all be like this. Then we let her take a nap in the other twin bed in my bedroom for about two hours only. Bodies with jet lag must adjust slowly.

After dinner in the apartment, we walked to a local music festival in the little town of Wehrda. There was almost no one but teenagers there, all drinking beer of course. We had a beer and went home. Marsha went directly to bed. I decided to read, but Barbara and Frank wanted to go to

122

the camp bar for a nightcap. There they met "Mississippi", an African American, ex G.I. He had been at the camp since we arrived, and we had chatted with him often. He and his German wife lived in a mobile home at the camp all summer long. I think they had a home somewhere else in the winter. They were retired and living the life of leisure, just like us. They all got smashed with impunity, since no one had to drive, and didn't get home until after two A.M.

SAT. JUNE 27 DRESDEN, (EAST) GERMANY

Today was the worst driving day since we started. I guess we wanted to break Marsha in properly. We had only planned to go half way to Dresden, but once we were in what used to be East Germany, we couldn't find any of the camps in the camping book. We started driving through all the little towns along the highway looking for hotels, but there were none. We came to the conclusion that in Eastern Europe we would have to go to larger cities if we wanted to find accommodations.

When we crossed into Eastern Germany, which by border boundaries, no longer exists, we could immediately see the difference. The houses were now Soviet style apartments. All four of us had been to Russia, so we were well acquainted with the lack of aesthetics in their designs. Soviet style means huge, drab, gray, high-risers. There is no comeliness whatsoever. It is simply utilitarian. Around six P.M., way past our limit of endurance in the car, we got to the Dresden area. Surprisingly, no one lost their temper and there was not even very much bitching. I'm sure this was because Marsha was with us. No one wanted to scare her off the very first full day.

We found the campground fairly quickly. By the look of the bungalows that we could see, we expected the worst. However, the camp was on a small lake and had lots of trees. The manager of the camp showed us to a bungalow that was very old and really quite horrid. One of us would have had to sleep in the kitchen. I had done this before, but the cabins had been a lot nicer. The worst camp apartment we'd had up to this point was the one outside of Palermo, Sicily in Italy. This one topped the Sicilian one for absolutely awful.

The cabins were $53 each, so we decided to take two. That way no one had to sleep in the kitchen. We started to unload the car, groaning and moaning about going from the sublime to the ridiculous again, when the manager came running up to us. He spoke English very well and said he had found a cancelation in the computer. He had a newly refurbished bungalow with three bedrooms, two baths and a big dining room, living room combination. We nearly jumped up and down for joy.

As he was showing it to us, he said we could only use two of the bedrooms. We agreed, as long as he would agree not to rent out the other bedroom. We were getting smarter as we went along, remembering our first apartment in Ischia, Italy where that had happened.

In all of these camp bungalows or apartments, the tenants must do their own housekeeping. So far no one from the camp had ever come into an apartment after we rented it. In most of them, the beds were bare when we arrived. They gave us the sheets and towels after we told them we wanted the place. This one had the sheets and towels folded neatly on the ends of the beds. One of the sheets was a bag. Marsha and I started making the beds by putting the mattress inside the bag. It was a weird way to do it, but nothing else occurred to us. Barbara came in and said that if these beds were like the ones in the little house in Wehrda, where for once the beds had been made when we got there, then the sack would go around the comforter and the flat sheet would go on the bed. "You're brilliant!" I said. Then just to emphasize my lack of vision, Marsha said, "Since we have to make the beds anyway, why don't we make one in one room and one in the other. When we leave, we can put all the sheets and towels in one room. It shouldn't make any difference to them in which bed we sleep." So Marsha and I each had our own room. We were careful to make sure that one room looked untouched when we left, and everyone was happy. Marsha left her bed made with the sheet around the mattress. I was sure the cleaning people would get a good laugh out of this until they had to struggle to get the sheet off the mattress, then they probably would cuss us out. The remodeled cabin cost the same $53 a night as the ugly, old ones.

We had dinner down by the lake in the camp restaurant. It was too late to cook. Found out that the camp was located about a half hour outside of Dresden. We could take the local bus into the city. This was perfect. Although the Germans were better drivers than the Italians, Frank was still happy that he didn't have to drive and park in the city. At least we kept telling him he was happy!

*Reichenberg, Sachsen (Dresden). Camping Bad Sonnenland. Directions: Highway exit Dresden-Wilder Mann, direction Moritzburd, 5 km. Tele: 03 51/4 72 77 88.

SUN. JUNE 28 DRESDEN, GERMANY

Took the bus to the city today. Round trip cost twenty Deutsch Marks, about $12 for all four of us. It said "Family Group" on the ticket. Dresden is an amazing city. It was bombed during the second world war and almost all the buildings downtown were left in rubble. Evidently the women of the city dug out the rubble after the war. The men were either dead or had not yet returned. The city was put back together piece by piece. It was hard to believe they could do it so well. Even when under Soviet rule they continued to rebuild. Now the restoration was going on in earnest. They set themselves a deadline to be finished by the year 2006.

We walked everywhere. We saw all the blackened buildings and the buildings surrounded by scaffolding. The old buildings were hauntingly beautiful. The main bridge over the River Elbe was a work of art. We all had knockwurst, a German hot dog, for lunch in a sidewalk cafe, and continued to walk until it was time to go back to the camp. Another wonderful day.

MON. JUNE 29 DRESDEN

Marsha and I took the bus into the city again while Barbara and Frank took the car to be fixed. One of our tires seemed to be wearing very unevenly. They went to a tire place where they were told that the front axle rod was broken, which was why the tire was so bad. The tire people sent them to a mechanic that had about twelve old VW busses that he perpetually cannibalized for parts. He put in another axle rod and another side piece on the front bumper, which had been broken when we crashed into the little house.

When we'd had the gas line fixed in France the first week of the trip, they didn't attach the hose correctly. Since then, Frank had been putting Italian duct tape on it to keep it from touching the ground where it hung under the car. He had to do it a number of times because Italian duct tape didn't stick very well. When the mechanic saw the duck tape, he just shook his head. Germans don't use duct tape. They do it right the first time, but Italians are lovers and singers, not mechanics. Besides they are too busy crashing cars. They don't have time to fix them properly. So the mechanic fixed it all. It cost us only $88 for all the repairs and two slightly used tires.

Meanwhile, Marsha and I were enjoying another day in the city. This time we decided to take the trolly from the bus stop over the bridge to the city, about a mile and a half walk otherwise. Unfortunately, we were supposed to buy tickets before we got on the trolly, but we didn't have any change. The trolly started up as soon as we were aboard and we tried to give a D.M. bill to the driver. He didn't want money. He wanted tickets, so he made us get off at the next stop. We were already halfway there and three quarters of a mile is better than a mile and a half, so we were happy. We stopped at a fancy hotel to use the bathroom. One of the nice things about being foreign is that hotel personnel never question your right to be in their establishment or use their facilities.

Once in the city, we took the open air bus tour of Dresden. The driver gave us earphones so we could hear everything in English. First we toured

Old Town. Then we went outside of Old Town to the area that hadn't been bombed. Here there were beautiful old homes. Some of these would qualify as mansions, and had been the homes of the Soviet leaders just a few years before. There were also many lovely parks. We went back to the camp after lunch. We'd spent $22 each which was not included in the budget. We probably would have felt guilty taking the money out of the kitty when Barbara and Frank were slaving over a hot car back at the camp.

In the afternoon, we all walked through the woods to the next little town of Moritzberg. Checked it out, and looked for a palace that was supposed to be there. Couldn't find it, so we bought ice cream and walked home.

TUES. JUNE 30 DRESDEN

All of us went back to the city today to see some of the museums and art galleries. This time the bus cost 21 D.M. and it included the trolly. It did not say "Family group" on the ticket.

Went to the Landhaus-stadt or City Museum where the story of Dresden from its beginning was told. There was special emphasis on World War II. None of us could understand exactly what was bombed or how they could possibly put it back together again with practically all the same stones. The pictures in the displays helped a lot. Many building had been burned and many were leveled. It was an amazing feat to make it look like a city again and truthfully, I was still not really sure how they did it. The Albertinium or art museum was also quite good.

On the way back, we walked to the bus instead of taking the trolly and, when we wanted to get on the bus to go home, we had to pay another 21 D.M. There was no rhyme or reason. It was as bad as Italy!

WED. JULY 1 MICHENDORF (BERLIN), GERMANY

Today was another appalling day, after our morning drive into the Berlin area. We were now fully into the summer season. Finding a camp with a bungalow that was not booked for the entire summer was an impossibility. We spent the whole afternoon driving from camp to camp. Even many of the camping sites were filled.

Along about five P.M., we spotted a new hotel with a banner outside saying the equivalent of $58 a room with breakfast. We took two rooms. We were in the tiny town of Michendorf in what used to be East Germany, somewhere southwest of Berlin. A young man named Henry seemed to be in charge. He spoke English fluently and tried to help us get a cabin for tomorrow by calling around for us. There were no vacancies. Then he got a train schedule for us so we could take the train into Berlin from the hotel. We decided to stay three nights. The hotel was brand new and very nice. He was delighted because it was evidently his job to keep the hotel filled. We had dinner at the hotel. Unfortunately, it wasn't very good.

*Sol Melia Inn, D-14552 Michendorf, Germany. Tele: 033205-780.

THURS. JULY 2 MICHENDORF, GERMANY

It was very easy to take the train into Berlin. Henry gave us a ride to the train station. It was only about a half mile from the hotel, so we planned to walk back. We had to change trains at Wannsee, but Henry had written everything down for us, and there were no problems.

Took our usual overall bus tour of the big city. The building that was going on here was like nothing I'd ever seen in my lifetime. Berlin was once again going to be the capital of the new unified Germany, and there were miles and miles, and acres and acres of construction going on everywhere. After the bus tour, we walked for about a mile to see Checkpoint Charlie. Every building on the street was brand new and empty. It was like being in the Twilight Zone, eerie to say the least! When we got to the corner where Checkpoint Charlie had been, there was nothing there but a sign saying, "Checkpoint Charlie."

In the evening, we had dinner at a local pub. The people were very friendly and the food was better than at the hotel.

WEEKLY BUDGET # 13 JUNE 26—JULY 2
LODGING
Camp Apts. (5)	$ 265.00	(Budget for Four People)
Hotels (2)	234.00	

FOOD
Restaurants
Dinners (3)	129.50
Lunches (3)	60.50
Groceries (15 meals)	46.00

ENTERTAINMENT
Cafes & Bars	35.50
Tour of Berlin	70.00
Museums	9.50

CAMPER
Camper payment	168.00
Gas	120.50
Car repairs & tires	88.00
Parking	1.00

TRANSPORTATION
Busses to Dresden	37.00
Trains to Berlin	9.00

INCIDENTALS
Books (We are running	28.00
out of novels)	$1273.50

WEEKLY BUDGET # 13

Fri.	$166.00
Sat.	161.50
Sun.	119.00
Mon.	165.00
Tues.	151.00
Wed.	234.00
Thurs.	276.50
	$1273.50

($44 Trip to Dresden with just Marsha and me. Not included in budget, $22 each)

$1273.50 divided by 7 days = $181.92 per day. $181.92 divided by 4 people = $45.48 per person, per day.

HOT AND SOUR SOUP
(We were only able to get the ingredients for this in Germany)

SOAK IN SHALLOW WARM WATER FOR 1/2 HOUR
2 medium-sized Oriental dried mushrooms. After soaking, discard stems, squeeze tops dry in paper towel and slice thinly.

SOAK FOR 10 MINUTES:
2 teaspoons dry sherry
1/8 lb lean pork, sliced into thin strips

BRING TO BOIL IN LARGE POT:
2 cups chicken broth (fresh or canned)

ADD:
mushrooms
pork with sherry
1/4 lb chicken breasts, cut into small pieces
2 cups fresh spinach
STIR,COVER AND SIMMER FOR 5 MINUTES
ADD:
1/4 lb tofu, drained and cut into small cubes
1 Tablespoon white wine vinegar
2 teaspoons soy sauce
SIMMER FOR 1 MINUTE
STIR TOGETHER, ADD TO POT AND COOK UNTIL SLIGHTLY THICKENED:
1 Tablespoon cornstarch
1/8 cup water

REMOVE POT FROM HEAT AND ADD:

1/2 teaspoon white pepper
1/2 teaspoon sesame oil

LIGHTLY BEAT:
1 egg and slowly add to pot, stirring constantly

SEASON TO TASTE WITH SALT AND GARNISH WITH
SLICED GREEN ONIONS

SERVES:
3 for dinner and 3 for leftover lunch

Week 14 Michendorf to Gdansk

BALTIC SEA

RUSSIA

Gdansk

POLAND

Szczecin

Ustronie
Morskie

Poznan

GERMANY

Berlin

Michendorf   Potsdam

Wroclaw

CZECH
REPUBLIC

Week Number Fourteen July 3 Through July 9, 1998

FRI. JULY 3 MICHENDORF (BERLIN), GERMANY

Today we bought an all day pass on all public transportation in and around the city of Berlin. Yesterday the train tickets expired before we caught the last train back to the hotel. These new tickets allowed us to ride any train above or below ground and all public buses, but we were not really sure about any of this.

Today we also found out that if we had walked just one more block yesterday, we would have come to the Checkpoint Charlie Museum. We went there today. Out in front was a large piece of the Berlin Wall. I have to admit that I was not taken with the museum. It was not that it wasn't moving, but it was in a very tiny building and hundreds of people wanted to see it. It was so crowded that it was hard to move or even breath. Whoever put the museum together, tried to put in things about oppressed people all over the world. They had barely enough space to tell the story of the iron curtain and the Berlin wall. There were whole walls covered with newspaper stories, reprinted in inch high letters, so that one was almost compelled to stand there and read the whole article. In my opinion, if they had just done stories and displayed paraphernalia about Checkpoint Charlie it would have been one hundred percent better. We had a Greek lunch and walked all over the city in the afternoon. Berlin is a fascinating place.

SAT. JULY 4 MICHENDORF (BERLIN), GERMANY

We had decided to stay until Monday night, six nights altogether. There was a lot to see and we didn't want to deal with finding a new place to live in East Germany. Tuesday morning, we will drive straight to Poland. We also had to call home on Monday night, as my nephew Gary was expecting to hear from us then. It was much easier to make phone card calls in the comfort of a hotel room.

We bought an all day transportation pass again this morning, as it worked very well yesterday. We started our day at the flea market next to the Tiergarten. You can buy anything and everything in these markets and we all enjoyed them, though we seldom bought anything. Next we went for a walk through the Berlin Tiergarten, which also houses the zoo. It was lovely. However once you enter it, you can never escape. We went in circles all morning. Stopped in a tea garden because it was raining and cold, and we wanted something to warm us up. Then we walked for another hour and found ourselves right back at the same tea garden.

Our destination was the Brandenberg Gate, on the other side of the Tiergarten, as Marsha wanted to take some pictures. However, after another hour of traipsing around in the now very muddy park, we once again came to the zoo by a small bridge. We had passed this place three times already, and it was ridiculously close to where we had first started. Decided to give up for a while. Found a dry spot under the bridge and sat down to eat the lunch we had been carrying around with us all morning. We arrived at the Brandenberg Gate at 3:30 P.M., after starting at 10:00 A. M. It was really only a short walk from where we got off the train, but we certainly got our exercise for the day.

SUN. JULY 5 MICHENDORF (BERLIN), GERMANY

Barbara and Frank took an R & R day today. They said Marsha and I should use the kitty for our excursion because they drank more than we did. They took some money for lunch, so everything was included in the budget. Marsha and I went back to the city to see two history museums, which were free on Sundays. We had a nice lunch at a very good pizza parlor, did some shopping and walked all over looking for a boat tour along the Havel River. We saw lots of tour boats as we walked along the river, but could find no place to board one. We were getting tired, so I suggested we just get on a train and go as far to the northeast of Berlin as Michendorf was to the southwest. We did this and it was very educational.

Aside from the obviously well carved piece of the Berlin Wall we had seen in front of the Checkpoint Charlie Museum, and a couple of pieces left as monuments within the city, we had not really seen any of the wall in its original location. On this trip we did. It was a large block in the middle of a field that they either just hadn't gotten around to yet, or for which they had other plans. Both of us felt a chill when we spotted it from the train window. We also saw just as many drab Soviet style buildings on this northeast side away from Berlin as we had seen on the southwest side while riding to and from Michendorf.

In the evening, we went out to dinner again as we had every night in Michendorf. There were only three restaurants in town aside from our hotel.

None of them was very good. German food is mostly meat and potatoes. We seldom saw fresh vegetables anywhere, at least not in Eastern Germany. However the people in the restaurants were very congenial and seemed to be delighted to have Americans among them. We had some cheerful, semi verbal conversations in all of them.

MON. JULY 6 MICHENDORF (POTSDAM), GERMANY

Took a local bus to Potsdam this morning. Walked all over the old city. The houses there were particularly unusual and interesting. Had lunch in a Chinese restaurant thinking we might get some vegetables. There were very few, but more vegetables than the regular restaurants served. Went to an outdoor market where Barbara shopped needlessly. She just couldn't help herself. Now that we were staying in a hotel, we were not eating in the camper, but we were all missing Barbara's cooking.

Back in Michendorf, while the old folks were napping, Marsha and I went out to find a warning triangle for the camper. These are the things that you set in back of cars when they break down. The triangle has reflective lights to keep other cars from hitting you. Our book on Eastern Europe had a list of things that must be kept in the car while traveling in any Eastern European country. The book implied that if we were caught without any or all of these items, we would be ticketed or possibly put to death. This list included a first aid kit, a flashlight, a fire extinguisher, and a triangle. We had brought flashlights and the equivalent of a first aid kit with us, but all the fire extinguishers we had seen in Europe weighed a ton and took up more room than we had to spare, which was none. We decided to take our chances and just get a triangle. Went to gas stations, an auto store and an old car junk yard. They were either too expensive ($30 in one place) or they didn't have any. We consoled ourselves with ice cream. Finally we found a heavy metal triangle for $10.50 at the VW dealership in town.

Throughout the rest of the trip, we were never asked for any of the above mentioned equipment, nor did we ever use any of it. I brought the weighty triangle home and now carry it around in my car.

In the evening we went to a local pub for dinner. The meal was forgettable, but they had a dart board with automatic scoring. I beat Frank and it made my day. He was convinced that I cheated.

TUES. JULY 7 USTRONIE MORSKIE, (KOSZALIN) POLAND

Drove all day today. Crossed the German, Polish border near Szczecin in the northwest of Poland. The camp cabins all seemed to be full for the summer. However, all that we saw were nothing more than beds inside a small wooden structure.

It was very cold ! We were close to the Baltic Sea heading for Gdansk, or Danzig as the Germans called it. I couldn't believe that people vacationing on this coast actually swam here! I would have to wait until we got to the Baltic to see for myself.

Took a hotel and had a pajama party with all of us in one big room. That was all they had, and we were ready to stop. With dinner and breakfast included, we paid $79. For four people that was $19.75 apiece. I was going to like Poland.

WED. JULY 8 GADANSK, POLAND

Drove all day again to the Gdansk area. We stayed in a resort on the Zatoka Gdanska, a bay in the Baltic sea in the north of Poland, near Sopot. There was a camp near the hotel, but the cabins were just beds, so we took two rooms in the hotel. This place cost $66.50 a night for all of us, but that included secured parking for the camper and breakfast. Actually, almost every hotel and apartment we have stayed in has had secured parking.

There was a promenade by the sea that was full of Polish tourists. We walked along it to get a feel for the place, found an outdoor cafe selling roasted chicken dinners, and we all ate there for $10. I couldn't believe how cheap everything was here. Walked all the way down to the other end of the promenade, watching one of the most incredible sunsets I have ever seen, and I have seen some spectacular sunsets on the California and Arizona deserts. This one was all in different shades of purple hues. The sun doesn't set until after 10 P.M. here. Maybe that and the fact that we were so far north had something to do with it, but this sunset alone would have been worth the two day drive it took to get here.

At the other end of the promenade there was an International Folk Festival going on. We found someone who spoke English and they told us the festival was on all week. It was free. All we had to do was buy a drink or something to eat and we could sit in the outdoor cafe and watch. We decided to come for dinner one night before it was over, and to come early enough to get good seats. Mind you, this was right on the water and it was absolutely frigid for my California blood, but we would wear everything in our suitcases at one time.

*Pension. Direction: coming from the center take direction to Helsinki—Ferry. 0.5 Km. from the beach.

THURS. JULY 9 GADANSK, POLAND

At breakfast this morning, they made the coffee by throwing the grounds into the cup. When they poured it, we had to wait for the grounds to settle. It was a little disconcerting at first but the taste wasn't too bad. It did take a little getting used to though.

Took the trolly into the city of Gdansk after breakfast. The city was rebuilt after the Second World War by the Soviets. We were amazed that they did such a nice job. It was certainly more beautiful than Moscow.

Unfortunately the main tourist street reminded me a lot of Universal Studios, and one building we saw looked just like "Small World" at Disneyland. In spite of the deja vu effect, we all enjoyed walking around the city. Stopped in a sidewalk cafe to have gyros for lunch and were given only two plates. All portions are weighed here and plates are sold by the grams.

This was probably not why we only got two plates though. Our Polish was non existent. Since we didn't want to wait for another order, we just shared what we had. It was not like any gyro I had ever eaten before. There was no pita bread, or bread of any kind for that matter. The meat, which was pork, had ranch dressing all over it, and it was served with cold slaw. The people all around us were eating it with a ton of ketchup. Three little kids at another table were sharing a pizza that was completely covered in ketchup. Ketchup is very popular here. All in all, our meal was not too bad, but we all decided to be very vigilant in making sure no one slopped ketchup on anything that passed our lips in the future.

When we got on the trolly to go home, there was a young man blocking the entrance way. I had to push to get by him. There was no reason for him to be there as there was plenty of standing room. Barbara and I got seats, but Marsha and Frank had to stand. I had noticed on the trolly going to the city how polite the young people were here. They immediately gave up their seats when someone older got on the trolly. This was true of both young men, women, boys, and girls. I was impressed because I saw it happen many times on that one trolly ride. So I was a little surprised that this young man was so rude.

I began looking out the window and forgot about the rude young man until a little while later when I heard Barbara call Frank over and say, "Your backpack is opened! Is your wallet still inside?" Of course it wasn't. At that point, out of the corner of my eye, I saw the rude young man slipping off the trolly just as we started going again. Everyone on the bus started talking at once when they realized that Frank had been robbed. A man who said he was the trolly policeman, or something like that, wanted to know what had happened. He had been standing right there the whole time, but hadn't seen a thing. Barbara explained to all of us that the thief, who was also the rude young man, had had a coat on his arm which he had sort of draped over Frank's backpack. Frank, who had been facing away from him, said he felt the man push every now and then, but he just thought it was because the bus was crowded. The trolly policeman probably didn't understand any of this, but when he found out where we were going, he said we were on the wrong trolly. Talk about adding insult to injury! He got off with us and flagged down a local police car. Frank told them what had happened without being sure of how much they could understand. They wanted to know what he lost. Luckily we were all wearing money belts under our clothes. Frank had only had about $50 in cash, not kitty money, and a $50 traveler's check.

Afterward, the trolly cop showed us where we had to wait for the trolly to take us home, and we were once again on our own, somewhere in the Gdansk area. We started rehashing all that had taken place. Barbara and Marsha thought maybe the trolly cop was in on the heist because he saw the whole thing happen. I didn't think he would have taken us to the cops if he was in on it, but who knows. I also thought that the thief was pushing against all of us as we entered the trolly, so that he could feel our backpacks. I had my heavy coat inside my pack, as the day had warmed up considerably. There was no way he would have tried to rob me. Frank had very little in his and the material of the backpack itself was very thin. The guy could have felt the wallet right off. We all learned a lesson from this. The bad guys were much better at stealing than we were at protecting ourselves! We vowed to be more vigilant and watch each other in tight places. People always shut the barn door after the horse is gone!

WEEKLY BUDGET # 14 JULY 3—JULY 9
LODGING

Hotels (7)	$641.00	(Budget for Four People)

FOOD

Restaurants:

Dinners (6)	190.50
Lunches (4)	73.00
Breakfasts (1)	12.50
(Usually inc. w/hotel)	
Groceries: (4 meals)	75.50

ENTERTAINMENT

Cafes & Bars	36.50
Checkp. Char. Museum	15.00

CAMPER

Camper Payment	168.00
Gas	55.50
Safety Triangle	10.50
Parking	2.00

TRANSPORTATION

Busses & Trollies	12.00
Trains	47.00

INCIDENTALS

Postage	3.50
Newspaper	1.50
Backpack check at	
Museum	1.00
Potty Fees	3.00
	$1348.00

WEEKLY BUDGET # 14

Fri.	$249.00
Sat.	219.50
Sun.	205.00
Mon.	264.00
Tues.	118.00
Wed.	164.00
Thurs.	128.50
	$1348.00

$1348 divided by 7 days = $192.57 per day. $197.57 divided by 4 people = $48.14 per person, per day.

Week 15 Gdansk to Sochaczew

POLAND

Week Number Fifteen July 10 Through July 16

FRI. JULY 10 GDANSK, POLAND

The Baltic Sea resort area was quite nice. The sand was lovely and white. The scenery was kind of flat and uninteresting, but we could see Sweden and Finland when it was clear. Unfortunately it was seldom clear and, it was freezing. We kept telling each other that it was July, but it was hard to believe. Nevertheless, I had actually seen people swimming in the Baltic Sea. I couldn't understand why they didn't have hypothermia.

Went back to the city of Gdansk today on the trolley. All of us were ready and waiting for pickpockets, determined that it wouldn't happen again! After visiting the Maritime Museum in the in the morning, we had "peroge" for lunch. It was a lot like ravioli, without tomato sauce, and fried in butter. I had heard about it years ago from my Slavic friends in Peace Corps, and had wanted to try it ever since. Little piggy that I am, I loved it, Marsha and Barbara did too. Frank decided it really wasn't worth eating because it didn't have a tomato sauce. Any variation in his pasta is sacrilege!

After lunch, we went back to the Maritime Museum on the ferry and climbed all over an old freighter docked in the harbor. Had to walk through the tourist section of town back to the trolley, so we did a little souvenir shopping along the way. I bought a dried flower picture from a little boy who assured me that his mother had made it. He was about twelve years old and was working very hard to help his family earn a living.

Back at our hotel in the evening, we walked to the small outdoor restaurant at the end of the pier to see the folk festival. Had two delicious fish dinners for the four of us. We thought we had ordered four again, but only got two. However, it was more than enough. They had very large portions in Poland. The free folk show we came to see was quite amateurish. Everyone was having a great time because they kept bringing people from the audience onto the stage. Luckily, we were sitting towards the back and thus were not required to do any of the entertaining. All of the entertainers were from other countries and no one spoke the same language, but when people were having fun, this was a very minor problem.

By ten o'clock, Marsha was turning blue from the cold. She had brought only summer clothes because, after all, she would only be in Eastern Europe in the summer. I had winter clothes, but I'm always freezing, so the two of us returned to the hotel. Barbara and Frank stayed out until about two in the morning. They said the party didn't really get going until after Marsha and I left, the story of my life! Frank claimed that he and Barbara and a few hundred others, danced two hundred yards down to the end of a second pier that jutted out from the restaurant. Frank was sure he would die of a heart attack, but he made it to the end and back. About midnight, they started back to the hotel only to be stopped by guitar music coming from a little cafe very close to the hotel. Of course they went in and met the Polish guitar player and his wife. They stayed until two A.M. and were invited to come back to the couple's apartment to look in on their sleeping children. They went, probably because they were either too drunk to refuse or they didn't know how to decline the invitation in Polish. They were invited back for breakfast the following morning. They agreed to do this. They were all pretty looped.

SAT. JULY 11 TURUN, POLAND

This morning Barbara and Frank related their nights adventure to us. Barbara insisted that she had to go to the couple's apartment and tell them that they wouldn't be coming for breakfast. Since it was included at the hotel, they had already eaten. She was afraid that the couple would have everything ready for her and Frank. I went with her. The man was up, but there was absolutely no recognition of Barbara on his face. He woke up his wife. They were both very polite, but seemed to have no memory of theprevious night, let alone a promise of breakfast. Barbara thanked them and we chuckled all the way back to the hotel.

Stopped in Chelemno on the way to Turun to see a World War II museum. It took about fifteen minutes to see the whole thing. The Poles didn't put up much resistance to the Nazis. We came on this particular route just to see this museum. Oh well!

Drove to the small medieval town of Turun. Had our usual trouble finding a hotel and wound up in another dump, two rooms for $63. The hotel staff was very accommodating which helped make up for the ugly Soviet style rooms. The parking lot was behind the hotel. Frank had to drive the camper through a tunnel type entrance that left barely an inch on either side and less than an inch at the top. We all sucked in our collective breaths to make the camper skinnier. It was very safe though. No one in his right mind would try to get it out again.

The city of Turun was never bombed, so it is still in its original state. This was the first time we actually stayed right in the heart of a city, actually right in Old Town. Fortunately it was a very small city, so no one panicked in the traffic. Walked all over Old Town. It was fascinating and well worth seeing. Had a simulated Chinese dinner. Better than Polish meat and potatoes, but not very good.

*Hotel Pod Orlem, ul. Mostowa 17, 87-100 Torun, Pol. Tele: (0-56)250-24.

SUN. JULY 12 TURUN, POLAND

Breakfast, not included with the hotel, was lacking in just about everything, especially food. Decided not to eat at the hotel again! Walked over the bridge on the edge of town to the other side of the Vistula River. Wanted to have a look at the local campground in case we had to return this way later. There was not much hope of taking a cabin in Poland. The cabins, unfortunately, had only two beds and a table, no bathroom and no kitchen. The glory days of Italy and Germany were gone.

Had Polish sausage for lunch, served without bread or mustard, but still very tasty. After a nap, we walked all over town and saw everything we had missed before. Had pizza for dinner then walked some more. Met lots of people and dogs out for a stroll. Came across some little kids painting pictures on a man hole cover. Wanted to tell them it was very nice, but of course had no way of conveying a message. A little boy made a circle of his thumb and index fingers and said, "Ok?" We all laughed and replied with a like gesture and word. Thanks to the American space program or the movies, we could all communicate on a very basic level. It was better than nothing.

MON. JULY 13 WARSAW, POLAND

This morning we had breakfast at Mc Donald's. We figured it couldn't be as bad as the hotel breakfast. However, at this Mc Donald's they didn't serve breakfast, so we had chicken sandwiches. It was a decided improvement. Everything in the restaurant was spotless. There were even young people polishing the leaves on the plants. We also noted that they didn't weigh the food here as they did everywhere else.

Drove on towards Warsaw. Had a picnic lunch on the way. Warsaw was a nightmare. Once again the streets were being torn up and the traffic was overwhelming. Looked for a hotel right downtown again, but there was absolutely no place to park. Wound up on the outskirts of town, at the last hotel on the list from the various books we were carrying. The hotel was not too bad, two rooms for $97. In fact, it was a major improvement over the flea trap we had been in for the past two nights.

As Barbara and I were getting the last things out of the car, and she was making hot water to have coffee back in the room, an altercation started on the street. I climbed back into the camper because I didn't want to leave her alone. A man was screaming at someone down the street whom we couldn't see. Suddenly he ran over to the camper and put a package on the floor inside our sliding door which was still opened. He said, Prosze, which means, please, and he ran off. The bundle was wrapped in a plastic bag and looked like a bunch of postcards. I picked it up. It was soft and squashy on the bottom. The first thing that entered my mind was "Drugs!" I got down from the camper and took the package over to an electric box hanging against the side of the hotel building. I placed it on top of the box. It was right about eye level.

Just as I got to the camper to tell Barbara that we needed to get out of there quickly, the cops pulled up in a squad car. I jumped back into the camper and slammed the sliding door shut. We watched all the action through the window.

The man that had delivered the package to me came running back into view and the cops immediately nailed him. This all took place about two feet from the camper. The police frisked the irate man, who resisted their every effort and screamed at them throughout the search. It took four cops to subdue the suspect enough to put cuffs on him. I noticed that the police were very gentle with the man. They did not harm him in any way. I had seen a cop apprehend an alleged criminal in Turkey once, and he had beaten the shit out of him with a rubber hose. From what I had seen in the United States, "gentle" was not a word I would have used to describe the police there either.

The officers seemed to be firing questions at the man while they worked to get him into the police car. He seemed to be screaming back answers, but this was all conjecture on our parts as we couldn't understand any of the tumultuous conversation. However, the package was in plain view throughout the whole ordeal, and no one saw it. Barbara and I were too scared to say anything. As soon as the police car pulled away with the alleged criminal inside, we ran into the hotel and up to our rooms. There the four of us had a huge debate over what to do. I wanted to go down and tell the woman at the desk what had happened. She understood English and I figured she would know the appropriate next step. Barbara wanted to forget the whole thing. She said they might misinterpret what we were doing with the package and we could get into a lot of trouble. Frank and Marsha voted with me, so the three of us went downstairs to talk with the clerk.

I told the desk clerk what had happened and showed her where the package was located. I also told her I was afraid that it might be drugs. She turned a little pale, and immediately called the police to convey my message. After she hung up, I told her we might not want to stay more than one night because we were afraid the man, whom we now collectively thought of as the "Drug Man," might come back if the police decided not to hold him. She said she understood completely.

Well, to quote The Bard, it turned out to be Much Ado About Nothing. We later found out from the desk clerk that the verbal altercation had been over a woman. The package, which the police returned for and showed to the desk clerk, contained nothing but pictures of said woman. The "squashy" part of the package was evidently excess plastic bag. Guns and drugs were still only in the movies in Poland. Even the police were not armed. Lucky people!

*Hotel Maria, 71 Aleje Jana Pawa II, Warsaw, Pol. Tele: 384062

TUES. JULY 14 WARSAW, POLAND

We took a seven mile hike all over the old part of Warsaw today. Frank had read just about every book ever printed about World War II. I also had read a great many such books. One of our favorites was Leon Uris'

Mila 18 a horrendous story about the Jewish ghetto in Warsaw. For some unknown reason, I was under the impression that the Ghetto, or at least parts of it, had been restored as a memorial. We were very disappointed to find out that I was wrong. Nothing was left but one monument and a map showing where the ghetto had once been.

With the help of the map, we followed the borders of the ghetto where there were now many Soviet style apartment houses. I really had wanted to relive *Mila 18*, but there wasn't a trace of the plight of those long ago heros, except for a few pieces of the original wall that had surrounded the ghetto. We went to the Jewish cemetery which was just outside of the ghetto border. Many of the graves were nothing more than headstones. So many people were killed in the concentration camps. Relatives that survived had nothing to bury, so they just erected headstones or monuments to commemorate the lost lives. It was all very poignant and the reality of it left each of us in silent reflection.

Walked from our hotel to a local Chinese restaurant for dinner. They had delicious Szechwan food. It was the best meal we had had in Eastern Europe. The people running it were Chinese. That helped a lot.

WED. JULY 15 SOCHACZEW, POLAND

Headed out the west side of Warsaw toward Blonie and Sochaczew. We immediately labeled the first Baloney and the second Such-a-screw. We wanted to see Chopin's home which was between these two small cities. The town of Baloney had a main park like square, with a quaint little town built around it. Found a nice hotel just outside the town and took two rooms. There were about fifty very loud men, women and children all over the driveway and in the lobby, speaking a strange language that was not Polish. They had an abundance of rolled up carpet that we thought they were laying, and we figured they would be gone soon. There were about five or six very expensive cars, obviously belonging to these people, parked in the circular driveway, and they evidently felt the entire driveway belonged to them. One of them didn't like where Frank parked the camper and got very obnoxious about making him move it. This in turn made Frank very belligerent and he refused. I guess it's a male thing. They acted like two cocks circling for the fight. Meanwhile a man and woman inside were having a screaming match and were about to go at it tooth and nail.

The young woman who showed us the rooms spoke English. She was very nice and truthful. When we asked her if these people were leaving soon, she told us they were staying at the hotel. We asked her if we could have our money back. We figured Frank was going to get into a physical altercation at any moment and that we'd never get any sleep with this cacophony going on. The young woman was very apologetic and told us that this happened all the time. No one wanted to stay at a hotel with constant commotion. She returned our money and we left as quickly as possible.

Next we went to Such-a-screw. There we found the newly built Chopin Hotel. We took two rooms with a buffet breakfast included for $94.50. This town was not as nicely laid out as Baloney. There was a lot of traffic and it was more difficult to just stroll around. Nevertheless, there were no loud people and the hotel rooms were large and luxurious.

*Hotel Chopin, ul Traugutta 21, 96-500 Sochaczew. Tele: (0-46) 862 59 99.

THURS. JULY 16 SOCHACZEW, POLAND

This morning we went to Zelazowa to see Chopin's birth place. It was definitely worth the trip. There were acres of beautiful gardens and a lovely little house full of family momentos. Chopin's delightful piano concertos radiated from the cottage to the surrounding gardens. The music was only a tape, but it was very apropos. Barbara and Marsha knew and loved Chopin's music. Frank used to play it on the piano, but didn't love it, and I knew nothing about it. None of us knew much of anything about the young artist who died at age thirty nine. We determined to look him up in the encyclopedia upon our return home.

After lunch in our hotel room, we went to the local war museum in town. It was only slightly more informative than the one in Chelemno. We spent the afternoon walking through the marketplace looking for ice cream and just enjoying the ambiance. This was Marsha's last full day with us.

WEEKLY BUDGET #15 JULY 10—JULY 16
LODGING
Hotels (7) $575.50   (Budget for Four People)

FOOD
Restaurants:
Dinners (7)   190.50
Lunches (3)   29.00
Breakfasts (2)   20.00
Groceries: (9 meals)   49.50

ENTERTAINMENT
Cafes & Bars   42.50
Museums   29.00

CAMPER
Camper payment   168.00
Gas   36.50
Propane   3.50
Parking   14.50

INCIDENTALS
Map of Warsaw   1.50
                     $1160.00

WEEKLY BUDGET # 15

Fri.	$147.50
Sat.	128.50
Sun.	128.00
Mon.	196.50
Tues.	197.00
Wed.	196.00
Thurs.	166.50
	$1160.00

$1160 divided by 7 days = $165.71 per day. $165.71 divided by 4 people = $41.42 per person, per day.

Week 16 Sochaczew to Nisko

POLAND

Week Number Sixteen July 17 Through July 23, 1998

FRI. JULY 17 KIELCE, POLAND

After a fairly good buffet breakfast, we drove to the Warsaw Airport and dropped Marsha off without a hitch. Then we started driving south towards Krakow. Planned on going just halfway. We were only three again, so we could camp.

Couldn't find a decent campground. As it got closer to five o'clock, we started looking for a hotel in Kielce. All we could find was another Soviet style monstrosity. This one was really awful. The woman at the desk was very surly because we didn't speak French. French, it seems, is the language of the so called upper-class in Poland. The woman showed us a room for three which she said was all she had. Unfortunately, we didn't notice how bad it was until after we had rented it. The toilet was in a room by itself and no one had bothered going into it. We didn't notice the smell of urine until it was too late. But that wasn't the worst of it. The toilet wasn't actually connected to the floor. When you leaned over to get paper, the whole commode came with you. These Soviet style hotels never used light bulbs of more than forty watts. They were dusty and stinky and the furniture and drapes were usually dingy and torn. In short, they were an abomination!

We were forced to eat at the hotel because there was nothing around it within walking distance. As always the food was very basic and cheap. The woman who ran the restaurant was a jack of all trades. She cooked,

157

served, did the dishes and took the money. In other words, she was the only one there. She was very pleasant as we have found all but a small minority of the Polish people to be.

SAT. JULY 18 KRAKOW, POLAND

The same woman was in the restaurant this morning. She gave us a menu with three different breakfasts on it, and we each chose a different one. She must live at the hotel because we had dinner late and breakfast early, and she was still there. As before, she was in excellent humor and made breakfast an enjoyable happening.

Drove on to Krakow. There were a number of camps in our book. The first was in a nice setting, but the bathrooms smelled of urine and the whole place had an aromatic sewer odor. The next two camps were also rejects. The second one was too far away from the city, and the third one had no clothes washing facilities. I am speaking here of a scrubbing board and large sink, not a washing machine. The third camp was actually quite nice, but we really needed to wash clothes.

Drove on to Camping Korona. Here they had spotlessly clean bathrooms with washing facilities for clothes, dishes and bodies. It was perfect! They even had a mini bus that would take us to Krakow and the Woeklicka Salt Mines, and the owner's son spoke a fair amount of English. Most of the other campers were Dutch and also spoke English. Everyone was very friendly. Campgrounds were the best place to get and give needed first hand information. We spoke to people who had been south, where we were going, and people who were going north, where we had been. The general consensus was that Poland was the most expensive of the Eastern European countries. We found this hard to believe. Our campground only cost $13 a night. Two or three course meals in fancy hotels, with drinks included, had never been more than seven or eight dollars a person.

*Camping Korona. Directions: Take E-77 from Krakow (Road to Zakopani)

SUN. JULY 19 KRAKOW, POLAND

We were eating Barbara's cooking again and it was heavenly. We were all very tired of meat and potatoes. This morning we took the mini bus into the city. It was about a thirty five minute ride and cost $8.50 for all of us.

Krakow is a beautiful city. There is a tree laden park running in a ring around the Old Town. We started out by walking this path with an occasional foray into the downtown area. The architecture was unusual and charming. Went to two art museums and had lunch in an outdoor cafe. Had a very enjoyable afternoon. Did a little grocery shopping and returned to catch the mini bus at four o'clock.

When we returned to camp, we spent the cocktail hour in the camp bar with our new Dutch friends. Barbara made pasta for dinner for the first time in weeks. It was the perfect ending to a perfect day.

MON. JULY 20 KRAKOW, POLAND

Took the mini bus to the salt mines today. Marsha had told us about this place. She had really wanted to see it, but unfortunately, she was no longer with us. The first thing we had to do was climb down 500 steps to the bottom of the mine. It was a very hot day up top, and we were all happy to descend into the cool earth. Most of the Polish people are Catholic now that they are no longer under Soviet rule. Many years ago, the miners had started carving religious statues out of salt. Most were crudely done saints, but the Christ on the cross was really noticeably better than the rest. It was fascinating to think that unskilled miners had created this underground art gallery.

We had lunch in the little town outside the salt mines, and then took a nap in the park because we had to wait for the mini bus to return at four o'clock. This was our first really hot day of the trip. It was over a hundred degrees, and we pooped out quickly.

In the evening, Barbara said dinners were getting more difficult to make. The only readily available vegetables were cabbage and potatoes. Frank, who was not fond of either one, complained loudly. Sometimes I wondered why we brought him. Then I remembered that he did all the driving.

TUES. JULY 21 KRAKOW, POLAND

I have read at least a hundred books about Auschwitz and World War II, but there was nothing like seeing it in person. We had to drive ourselves because the mini van didn't go there yet. Next year it will. The family that ran our camp was trying very hard to get everything in the camp up to western standards. There were some Dutch camp owners staying at the camp this week just to help them modernize. But I digress. Back to Auschwitz, which was not unlike a campground or army barracks. It too was run very efficiently by the Germans. At first it was a place to put Polish dissidents, but by 1943 it was a death camp for Jews.

There is a sign in German over the entrance to the camp that says, "Work Will Make You Free." Those that were unable to work were sent to Birkenau about three miles away, to be exterminated. Those that could work were worked to death. Maybe the Nazis meant "Free" in a spiritual sense. There were many moving things to see in the acres of the museum that comprised Auschwitz. In one of the buildings was a display of the actual hair, bones, and shoes of the people who died there, but one of the most heart wrenching displays was the photographs of the actual people. The Nazis took head shots of each prisoner, and the pictures lined the walls in every building. The majority were able bodied young men and women, mostly men. They evidently didn't bother to photograph the children and old people that were exterminated in the gas chambers. It was truly horrible to realize how cruel and inhumane people could be. We did not have time to go to Birkenau. We didn't even have time to see all the memorials from all the different countries. The ones we did see were very moving. We'll have to come again. Barbara would rather not come back, but I needed to see it all. I think everyone should.

Our camp had people from many countries. Most of them spoke English. That seems to be the common language of the world now. A Dutch man told us we should not go to Romania or Bulgaria. He said they were having a lot of unrest there. He also told us there were some young people in the camp from Lithuania and that they spoke English. I went over to talk to the Lithuanian kids. There were four of them and sure enough they all spoke English. They of course told me that the Baltic States, Lithuania, Latvia, and Estonia were well worth seeing. They said everyone spoke English, the countries were beautiful, and that we shouldn't miss any of them. However, they were adamant that Lithuania was the best.

WED. JULY 22 KRAKOW, POLAND

Took the mini bus into Krakow again this morning. This time we went to the old Jewish part of town. Saw two synagogues. One was a museum and the other was still being used, though there were not many Jews left in Poland. Evidently the Poles also mistreated them after the war and most of them left. I guess it never ends. We also went to the Ethnic Museum. It was full of Polish costumes, houses, lace, etc. Very interesting and a welcome break after all the murder and mayhem. We had definitely decided to change our plans and head north to the Baltic States the next day. We would see the rest of Auschwitz when we returned in a month or so.

THURS. JULY 23 NISKO, POLAND

I have a Peace Corps friend who has an aunt who lives somewhere in the city of Nisko. Before I left home, I called Mary who lives in San Antonio, Texas, and asked her for her aunt's address. She said she would get back to me after she looked for it. As it turned out, we left before she called, so she left the name and address on my answering machine where my nephew Gary, house sitting in Lakeport, received it. Gary in turn gave it to his mother, Barbara, when we called home. He wasn't sure if he had written it correctly because the message had not been clear. Nisko was as good as any other way to drive back through Poland, so we headed East and then North. There's a lot to be said for spontaneity when traveling. The following is a copy of the letter I wrote to Mary and her husband Jose, whom she met and married while in the Peace Corps in Honduras.

July 31, 1998

Dear Mary, Jose and kids,

I am now in Lithuania. I want to relate to you what happened about a week ago when we drove through Nisko on our way north. The drive from Krakow was hair raising and tedious. About five kilometers outside of Nisko proper we decided to stop at a tiny roadside cafe for a cup of fortitude. We were sitting in a little outdoor patio when a nicely dressed Polish man asked us where we were from. We of course spoke no Polish and he no English, but we understood what he meant. He smiled a lot and seemed very interested in us, so I thought I'd show him your aunt Waleria's name and address. I was thinking he might tell us how many kilometers or whether or not she lived right in the town of Nisko. He looked at the paper and said, Tac, tac! ("Yes, yes!") and he indicated that this dirt road we were on was the street in question. He started speaking very quickly and we gathered that he knew your aunt personally.

Next thing we knew, he left his cold beer on the table, got on his bicycle and rode off down the street. We waited, telling each other that this was not possible. We had been planning to go to the post office to see if it was even conceivable to find this person for whom we had no phone number and a somewhat dubious address relayed to us by phone through three different people and machines.

About ten minutes later, the man came back walking his bike because an elderly woman accompanied him. She also spoke no English. She looked at the paper and said, at least we thought she said, "Tac, this is me, Waleria. I said, "Mary, America?" No recognition! I couldn't remember your maiden name. I thought it was Noel. When that didn't work I tried Novak, but nothing rang a bell. She indicated that we should finish our coffee while she went to get someone who spoke English. We sat.

Soon a half naked, barefoot man came barreling onto the patio. He was quite rotund with a beetling belly that hung over a skimpy pair of shorts, his sole garment. He spoke loudly and with great animation, but we had no idea what he was trying to tell us. The first man, who had accompanied Waleria to the cafe, was now quietly sipping his slightly warmed beer and paying no attention to the intruder. I kept looking at him for help, but he ignored everyone. Naturally, since we didn't understand the screaming man, he yelled louder. Then he took me by the arm and started leading me out of the patio and across the street. My brother and sister-in-law followed us.

Across from the cafe was a little house with a woman sun bathing in the back yard. We all thought, Oh good! Someone who speaks English lives here, but no, she didn't! She went into the house and dragged out a little old lady who could hardly walk. It was all very exciting to have visitors from America, but no one could communicate! Finally another older woman came riding up on her bicycle. The fat man breathed a sigh of relief, and said, Zgfth pzhrng! (There are no vowels in the Polish language.) I interpreted his exclamation to mean, "Ah, here she is! Now we can find out who the hell these people are."

The woman got off her bike and said, Dzien dobry. Which means, "Good day" and were the only words we could understand. Then she proceeded with a veritable flood of Polish words while the three of us stood with our mouths opened. When she saw our reactions, she switched to very heavily accented French. We all started shaking our heads and laughing.

The rest of the people realized the hopelessness of the situation at the same time, and they started laughing too, while talking incessantly at each other and at us. At this point, the first little old lady, Waleria, returned with a bag full of family pictures. If your picture was in there Mary, I didn't recognize you. I wrote "1974" on her bag and told her that was the year when Mary had been in Poland. She seemed to understand, so I wrote "21" and said Mary was this age in 1974. She kept saying, Tac, tac. like she understood everything, but she still didn't remember who Mary was.

I decided we must have the wrong Waleria, and I told her we had to leave. She got very upset and said we must walk to her home with her because someone who spoke English was coming. Of course, she said all this in Polish so I'm giving you a very loose interpretation.

We said good-by to all the people who had tried to help, crossed the street again and reluctantly followed her down the dirt road. We hadn't gone very far, when a car pulled up and two guys jumped out. Waleria was very happy to see them. One of them was her son and the other was her son's brother-in-law who lived in Brooklyn, New York and had come home for a visit. Your aunt started to tell them how she didn't know who Mary was. Your cousin said, "Mary Novacheski." (You could have told me you had Americanized your name, Mary!) The brother-in-law said, "She wrote you a letter to tell you these people were coming." Your aunt said, "Mary, Honduras!" like a little light bulb had gone pop in her brain. I said, "Yes, Honduras, that Mary!" We walked to their house where they broke out a bottle of champagne. They were so hospitable. We really enjoyed our visit.

When we finally left, we drove through Nisko and realized that the city is quite large. If we hadn't stopped for coffee, we probably never would have found your family.

Love to all

D

WEEKLY BUDGET #16 JULY 17—JULY 23
LODGING
Hotels (2)	$80.00
Camping (5)	65.00

FOOD
Restaurants:
Dinners (2)	22.00
Lunches (3)	31.50
Breakfasts (1)	8.00
Groceries: (15 meals)	44.50

ENTERTAINMENT
Cafes & Bars	27.00
Salt Mines	20.00
Museums	8.00

CAMPER
Camper Payment	168.00
Gas	43.00
Oil	2.00
Car Wash	4.50
Parking	1.50

TRANSPORTATION
Mini Bus	34.00

INCIDENTALS
Auschwitz
Booklets	2.00
New Coffee Cups	3.50
	$564.50

WEEKLY BUDGET #16

Fri.	$67.00
Sat.	83.00
Sun.	57.00
Mon.	92.00
Tues.	47.50
Wed.	91.50
Thurs.	126.00
	$564.50

$564.50 divided by 7 days = $80.64 per day. $80.64 divided by 3 people = $26.88 per person, per day.

LENTILS WITH HAM HOCKS AND MACARONI

RINSE AND DRAIN:
1 package lentils, take pebbles out first

IN LARGE POT PUT:
3 cups chicken stock, (canned or homemade)
3 cups water
1 1/2 large onions, finely chopped
2 large carrots,
1/2 teaspoon thyme leaves
2 lbs ham hocks
BRING TO A BOIL, COVER AND SIMMER, STIRRING OCCA-
SIONALLY, FOR ABOUT ONE HOUR AND FORTY FIVE MINUTES,
OR UNTIL MEAT PULLS AWAY FROM BONE

ADD:
1/4 lb macaroni (any short fat kind will do)

COOK:
for another ten minutes or until macaroni is done

SERVES:
3 or four for dinner, and again for leftover lunch

Week 17   Nisko to Traki

LATVIA

LITHUANIA
Vilnius
Traki

BALTIC SEA

BELARUS

POLAND
Poznan
Warsaw

Nisko

Wroclaw
Krakow

Week Number Seventeen July 24 Through July 30, 1998

FRI. JULY 24
SAT. JULY 25 DROVE FROM POLAND TO TRAKI, LITHUANIA
SUN. JULY 26

Nothing eventful happened for these three days. Stayed in Soviet style hotels each night because we could find nothing better. In one place we went to an Italian restaurant with no spaghetti and no Italian food. One night the walls were so thin we could hear people peeing in the next room. No one got any sleep with all the hotel noise. However, eating and sleeping was at a budget wise all time low. Two rooms with full breakfasts cost between $30 and $60. Dinner and a considerable amount of beer for all of us together had not exceeded $15.

On Sunday we crossed the border from Poland into Lithuania. While waiting for the papers to be processed, we noticed there was a barrier of orange cones across half of the road where cars and trucks had to pass. Trying to avoid this barrier, a huge semi truck sideswiped us. It didn't do much damage, knocked off a piece of the front bumper, but Frank became very irate. He was not mad at the truck driver. He was mad at the border police because they had erected the barricade leaving half the passage way blocked off for no apparent reason. In the truck driver's mind, he had no choice but to squeeze between the orange cones and us. Eastern Europeans did not seem to question authority. Frank, being a Westerner with no inhibitions about negative attitudes towards authority figures nor, evidently, anxieties about being perceived as an ugly American, picked up the cones and threw them forcefully, conducting each one with a loud expletive to the other side of the road. There were nothing but looks of astonishment on the faces of the border guards and the truck drivers who had, up to that time, been waiting patiently to pass through the border. Nevertheless, once the dastardly deed had been done by the ill mannered foreigner, none of the truck drivers even hesitated to pass through the border area on the newly opened street, and the border guards did not interfere. They were probably in shock.

Went to a fairly nice camp on the beautiful lake in Traki. There were people there from just about everywhere in Europe. It was very noisy and the bathrooms were not too spiffy, so we decided to stay only two nights.

* Kempingas Slenyje (International Camping), 4050 Trakai, Lithuania. Tele: (307-38) 51387.

MON. JULY 27 TRAKI, LITHUANIA

After the usual clothes washing chores this morning, we rented a rowboat and Frank and I took turns rowing across the lake. Barbara's wrist was hurting, from some unknown cause, and she couldn't row. It was a beautiful day with a gorgeous blue sky up above. It took us about forty minutes to get across to the town of Traki. When we arrived, I stayed with the boat while they shopped for food. I had brought a book along to amuse myself. However, people watching in this little town with its nicely renovated castle off to the side of the boat dock, would have been entertainment enough. When Barbara and Frank returned, they said the people in the stores still used an abacus to figure the bills. They also found out that the word 'Ah chew" means "Thank you" in

Lithuanian. Now whenever anyone sneezes, one of us answers "You're welcome." You do get a little dingy after four months of traveling. We were gone for a little over two hours, but the boat only cost us about three dollars and four blisters.

The camp was very crowded and noisy. Late in the afternoon a busload of Germans pulled in. The bus had beds like the Pullman cars of a train. It also had camping equipment, tables and chairs. It had no bathroom. The people on this tour all helped with the work. They set up the tables and chairs, cooked their dinner, cleaned up and did the dishes as a group. It was evidently very inexpensive to travel this way. The majority of the people on this particular bus were upper middle age to elderly. German's are a very hardy group of people. Camping is by no means a luxurious or easy way to travel. After dinner they played cards, read or went to the camp bar to visit with other campers. Many of them spoke English as well as other languages. They were all very friendly and we enjoyed talking to them. However there was an obnoxious American man traveling with them. He spoke German fluently, and thought he was God's gift to the campground. It was my contention that he single handedly contributed to 20 per cent of the noise pollution. The other 80 per cent was brought about by some people in the camp who hired a hot air balloon. The noise that was made filling it up with air was unbelievable. I seriously thought about running away from home. After the balloon took off, people started going to bed, so things quieted down.

TUES. JULY 28 TRAKI, LITHUANIA

Left the camp this morning long after the elderly Germans. Drove to the other side of the lake to look for a hotel in Traki. We kept telling ourselves that we had more than enough money to live comfortably, but we always seem to find ourselves in Soviet style rat traps. Actually, the camp wasn't really that bad, unless we compared it to the Italian or

German camps. But the bathrooms were woefully wanting in privacy and cleanliness.

First we went to the tourist agency in town. The young people in charge were very friendly. They told us of an apartment for rent for $60 a night. It was just around the corner, so we walked over expecting the worst. It was attached to a brand new bank building. There were four or five apartments in the bank complex and it had obviously just been built. The woman in charge of the apartments spoke no English, but she smiled a lot and with Barbara's five words of German, added to the woman's five words of German, we were able to rent a two bedroom apartment for four nights. As in all the other places, the apartment was fully equipped with linens, towels, dishes, pots and pans, and silverware. What luxury! Even though it was now well into summer, the rest of the apartments were empty.

In the afternoon, I went out to get a haircut. I had cut my hair short before I left California, but it had been four months. Barbara always cuts Frank's hair because he doesn't really have any, and she had started cutting her own a few weeks before. In Peace Corps, I used to cut everybody's hair including my own because I found a magazine article that told how to do it step by step. But I was now a person of more means than the $150 a month I received in Peace Corps. I felt wealthy enough to have someone else cut my hair. Setting off in pursuit of a beauty parlor, I walked for about a mile with no luck. I asked a lady on the street by holding out a hank of hair with one hand and pretending to cut it with the fingers of my other hand. Then I shrugged my shoulders to show her I didn't know where to go. She laughed and pointed me back the way I had come. By repeating this pantomime along the way, I finally found the beauty parlor right across the street from our apartment. It was behind the stores on the street.

I went inside. There was a long line of men and women waiting on the right. On the left was a young woman just finishing up with an almost bald man. I did my pantomime for her and she motioned me to her chair. My inner intellect was telling me that there had to be a reason why all the other people were waiting for the woman on the right side of the shop, but my inner idiocy was telling me it was a crap shoot either way. I sat in the chair with much trepidation. The first thing the young woman did was to take a dripping comb out of a bucket of dubiously clean water and wipe it on a definitely grubby towel. I cringed as she began to comb my hair. I pantomimed again that I just wanted it washed and for her to cut a half inch off all over my head. She then took me to a Soviet style sink (not really attached to the wall) and washed my hair. She took great care in cutting it and I must say it wasn't any worse than some cuts I'd had at home. It was a little lopsided, but because it's curly, it really didn't show much. I didn't even get lice.

In the afternoon we met one of the young people from the tourist office on the street. He asked if we were going to the concert that evening. We didn't know anything about it, so he dragged us to the tourist office and sold us tickets. He said this concert was Lithuania's rendition of the Three Tenors in America.

Naturally it started to rain as we walked to the castle for the outdoor concert. By the time we were settled in the courtyard, it was pouring. The place was packed with people and everyone had umbrellas. We couldn't see much of the performance because of the umbrellas, but the singing was wonderful. After a while the rain let up and everyone put their umbrellas down. One of the tenors turned out to be a baritone. The people watching the show went wild with enthusiastic applause. It was an evening to remember.

WED. JULY 29 TRAKI, LITHUANIA

Took a bus into the capital city of Vilnius this morning. The bus station was in a part of the city that made my Peace Corps experience in Honduras seem like Shangri-la. I hadn't seen anything this bad for a long time. There were people begging everywhere, and everything and almost everyone was filthy dirty. The public bathroom was an experience none of us cared to repeat.

There were three things we needed to do in the city, and we had to go all over the entire city to get them done. Actually, this was a good thing because Vilnius is really a beautiful city if you stay away from the bus station. The parts they have renovated are quite lovely. It was obvious that they were working hard to repair and reconstruct. The first of our tasks was to find an ATM. In Traki, the bank didn't have ATM or cash advance services. The second task was to find out if we needed a visa to go to Latavia. The decision to visit the Baltics had been made rather hastily and we had very little information other than what was in our Eastern Europe book. The third, and most important task, was to find a supermarket that had imported food from Italy. We were out of everything we needed to make pasta.

There were ATMs on every corner in Vilnius, so that was no problem. A local travel agency found out for us that none of the Baltic States required visas from Americans, and a taxi took us to a grocery store that had everything. It was on the other side of the city. We took another taxi back to the bus station with all our gastronomical treasures. Between the taxi and walking at least five miles, we saw most of Vilnius. Had a surprisingly good lunch too.

THURS. JULY 30 TRAKI, LITHUANIA

Traki is the most beautiful little town. It's on a peninsula with lakes all around. The weather is always around seventy degrees in the summer, according to the local tourist agency. There is a path with many trees all around the lake. We took long walks along the water. The local castle and museum were quite interesting.

Our landlady was very sweet. We met her walking in town today and she blew us a kiss, a nice gesture when you have no common vocabulary. She came in every day and cleaned the apartment. This was the first time we had ever had our apartment cleaned. She gave us new bath and dish towels every day. Even the hotels didn't do that. Though there were many flaws in the workmanship, the apartment was very nice. The dish cabinet full of dishes did fall off the wall yesterday, but we were able to catch it as it fell, so no harm was done.

WEEKLY BUDGET # 17 JULY 24-JULY 30

LODGING

Hotels (2)	$91.50
Camps (2)	34.00
Apartment (3)	180.00

FOOD

Restaurants:

Dinners (2)	27.00
Lunches (1)	11.50
Groceries(18 meals)	71.00

ENTERTAINMENT

Cafes & Bars	18.00
Row Boat Rental	3.00
Concert	22.50
Museum	5.50

CAMPER

Camper Payment	168.00
Gas & Oil	48.00
Parking	5.50

TRANSPORTATION

Busses	4.00
Taxis	6.00

INCIDENTALS

Postage	3.00
Border Charge	7.50
Maps	6.00
	$712.50

WEEK # 17

Fri.	$126.00
Sat.	101.00
Sun.	81.50
Mon.	53.00
Tues.	127.00
Wed.	131.00
Thurs.	93.00
	$712.50

$712.50 divided by 7 days = $101.78 per day. $101.78 divided by 3 people = $33.92 per person, per day.

Week 18 Traki to Segulda

Week Number Eighteen July 31 Through August 6, 1998

FRI. JULY 31 TRAKI, LITHUANIA

Today we walked all over Traki again and had lunch in a touristy little restaurant down at the lake. The food wasn't very exciting, but the view was magnificent. We met an English couple about my age who were riding their bikes all over Eastern Europe. They had biked almost everywhere in the world, and I knew instinctively that they were a lot tougher than I would ever be.

I would have liked to have seen a little more of Vilnius, but Barbara and Frank voted for a day of rest and I was too lazy to go by myself. I knew I would get lost and spend most of the day trying to find myself again, so I settled for a lazy day.

SAT. AUG. 1 PANEVEZY, LITHUANIA

Drove northwest towards Latvia until about four thirty. There was only one hotel in the town of Panevezy. It was Soviet style naturally, and overpriced (for Eastern Europe). It cost us $70 for two rooms. Across the street from the hotel was a lovely park with lots of ducks. There was a wedding taking place as we passed through. Watching the wedding and walking all over the little town was our evening entertainment. We had Lithuanian pizza for dinner. It too was served smothered in catsup as in Poland, but we managed to convey to them that we didn't want any on ours.

SUN. AUG. 2 JURMALA, LATVIA

Crossed over the border into Latvia. Only had to wait about a half hour. We drove to Jurmala, thinking we'd like to stay near the beach as we did in Gdansk, Poland. Unfortunately, we were now in the high season, and getting a place at the beach was just about impossible. The campgrounds here were really the pits. We wanted to camp so we could have pasta for dinner. It was Sunday after all, but the bathrooms in the camps were beyond usable. We were all ex Peace Corps, so when I say bad, it really had to be disgusting.

We wound up in a Soviet style hotel near the beach. The walk to the beach was nice, but the hotel was really hideous. Soviet style hotels were unbelievable. They were almost always nineteen or twenty stories high. There were never more than two small elevators, undoubtedly installed when elevators were first invented. Each elevator moved erratically from side to side as the gears ground noisily pulling the box up or down.. The staircases were almost always blocked off, so that if there was a fire, you would be sure to die. The peeling linoleum or frayed carpets could and would entangle your every move. The plumbing invariably leaked and the unenclosed showers allowed the water to run all over the bathroom. Some of the toilets were stuck to the floor with globs of cement that looked like they were thrown there from at least five feet away. Others were not stuck to the floor at all. If you leaned over to get paper while sitting down, the whole toilet came with you. The plumbing pipes were always on the outsides of the walls, patched up and down the wall with globs of cement. The water pipes screamed day and night, and you could hear clearly every toilet on the floors above and below when they flushed. Beds were always single day beds covered with rough dark material. The sheets never fit, so that in the morning you body inevitably would be lying on the well used dark material. The lighting was comical. I was sure there was no wattage higher than forty in all of Eastern Europe. The curtains were thinner than sheets, and the sun came up at four A.M. in the summertime this far north. In short, Soviet style hotels were vile. If it wasn't for the fact that there was nothing else in many cities, I would never have paid good money to stay in one.

*Liesma Hotel, Dubultu prosp. 101, Jurmala (Pumpuri), Lat. Tele: 767032.

MON. AUG.3 RIGA, LATVIA

As much as we wanted to stay at the beach, none of us wanted to stay in the "Soviet Hell Hole" for another day, so we drove on to Riga. Riga is the capital city of Latvia. It sits on a large river and is rather attractive. We stopped to have a picnic lunch at a local park, and shared our chicken sandwiches with an ungrateful cat who turned his cute little nose up at our generosity. About a block away from the park, we found a suitable hotel. The Hotel Omni was about a mile and a half outside the city. It was run by a German company and had an old world charm that was only slightly akin to the Soviets. It was situated on the opposite side of the city from the river. We had a two bedroom "suite" with a bath. Everything was small and the space was almost as tight as the camper, but it was clean and neat and was a large step up from last night. It was costing us $80 a night. This was the capital after all.

Walked into "Old Town" for dinner. It was four miles round trip on Barbara's pedometer. Chose a higher class restaurant than usual. Very small, but they had a piano and Clarinet duo. An exceedingly enjoyable experience. We were always hungry for the sound of good music. All of the other people in the tiny restaurant were also foreigners. One group was a mixed tour, all speaking heavily accented English, the common language. The food was mediocre, but the company was amiable, and the duet played many songs that everyone seemed to know and enjoy. As my favorite Aunt Sallie used to say, a good time was had by all. After exploring the old town, we walked back to the hotel in the dark. There seemed to be very little crime here. Of course, we couldn't read the papers, so this was pure conjecture.

TUES. AUG. 4 RIGA, LATVIA

Walked into town again this morning. Went to an unusual medical museum, a doctor's private collection, distinctive and provocative. The man had a strange spectrum of the bizarre. It was interesting to see some of the oddball instruments doctors used in the early days of medicine. It was a wonder that anyone survived. Had lunch in a local cafe. Could read nothing on the menu, so we asked the waitress to bring us what a woman nearby was eating, bratworst. Instead, she brought each of us a large plate of what seemed to be chicken nuggets covered with thousand island dressing. Maybe we pointed in a foreign finger language? Walked home by way of a different bridge, seeing another part of the city. Did five miles on the pedometer.

WED. AUG. 5 SEGULDA, LATVIA

This morning we decided we were too cramped in our hotel rooms and tired of eating out. So we set out for Segulda, about an hour northeast of Riga. We were determined to find an apartment. The downtown area of Segulda was small with lots of green vegetation everywhere, but the points of interest were spread out for miles around. It was not like the usual tourist town, possibly because there seemed to be no tourists other than ourselves. The campgrounds in the area were, as usual, not to our liking. After an hour and a half of tracking down places in our book, we decided to try the local tourist office. They sent us to a guesthaus that was more than difficult to find. No one in the neighborhood had ever heard of this place, and this was a very small town. We searched for an hour or so, and narrowed it down to an edifice that had no sign and looked totally deserted, but was too big to be anything but a hotel.

We found a man and his daughter working out back. He spoke very little English, but said his wife could speak to us and that she would be back soon. He showed us two completely renovated rooms with baths that were very spacious and cost only $40.50 for both. Nothing else in the guesthaus was finished. His wife, who was a teacher on summer vacation, came in about this time. I asked her about breakfast because it was almost always included. She said the kitchen was not yet renovated and couldn't be used. They weren't actually opened for business yet, but they really wanted us to stay. I told her we had our own kitchen in the camper and asked if it would be all right to cook our meals in the parking lot out back. The both of them were delighted at this prospect. They told us to make ourselves at home.

The only other tenant in the building was a man who had an apartment on the second floor with his very large and vociferous dog. They assured us that no one would bother us and that we could use the upstairs lounge if we wanted to watch television. They did not live at the guesthaus, and would only be there in the daytime.

We took it for three nights. Barbara made pasta for dinner. It had been more than a week since we'd had it. Most people don't know this but Italians, even those whose blood has been thinned on American soil, have withdrawal symptoms if they don't get macaroni in one form or another at least once a week. Twice a week is preferable, and three times is ambrosial.

*Hotel Vejupe, Televizijas iela 19, Sigulda, LV 2150, Tele:371 2 973121

THURS. AUG 6 SEGULDA, LATVIA

Went back towards Riga this morning to the Ethnological museum, nineteen hectares large. I didn't know what that meant, but my feet screamed that it was mighty big. Saw many different kinds of houses and farms, all from various parts of Latvia and all from before this century. It was a little like going to Williamsburg with fewer people.

The museum was interesting, but the weather was getting cold and rainy. We decided we should start moving faster to get through Estonia and Finland. Couldn't understand how people could live here. They have two months a year of semi warm weather and then it freezes again. We had seen many drunks on the streets both here and in Lithuania. The weather more than likely was a major factor.

WEEKLY BUDGET # 18 JULY 31—AUGUST 6
LODGING
Bank apt. (1) $ 60.00
Hotels (6)   355.00
    FOOD
Restaurants:
Dinners (4)   122.50
Lunches (2)   25.00
Groceries (15 meals)   53.00
ENTERTAINMENT
Cafes & Bars   20.00
Museums   6.50
    CAMPER
Camper Payment   168.00
Gas   55.00
Parking   4.00
INCIDENTALS
Border Crossing   6.50
Postage   7.00
                     $883.00

WEEK # 18

Fri.	$116.00
Sat.	133.00
Sun.	110.50
Mon.	177.00
Tues.	161.50
Wed.	78.50
Thurs.	106.50
	$883.00

$883 divided by 7 days = $126. $126 divided by 3 people = $42 per day, per person.

Week 19 Segulda through Estonia and back to Traki

BALTIC
SEA

ESTONIA

RUSSIA

Tallen

Parnu

Seagulida

Riga

LATVIA

Panevezy

LITHUANIA

RUSSIA

POLAND

Traki

Vilnius

BELORUSSIA

WEEK NUMBER NINETEEN AUGUST 7 THROUGH AUGUST 13, 1998

FRI. AUG. 7 SEGULDA, LATVIA

Went to Turaida's Castle outside of Segulda today. It was being restored in a rather haphazard manner. In many of the restorations we have seen, there has been a concerted effort to make the new look as much a part of the old as was humanly possible. This one seemed to be being restored without any knowledge or forethought about what it had once looked like. The archaeological digging, was being done by what appeared to be college students, but they were doing it with large shovels instead of spoons. I really know nothing about archaeological digs except what I have read, but it seemed to me that anything fragile would be destroyed by the force of the huge shovels.

The old parts of the castle and the grounds were very pleasant and we all enjoyed exploring them. Barbara wanted to see "Maya's Grave" because she had read about the fable when she was a child. In the tale, a peasant girl falls in love with a gardener. A rich Lord comes and takes her away. She tricks the Lord into killing her with a magic scarf, and the gardener buries her under a local tree inside the castle walls. In my opinion, when one dies in the effort to get even, it is contradictory to any satisfaction that might have been obtained by revenge. It was all very tragic and less than romantic as fairy tales go.

In the evening, we went to Segulda Castle. Only the walls were still standing. It reminded me a lot of Tintern Abby in Wales. In the mist, it was all very ethereal, and I looked around for a darkly robed priest or at the very least Darth Vader to materialize out of the haze. We went to dinner in the ancient restaurant at the castle. It was very expensive, $65 for the typical meat and potatoes we'd been getting everywhere in Eastern Europe. But the waiters, the ambience and the evening were very pleasant.

SAT. AUG. 8 PARNU, ESTONIA

Arrived at the Latvian, Estonian border just before noon. Waited five hours and fifteen minutes to get across. The line was ridiculous to say the least. Most people just sat in their cars and waited patiently. Because we were lucky enough to have a camper, we had lunch, took naps, read our books, and played cards. We didn't get into Parnu, a village on the Baltic Sea, until after six o'clock.

Looked at hotels in the area for about an hour. Everyone was tired and cranky, so we took the attitude of our favorite Uncle Micky, said, "The hell with poverty!" and took an expensive non Soviet style hotel for $110 a night. We had a family suite with a bedroom and bath upstairs and the same on the lower level. It was over budget, but there were so many times we'd had no choice. We decided that from now on, when there was a choice, we would take the first class over cheap every time. We always said that until the next time. The three of us were such cheapskates.

The weather was still rainy and cold. Had pizza for dinner with the usual catsup sauce under the cheese, but the restaurant was dry and warm and the people were very friendly. In looking back over my journal, it sounds like we never ate anything except pizza and pasta. This was not really true. Barbara made a wonderful variety of meals many days each week. When we ate out, we unfortunately had meat and potatoes much more often than pizza.

SUN. AUG. 9 PARNU, ESTONIA

Looked at hotels all morning. Couldn't find anything we liked for less money, so we decided to just stay one more night and leave the beach area. The beach in Parnu has beautiful almost white sand. We went out walking on it, and walked for miles until the rain started coming down in buckets. This happened long before we got near our hotel. Barbara was the only one who had thought to bring rain gear. Frank and I were mostly soaked by the time we got back. Took showers to warm up and read and slept until early evening.

Took the car into town because it was still raining. Then we went to almost every bar in the area eating snacks and drinking beer. It was fun and it sure beat another dinner of meat and potatoes. However, most of the snacks they served were just that, meat and potatoes. About nine P.M. the sun came out, and we were able to walk without our rain ponchos. The nights are very short here. It gets dark well after ten P.M. and stays that way only until about 4 A.M. when the sun comes up.

MON. AUG. 10 TALLEN, ESTONIA

On the drive to Tallen, the capital of Estonia, we picked up two teenage girls who were hitchhiking. They were selling cheaply made massage devices for the equivalent of about $18. This was a summer job, as they were still in high school. I questioned them about their new freedom because they both spoke a little English and I didn't get such an opportunity very often. One girl said she liked the new political system because they were free. The other said very emphatically that she hated it. She flashed pleading looks at the other girl, like she wanted desperately to make her admit the truth. She insisted that life was much harder under the new system and that it was very difficult to make a living.

Neither girl had a father. Both had mothers who had to work very hard to support the family, and the two of them were working to help out. Americans of the twentieth century have always enjoyed freedom, and most of us take it for granted. But freedom doesn't feed hungry kids. It seemed to me, it would be a long time before the majority of the common people in the former Soviet Union would be employed securely enough to take the time to stop and enjoy their freedom.

About ten minutes before we got to the town where they wanted to go, it started to pour. Luckily, we were able to take them right to their destination. They had no rain gear or even jackets. This was no light summer rain. It was damn cold up here.

Found an expensive hotel on the outskirts of Tallen, $92 for two rooms with breakfast. At least it was not Soviet style, and there was even English television. After settling in, we drove into Tallen to find out about the ferry to Helsinki, Finland. We really didn't want to drive back through the Baltic States in all this rain. We decided a more desirable plan would be to take the ferry to Finland, spend a week there, and then take another ferry back to Gdansk, Poland. We got acquainted with the layout of Tallen, but it was too late to get any information. Drove back to the hotel for dinner. I was able to get a movie with Segorney Weaver on my television, the first movie I'd seen since we left home.

TUES. AUG. 11 TALLEN, ESTONIA

Since it was almost impossible to park in the city yesterday, we took two busses this morning to go back there. A young woman at our hotel, who spoke English fluently, told us exactly how to do it, and we had no problems at all. The sun even came out for our journey. However, we all carried our rain ponchos. On one bus, we met an American woman whose husband worked at the American Embassy. The recent bombings of the embassies in Africa had made her very nervous and she wanted to take her children and go home. Her husband did not feel the same way.

She also was not looking forward to another winter in Estonia. I could certainly understand that. As far as I was concerned, it was already winter! She did say, as had many other people we had met, that this was a very unusual summer. They usually got almost two months of summer before winter set in. (I don't think there is a spring or a fall this far north.) But this summer they only had a few days of real heat.

At the ferry office, we found out that it would be no problem to take a ferry to Helsinki, but we would have to wait at least three weeks to get a ferry to Gdansk. It was cold and wet in Finland, so this was unacceptable to all of us. We decided we would drive back the way we had come, and just shoot the border guards!

Spent the day exploring Tallen. It seemed to be a nice city, but it was cold, and of course it started raining again. I think the three of us were in a slump. It was weather depression. We came across a movie theater after lunch, and decided to go inside and forget our doldrums for awhile.

Unfortunately, the movie was Fear and Loathing in Las Vegas. We left after forty-five minutes. It was really bad. We only stayed that long because I had fallen asleep and Barbara and Frank didn't want to disturb me. When they could stand it no longer, they woke me up.

Had a Chinese, Indian dinner. Not great, but better than the usual fare. Took the two busses back to the hotel about nine o'clock. It was rainy and dreary, but it was definitely still daytime.

WED. AUG. 12 RIGA, LATVIA

No one was looking forward to the drive back to Poland, but we had all forgotten how small these Baltic countries were in reality. For some unknown reason it only took fifteen minutes at the border this time. By five P.M., we were back in Riga, Latvia. We went right to the Hotel Omni where we had stayed before. It was full. Now it was six o'clock. It had taken awhile to find the hotel, and we were tired and cranky again. We drove out to the airport and found a Canadian run Best Western Hotel. This was the most expensive hotel we had had so far, $118.50 for two rooms, including breakfast, but the luxury was wonderful. It put all of us into a better frame of mind. We dined in extravagant affluence, and drank toasts to a better, dryer, warmer tomorrow.

THURS. AUG. 13 TRAKI, LITHUANIA

We were all in great spirts today because the sun was shining and we were headed to Traki, where our wonderful new apartment in the bank building awaited us. We decided we would stay four days and just enjoy ourselves on the lake without getting into the car again. The first clue that the day would not be as fortuitous as anticipated was when it took one and a half hours to cross the border from Latvia to Lithuania. Then unfortunately, there was a festival in the town of Traki, and every available space was taken.

Went back to the campground where we had stayed our very first two nights here. Decided to stay four days in spite of the bad omens, just to enjoy the festival, the lake, and the sunshine. By nightfall the campground was packed. Met a nice English couple traveling in a motor home with two small preschoolers. Went over to their campsite to share a bottle of wine and conversation. The man worked for the Thomas Cook travel company. He was writing a book about travel in Eastern Europe. Since we were traveling in opposite directions, we swapped stories and places to stay. I was also able to trade two books with them. This was a real bonus because I was just about down to nothing to read again.

WEEKLY BUDGET # 19 AUGUST 7—AUGUST 13
LODGING
Hotels (6) $563.00
Camps (1)   16.00
FOOD
Restaurants:
Dinners (6)   191.50
Lunches (2)   29.50
Groceries (7 meals)   50.00
ENTERTAINMENT
Cafes & Bars   23.50
Movie   13.50
Museum   7.00
CAMPER
Camper Payment   168.00
Gas   65.50
Oil   3.50
Camper Supplies   7.00
Parking   2.00
TRANSPORTATION
Busses   6.00
INCIDENTALS
Gift for Bro. Nick   2.50 (We didn't want to spoil him.)
Toilet fees   .50
Border Crossing   5.00
Newspaper   3.00
                $1157.00

WEEK # 19

Fri.	$146.50
Sat.	181.00
Sun.	171.00
Mon.	172.00
Tues.	197.50
Wed.	217.50
Thurs.	71.50
	$1157.00

$1157 divided by 7 days = $165.28. $165.28 divided by 3 people = $55.09 per person, per day.

LAMB CHOPS A LA BARBARA

BROWN IN PAN:
3 lamb chops
1 onion chopped
3 cloves of chopped garlic

ADD:
1/2 cup white wine
1/2 teaspoon curry powder

SIMMER FOR 1/2 HOUR. TAKE OUT ABOUT 1 TABLESPOON OF LIQUID AND ADD IT TO 1/2 CUP YOGURT. STIR IT TO WARM THE YOGURT. (Add a little warm water if too thick) POUR BACK INTO PAN AND STIR AGAIN.

ADD:
1/2 cup chopped cilantro

SERVE OVER COOKED RICE

Week 20 Traki to Sochaczew

Week Number Twenty August 14 Through August 20, 1998

FRI. AUG. 14 AUGUSTOW, POLAND

Woke up to pouring rain in the Traki campground, and the deluge continued all morning. It would have been difficult for one person to live in a small camper when it rained. Three was impossible. There was just no point sitting in the camper in the downpour as ill fortune continued to pursue us, so we decided to drive on to Poland.

Arrived in Augustow in the early evening, as usual. The last time we were in this town, we couldn't find any place to stay and had to drive on towards Lithuania. Nothing had changed. There was a campground here in a nice resort, but it was still raining. We kept that for a last recourse, and went looking for a suitable hotel.

Augustow is a nice little town in the popular lake area of northern Poland. It is surrounded by beautiful lakes and is very popular with Polish tourists. After trying every hotel in town, we went back to a crummy Soviet style hotel that we had turned down the last time we were here. This time they showed us two newly decorated rooms with baths. Our delight was immediately diminished by the fact that it was available for only one night. We had hoped to stay and rest for a few days, but it was not to be. Took it for one night. Walked all over town in the evening, lamenting the fact that we were being forced to move on. The town was so cute and interesting, but this happened to people who preferred whimsical freedom of movement to making reservations. Depressing as it was, we all agreed that spontaneity was more important to each of us than security.

SAT. AUG. 15 MIKOLAJKI, POLAND

Bid good-by to Augustow and drove on through the heart of the lake country. The scenery was smashing. There were glacial lakes among the rolling hills in every direction. I can only imagine how much more beautiful it would have been if we had not been besieged by rain.

Our camping book said that the camp in Mikolajki had cabins with varying degrees of facilities. Unfortunately, the cabins with kitchens were all full. Took one with just two bedrooms and a bath. It was hideous and squalid. However, this was the only Polish camp that we had found to have any amenities at all in their cabins, other than beds and a table. At least there was a bathroom. The lady in the office was very sweet. She promised she would get us a cabin with a kitchen after the weekend.

SUN. AUG. 16 MIKOLAJKI, POLAND

Spent the morning looking for a better apartment. There was nothing in town with a kitchen, though there were some nice clean rooms in people's homes. Barbara had been cooking in the camper outside our cabin. It would have been all right if the cabin had been clean. Instead, it was grimy, and nothing short of burning it down could have sanitize it.

Mikolajki was another nice little town on a beautiful lake. Many Polish and other European tourists were here. We seldom heard English spoken, except with an accent, when it was used as a common language between Poles and other Europeans.

The woman in the camp office worked long hours, as did the other hotel and camp workers we had met. She had to be there from 8 A.M. until 10 P.M., with a half hour off for lunch and dinner. Her brother leased the camp from the owner, and she worked for him. She was about sixty years old. I went to get some towels from her, and she was almost in tears because she was so tired. I felt very badly for her.

*Camp: There was only one in Mikolajki.

MON. AUG. 17 MIKOLAJKI, POLAND

Got a cabin with a kitchen this morning. It was much bigger, but almost as wretched as the last one. It only appeared to be a little cleaner because there was more space. The weather had been cold, rainy and gloomy since we arrived in Mikolajki, but today it was beautiful.

Went for a boat ride on the lake to take advantage of the beautiful weather. Thought we were going to see the whole lake, but at the first stop, they made us get off. The captain went up and down the boat looking for us. We evidently bought tickets for only a short ride, but we had no idea that we were the fugitives he was seeking. We couldn't understand anything he said to us, and we were getting upset because he wanted to put us off in the middle of nowhere. Luckily some of the other passengers spoke English and they assured us that another boat would come in about ten minutes. Twenty minutes later the boat arrived.

In the afternoon, I walked into town while Barbara and Frank took a nap. I loved this little town and I loved the Polish people. They were outgoing, friendly and jovial. As I was walking past a bus stop, I saw a little old lady on the bench. She smiled at me and held out her hand. We had not seen very many beggars on this trip. I am always appalled when I see old people begging. It seems very unfair that they should be reduced to asking favors from strangers when they should have been resting on their laurels, or at least on social security. I sat down next to the old woman and smiled at her. I gave her some money and she did an astonishing thing. She took my hand and kissed it. Found out later that this is a Polish custom. When one meets someone new, or when something is done for someone else, the hand is kissed in appreciation.

I did some shopping, had tea in an outdoor cafe while writing postcards, and thoroughly enjoyed my afternoon of solitude.

TUES. AUG. 18 MIKOLAJKI, POLAND

It poured all morning. We stayed home, washed clothes, and hung them on the porch to drip. They sure weren't going to dry. About eleven thirty the sun came out, and we walked into town to shop for groceries. While walking through the outdoor market, we tried blueberry waffles with whipped cream, a specialty here. Well worth the thousands of calories.

After lunch, we walked along the shore of the lake as far as the road went, about two miles. This was when we came across the place where the boat captain had forced us to disembark. Had we walked for the twenty minutes that we had waited, we could have been home. This area reminded me greatly of beach areas in California. There were houses all along the water and boats tied up along the shore. Neither were as ostentatious as Newport Beach or Balboa Island, but you could tell that the enjoyment of the water was appreciated every bit as much and maybe even more.

WED. AUG. 19 MIKOLAJKI, POLAND

Went to a petting farm today. It was wonderful to be so close to animals again. With a large group of people, we took a tour to the four corners of the farm. Saw reindeer, moose, goats, wolves, and all kinds of birds. Most of the animals were quite tame. Everyone was petting them and taking pictures with them. The wolves were kept apart in a large fenced off area. The hike through the mud was quite rigorous. There were stiles over the fences that we all had to climb. The only time I ever heard of a stile was in the children's poem, *There was a Crooked Man.*

This was the first time I had ever seen one, let alone climbed one. It was a delightful day.

It was still rainy and cold in the afternoon, so we decided to cut the week short and head south tomorrow.

THURS. AUG. 20 SOCHACZEW, POLAND

Spent the day driving to Such-a-screw. This is near where Chopin's home is located. We were here before with Marsha. Came back because we remembered that the Hotel Chopin was very nice, and we had to come this way anyway. The best part was that they actually had two vacancies. We also got the car washed again as the hotel had this service.

It was still raining. Decided to explore a part of the town we missed last time. There is an unwritten law in Poland, and for that matter all of Eastern Europe. The rule is that you must never walk without constantly looking down at your feet. If you let your eyes wander for even a few seconds, you will fall and break both ankles, or worse, step in a pile of dog shit. This rule is in effect because there are no sidewalks or streets that are not broken, have cut off tree roots lifting the pavement, or have sewer covers rising at least six inches above the walkway. Take it from one who has walked many miles on foreign soil. Not to say that all of our sidewalks are so great, but in the United States, you can usually walk a short distance admiring the scenery before falling. Here it was necessary to stop completely before taking your eyes off your extremities.

WEEKLY BUDGET # 20 AUG. 14—AUG. 20

LODGING

Hotels (2)	$138.00
Camp Apts. (5)	283.00

FOOD

Restaurants:

Dinners (2)	32.00
Groceries (19 meals)	71.50

ENTERTAINMENT

Cafes & Bars	36.50
Boat Ride	21.00
Petting Farm	4.50

CAMPER

Camper Payment	168.00
Gas	53.50
Car Wash	6.00
Parking	8.50

INCIDENTALS

Guide Book	3.50
Postage	1.00
	$826.50

WEEK # 20

Fri.	$118.00
Sat.	110.00
Sun.	87.50
Mon.	123.00
Tues.	110.00
Wed.	115.50
Thurs.	162.50
	$826.50

$826.50 divided by 7 days = $118.07. $118.07 divided by 3 people = $39.35 per person, per day.

Week 21 Sochaczew to Zakopani

Week Number Twenty One August 21 Through August 27, 1998

FRI. AUG. 21 KRAKOW, POLAND

The one night stands we were doing were killers, but we had already seen this area and were anxious to move on to uncharted territories. For variety we took a different route today through the city of Czestochowa, where the Black Madonna is located. Due to a total lack of religious convictions on all our parts, we didn't stop to see it. Outside the cities, the scenery was composed of rolling hills and lots of rivers. It was much nicer than the main road from Warsaw to Krakow that we had taken before.

Had to take a detour across one of the large rivers. The bridge we crossed on was so rickety that it was terrifying. As we looked down the river, we saw that the detour was created because the old bridge had fallen into the river. It looked worse than the Bay Bridge in San Francisco after the earthquake. If I were a religious person, I would have blessed myself. It was a frightening sight, and the bridge we were now on felt like it might be in worse condition.

When we got to Krakow, we got lost and wound up driving right through the city, a portentous experience, and I was just a passenger. Finally got onto the road to Camp Korona. This was the nice camp with good drinking water where we stayed before. The sun was shining. Unbelievable!

*Camping Korona. Directions: Take E-77 from Krakow (road to Zakopane)

SAT. AUG. 22 KRAKOW, POLAND

This morning we went back to Auschwitz. We had missed the memorials that each of the European countries had erected for the museum, and we wanted to take the bus to Berkenau. You really need two days to see it all. Belgium had a very heart wrenching memorial. It showed an ordinary family of four having dinner. Then, as you walked down the hall, one by one the family members disappeared. To depict the disappearance, there was a hole right through the life-sized photo and the board behind it. It was very effective.

Berkenau is about three miles from Auschwitz. The bus, like the rest of the museum, is free to the public. Berkenau is where the crematoriums were located. Auschwitz was a working camp. Those that were too old, too young, or too infirm were sent to Berkenaw to die. The Nazi's had tried to burn down the crematoriums when the allied forces were about to arrive, but they were only partially successful. Horrible as these death camps were, I think everyone should be required to see them. Maybe then history wouldn't repeat itself so often.

When we were about to leave Auschwitz, we met a couple from California. Carol Mickelsen writes camping books. She and her friend had a horrible robbery story to tell us. Somebody had evidently tied water bottles to the bottom of their car while they were off viewing something.. Later, when they got out to investigate the noise, another person was there to commiserate with them. They had left the keys in the car, and the thief just jumped in and drove away. They lost everything, passports, money, camping equipment, etc., and were left with nothing but the clothes on their backs. By the time we met them, they had wired home for money and had bought everything new. It will make a great story for her book, but it was definitely an expensive lesson to learn. We told her we had money belts on us at all times and that we never carried much cash. She wanted to know how we got money, and we told her about ATMs. We also explained about banking with an investment company to make interest on the money while we traveled. We exchanged names and addresses so we could get together and compare notes at home.

SUN. AUG. 23 ZAKOPANE, POLAND

Finally into new territory. Drove up into the Tatra Mountains today, actually, the low Tatras. It was beautiful, but cold. Zakopane is a mountain resort. Our luck must have been changing. Went to the tourist office as soon as we arrived in town. The first place they sent us to was marvelous. It was a cute little house. It had two bedrooms and a bath upstairs, and a living room, bathroom and kitchen downstairs. It cost $59 a night. We were in heaven and decided to stay for eight days. We all needed a rest.

MON. AUG. 24 ZAKOPANE

Hung out at the house all morning. It was about two and a half miles to downtown, so we could walk or take the bus. Today we walked for exercise. There was a folk festival in town. We got tickets for tomorrow. Groups from Georgia, Hungary and Poland will be performing in the *Festiwal Folkloru* 1998. Zakopane has this festival every summer.

TUES. AUG. 25 ZAKOPANE

This morning we took the bus to town and then walked all over exploring. Zakopane is as popular in this southernmost part of Poland as Mikolajki is in the northernmost part of Poland. We were very lucky to get such a nice place to stay as there were thousands of tourists here.

In the late afternoon, we saw the folk show. The Georgians did a spectacular dance with knives and swords. The costumes were as enchanting as the women dancers were beautiful. The Hungarians were also excellent if not as athletic, but the Polish part of the show was tedious. The show was two hours long and cost $4.50 for all of us. Every evening different countries performed, but the Poles performed every night. They tried to do skits about old world country life. However, a good percentage of the audience couldn't understand Polish. Their singing and dancing was very amateurish too. It was a shame because they really meant well and tried hard.

In spite of all this, we decided to buy tickets to the final performance on Saturday night. This will evidently be a presentation of all the winners. The final performance cost $13 for all of us, less than it would cost us to go to a movie at home. After purchasing the tickets, we had a good roasted chicken dinner and took a taxi home. Luxury!

WED. AUG. 26 ZAKOPANE

Took the funicular up to the top of the Tatra Mountains overlooking Zakopane today. It didn't rain at all and the view was wonderful. Unfortunately, Barbara took her eyes off the ground and fell very hard. She skinned her elbow badly and twisted her ankle. She's tough though. She got up and limped to the nearest bar. I had bandages and Neosporin in my backpack, so she went into the bathroom and doctored herself up before she drank her beer. The woman in the bathroom wanted to charge her even when she held up her elbow to show her the dripping blood. The bathroom Dragon Ladies are forever vigilant.

THURS. AUG. 27 ZAKOPANI

Today we took a 45 minute bus ride along a winding mountain road towards Poprad, Slovakia. We paid a small park entrance fee and, with about seventeen other people, boarded a horse drawn wagon. We rode further up the mountain for about an hour. After this, we disembarked and walked another one and one half miles up the mountain. The scenery was wonderful, though the air was very cold. Eventually we came to a beautiful lake surrounded by tall mountain peaks. Most of the people up there had walked the whole way. Some were elderly and some were close to crippled. The Poles, like the Germans, are a hardy group.

We had lunch and then took a walk part way around the lake. I had to admit this place was more beautiful than Clear Lake. In fact, it was even more beautiful than Lake Guarda in Italy. However, it was a lot more difficult to get to than either Clear Lake or Guarda.

While on our walk, we encountered an American family. The man was from North Dakota and had just married a Polish American woman. She brought him and his sixteen year old daughter to visit her family in Poland. It was really a great experience for all of them because the woman had been born here and spoke Polish fluently. We talked for quite a while. They had been to see one of the folk shows we had seen in Zakopani. They raved about the Zulu's performance. The teenager described the Polish performance as "Embarrassing." We had to agree with that, but said we were looking forward to seeing the finals on Saturday. We exchanged E-mail addresses for future contact.

We walked down the mountain to the bus. According to Barbara's pedometer, we walked just short of ten miles, and we only went one way. I really respect these Poles. They might not be great entertainers, but they are a very fit group.

WEEKLY BUDGET # 21 AUG. 21—AUG. 27
LODGING

Camps (2)	$ 27.00
Little House (5)	295.00

FOOD

Restaurants:

Dinner (1)	10.00
Lunches (2)	15.00
Groceries (19 meals)	51.50

ENTERTAINMENT

Cafes & Bars	29.50
Int. Dance Festival	4.50
Gondola	10.50
Int. Dance Fest. Finals	13.00
Horse Drawn Wagon	17.00
Park Entrance	1.50
Spending Money	14.00

CAMPER

Camper Payment	168.00
Gas	41.50
Parking	2.50

TRANSPORTATION

Busses	12.50
Taxis	3.00

INCIDENTALS

Toilet Fees	1.50
	$717.50

WEEK # 21

Fri.	$ 60.00
Sat.	79.00
Sun.	95.00
Mon.	119.00
Tues.	102.50
Wed.	134.50
Thurs.	127.50
	$717.50

$717.50 divided by 7 days = $102.5. $102.50 divided by 3 people = $34.16 per person, per day.

Week 22 Zakopani to Eger

POLAND

Krakow
Zakopane
Leuvca
Poprad • Kosice
Eger
CZECH
• Prague
REPUBLIC
SLOVAKIA
Vienna
Bratislavia
Budapest
AUSTRIA
HUNGARY
SERBIA
SLOVENIA
CROATIA
BOSNIA

Week Number Twenty Two August 28 Through September 3, 1998

FRI. AUG. 28 ZAKOPANE, POLAND

Took the bus to Kunice today. Could have walked, as it wasn't very far, but weren't really sure where it was located. Our objective was to take the gondola up to the 6,000 foot peak. We had to wait three hours in line to get on the gondola. Never again!

Didn't realize it at first, but tour groups took precedence over those who didn't purchase tickets ahead of time, a must do if we are ever here again. Also many people in line were letting people get ahead of them. We started standing in the path so no one could pass. Not a good thing to do in a foreign country. I think we wound up changing a way of life. The people in front of us, when they realized what we were doing, started questioning each person as to whether or not they had someone holding their place. They were really getting into helping us be guards. Many people had legitimately gone to the bathroom or left for a snack. Those that were just butting in were sent packing. The amount of people who thought they had a right to go to the front of the line was unbelievable. Some argued in an imperious tone of voice as if they had a God given right to intrude. We couldn't understand the words, but the condescending manner was unmistakable. When they weren't allowed to pass, they became hostile, but by this time all of the people in front of us, and there were at least thirty, were determined not to let anyone else pass. My guess is that in the old days high ranking people could just go to the head of the line, but Poland is free now and the people are just beginning to understand that.

Through the chain link fence, we could see a little old lady and her grandchild approaching from far away. They walked around the fence and came right up to the man made barrier expecting to be let right through. I think it is a Polish custom, like giving seats on the buses, to let old people pass to the front of the line. The three of us had nothing to do with this anymore. The thirty odd people ahead of us refused to let the old lady pass. She pleaded with them, but they were resolute. I felt like we had created a monster, but on the other hand, we had been waiting for almost three hours. A lady behind us let the woman get in line with her.

After a while, all of the people in front of us had gone on the gondola. Then they let us through the turnstile and stopped everyone behind us to let a tour group through, so we were separated from all the friends we had made in line. We went to the door of the entrance to the gondola and stopped, even though no one was there to stop us. At Disneyland, no one was ever allowed on the platform until it was time to enter the gondola because it was dangerous.

A Polish-Prussian man dressed in Alpine climbing clothes tried to push past me. I wasn't about to let anyone get in front of me again. He was about sixty-five years of age and carried himself just like a military general. He told me in English that he wanted to pass. Then he started yelling at me, "Excuse me. Don't you understand English? Let me by!" He yelled it three times getting louder and angrier with each outburst. I told him that we had been in line for three hours. He had waited less than ten minutes. He literally pushed me aside and went out on the platform. Everyone in the line behind him followed including us.

Frank got the bright idea that the gondola would be coming on the other side from where everyone was waiting. He thought this because he could see it coming. The three of us got out of line, where we would have been the second group to enter the gondola, and went to the opposite side of the walkway. Of course what Frank had seen was the last gondola going away from us. His vision is only slightly better than mine, and I am blind in one eye. We all started laughing. The Nazi on the other side of the platform looked haughtily down his nose at us. He had a knowing smile on his countenance that openly stated, Dumkoff Amerikanski! And in this case, he was right! When the gondola arrived, the Nazi and his wife and grandchild got right in front for a spectacular view. The rest of the people ran for all the surrounding windows. We were right in the middle. We could neither see nor move, but we were all still chuckling over Frank's brilliant move.

It didn't rain all day and the view from the top was spectacular. We had lunch up there and walked all over looking at the scenery from every side. After about two hours, we got in line again to take the gondola down. The line was very short because many people had walked down. It takes two and a half to three hours to walk. If we hadn't done ten miles the day before, I was sure Barbara and Frank would have forced me to do it, Ist Gut! Thank goodness they were tired from standing for three hours. Besides, we had round trip tickets, and we were all too cheap to waste them.

The Nazi was at the front of the line, of course. After a while a woman came and demanded to get in front of us. She spoke in Polish, but it was easy to tell what she wanted. I wasn't even going to object because I figured she was with someone up front, but it was a very narrow space and there was no place to which I could move. She was a rather large woman and I had on a backpack. She pinched me hard on my arm and shoved me backward while yelling, Mine man! Then she bulldozed her way to the front of the line and stood by the Nazi. Evidently she was his wife. I didn't remember her from our last encounter because I had been concentrating on him. Now I was mad. It takes a lot to make me mad, but deliberately pinching and shoving me will do it! So I said in a loud voice, "Oh, she's the wife of the Nazi! No wonder she pinched me and pushed me to get ahead. She is a Nazi too! Nazi's always think they are better than everyone else!" Most of the people in line only understood the word "Nazi," but there were a few who understood all of it, including the Nazi himself. It didn't change anything, but it sure made me feel better. Now I was an ugly American just like my brother.

Before long we got on the gondola and started down. At the half way point everyone had to get out and get into another gondola. Well, Mrs. Nazi had some sort of difficulty and was delayed. Thus Mr. Nazi couldn't get to the second gondola in time to be in front. He screamed at the guard and everyone else. He wasn't about to ride in the middle, with us. He dragged his wife and his grandchild, who was screaming Niet!, niet!, niet!, over to the gondola we had all just exited. He was going to go back up again so that he could be in front. This guy really had a problem. I could picture him in a death camp torturing people with unabashed pleasure. When we got to the bottom, Frank pointed out that there was now a guard at the entrance and no one was being allowed on to the gondola platform until our group had disembarked. That particular safety rule was evidently in effect here as well as at Disneyland.

SAT. AUG. 29 ZAKOPANE, POLAND]

We were very happy with our little Polish house. Between the two bedrooms there was only one thin board and you could hear a pin drop, but between the inside and outside of the house it was well insulated for winter with double paned windows. I appreciated this because, as far as I was concerned, it already was winter, even though it was August. It rained part of every day and it never got above fifty degrees. The mountains surrounding the town still had snow.

Went hiking in the nearby woods this morning. You must pay a fee to go on any trail. It was worth it though because the trails were fairly free of trash, unlike the roadside woods, and there was no traffic. The countryside was lovely. Young and old alike hiked here all the time.

Went to the folk dance finals late this afternoon. The show was four hours long. Most of this time was taken up by the Poles. We decided the city fathers must have paid off all the people who put the show together by letting them perform. There was only one group that was worse. We think they were Czechs, but couldn't understand anything that was said, so we weren't sure. Most of the other groups were fantastic. The Georgians and the Zulus took the grand prizes.

We were all going to miss Poland. We loved the people, in spite of their lack of musical talent. We found them to be a lot like the Italians. Most of them were friendly and happy, not counting the Nazi on the gondola. They had no talent for building anything that required plumbing or electricity and they didn't know the meaning of a straight line. Light switches and window frames were always crooked. They were actually worse than the Italians in this area. If that was possible. Also, unlike the Italians, with the exception of my brother, they drank too much. We often saw young men drunk in the parks, sometimes old men and even women too. But on the whole they were a generous, friendly fun loving people.

Around the whole country, we had seen accordion players from seven to seventy years of age, playing for coins on the streets. They all played the same song, "The Anniversary waltz." Why, I couldn't say. Evidently they all had the same teacher, and these are the people who helped produce Chopin! (However, I think he was half French.) The Poles may have been decidedly lacking in musical talent, but they never let that stop them from performing. It was really kind of refreshing. Singing and dancing just for the joy of it can't be a bad thing. It probably would be better if they didn't try to do it on the stage, but their enthusiasm was definitely contagious.

Now that we were about to leave Poland for the last time, I had to admit that I would miss the country and its people. After a month and a half, we were all starting to feel Polish. Barbara even thought she could speak the language. I was going to miss the sound of horses clip-clopping by on the cobblestone street outside our house, the long walks in the Polish woods, and the genuine joy in the laughter of the people. We had only one more day in this wonderful country.

SUN. AUG. 30 ZAKOPANE, POLAND

Did laundry and hung out around the house this morning. I took a bus into town by myself in the afternoon. I liked to look at everything and I hated it when someone was waiting for me. Needed some time alone anyway, and I was sure Barbara and Frank did too. I enjoyed my afternoon of solitude, even though I didn't buy anything. Everything I wanted was too big to carry.

MON. AUG. 31 LEUVCA, SLOVAKIA

Drove back to the Slovakian border the same way the bus to the lake had gone the other day. Arrived at the beautiful little walled city of Leuvca. It was only an hour and a half from Zakopane, but it was higher up in the Tatra Mountains.

Got a nice recently remodeled hotel right in the heart of town. The town only has about twenty streets. We had decided to stay here only two days instead of a week because we were all tired of being cold and, if we didn't hurry to Hungary, we would miss summer completely. The hotel was about $80 for two very nice rooms, though the light switches on the walls were not straight here either. We found out that foreigners were required to pay double what the locals paid. They had the rates posted when we entered. They made no bones about this rip-off. However, everything else was so unbelievably cheap that they probably had a right to make up the difference any way they could.

It rained hard most of the afternoon. Went to dinner in a fancy restaurant and had our first Slovakian food. We each had a three course meal with a great deal of beer and soda, and the whole thing came to $12.50.

The food was mostly meat and potatoes, but the flavors were good, though none of us knew exactly what we were eating.

*Arkada Hotel, Curila miroslav, nam. majstra pavla 26, Levoca, Slovakia. Tele: 0042/966/51 23 72.

TUES. SEPT. 1 LEUVCA, SLOVAKIA

The sun came out. Walked all over the walled city of Leuvca this morning soaking up the rays, through heavy coats of course. We followed the old wall as far as it went, more than halfway around the town. Any street you looked down had a beautiful view of the countryside because the town was in the middle of no where. It rained off and on, but lightly.

Almost everything we wanted to see in town was closed for the season. Three tour busses were here all morning, but it was September first and the season was over as of today. They did have a canned music show outside the Town Hall. It was fun to watch, and the audience had to follow the cast around the second story porch to different parts of the building. The actors all had on mediaeval costumes and mouthed the words to a tape for both talking and singing. This was good because no one could have heard otherwise. Of course, more than likely, none of the tourists could understand Slovakian anyway. The sun came out every now and then, but I never removed my coat. Had pizza with ketchup for dinner, ugh!

WED. SEPT 2 KOSICE, SLOVAKIA

This morning we set out for Kosice. On the way we came to Spisski Hrad Castle. It sat high on a hill and could be seen for miles around. We explored all of it for over an hour. I must say it was one of the most interesting castles I had ever seen, and I had seen a lot of castles by this time.

We had planned to stop in Presov, but it was so massive and loaded with Soviet style buildings that we just drove on to Kosice. We arrived about three o'clock. Kosice is another huge city, but it is nicely laid out. Went to every hotel in our book. They were either full or horrible. Wound up in the Hotel Hutnik. The book said to only stay there as a last resort and the book was right.

The old town of Kosice had been remodeled beautifully. We walked all over and had dinner in a nice restaurant. Had we had a nicer place to stay, I would liked to have stayed longer even though it was freezing.

THURS. SEPT. 3 EGER, HUNGARY

There was a K-Mart, called Tesco in Kosice, right across the street from our hotel. We were able to stock up on all the supplies we needed. They had bandages for Barbara's elbow, which got infected after her fall in Poland. Unfortunately, we couldn't get hydrogen peroxide. They had linguini, something we hadn't been able to find since leaving Italy. They had Parmesan and tomato sauce, neither of which we had seen since Germany. I guess the Italians from Italy, the real Italians, brought it with them when they traveled, but we had no excess room.

We drove across the Slovak-Hungarian border to a camp in Eger. Hotels were out of the picture because it was time to have pasta for dinner again. We had had pasta, with the last of our supplies, in the little house in Zakopani. But it had been four days since then, and withdrawal was once again consuming us. Found a fairly nice camp in Eger and settled in.

While exploring the camp, I came across a group of Kiwi kids (young people from New Zealand) traveling in an old van. I was delighted to be able to exchange two books with them. English reading material was always a problem. As I've said before, we brought nine books with us that none of us had read. I was down to two in Italy. Since my only job on this trip was to wash dishes and handle the money, I had more free time than Barbara or Frank. Marsha brought two books with her and left them with us. We were able to buy two English novels in Berlin, and I traded two that we had all read at the camp in Traki, Lithuania with the British couple that worked for Thomas Cook. With this trade in Eger, I would be able to read my sixteenth and seventeenth novels, and with luck, I would not finish them before I got back to California.

WEEKLY BUDGET # 22 AUGUST 28—SEPTEMBER 3

LODGING

Little House (3)	$177.00
Hotels (3)	232,50
Camps (1)	10.00

FOOD

Restaurants:

Dinners (4)	55.50
Lunches (2)	20.00
Breakfast (1)	4.00
Groceries (14 meals)	68.50

ENTERTAINMENT

Cafes & Bars	10.00
Gondola Ride	20.00
Hiking Trail	2.50
Castle Entrance	3.00

CAMPER

Camper Payment	168.00
Gas	38.50
Parking	3.50

TRANSPORTATION

Busses	3.50
Taxis	3.00
	$819.50

WEEK # 22
Fri. $130.00
Sat.   112.00
Sun.   89.00
Mon.   136.00
Tues.   124.00
Wed.   128.50
Thurs.   100.00
              $819.50

$819.50 divided by 7 days = $117.07. $117.07 divided by 3 people = $39.02 per person, per day.

My UNCLE JIMMY'S CHICKEN CACCITORI
(Barbara makes this to perfection)

BROWN IN OLIVE OIL:
2 1/2 lbs. chicken breasts (about 4 cups)
1 medium onion, chopped (1 cup)
3 cloves garlic, chopped or pressed

ADD:
1 cup white wine
1 cup chicken stock (can buy in can if traveling)
2 sprigs fresh basil leaves, or 1 teaspoon dried basil
1 sprig fresh oregano leaves, or 1/2 teaspoon dried oregano
1/2 cup whole black olives
1/2 cup whole green olives
salt, pepper and hot red pepper flakes to taste

SIMMER:
3 to 4 hours, covered

SERVES:
6 good sized meals (We ate it for two dinners)

Week 23   Eger to Szentendre

Week Number Twenty Three September 4 Through September 10, 1998

FRI. SEPT. 4 Romi, HUNGARY

Didn't leave Eger until almost noon today. First we walked from the camp all over town. It was a bit of a disappointment. The brochures the Hungarian Government had sent to us in California had beautiful pictures of the castle on the lake or a very wide river. The glories of both the castle and the river were greatly exaggerated.

Took the new toll road into Budapest. Budapest is really two cities, Buda and Pest, one on each side of the Danube. However, most people refer to it collectively as Budapest. The toll road was very fast and free because it was so new that they hadn't opened the toll booths yet. Went to a hotel in the Romi resort area north of Budapest. The woman behind the desk was really not interested in renting rooms. We had come to think of this as the "Soviet Attitude". We had run into it in a number of Soviet style hotels. The clerk would have a personal conversation on the phone, laughing and chatting with a friend, while we waited. Or they would tell us they couldn't leave the desk to show us the rooms, and would we please wait. After we waited awhile, they would decide, for no apparent reason, that they could show the rooms to us now, but we must hurry. This seemed to be all part of the plan to rush us through, not giving us a chance to examine anything too closely. This time Barbara decided to linger in

227

one bathroom and she discovered that the shower was nothing more than a hose connected to the sink faucet. We left.

At the next hotel, the woman in charge was very pleasant. She didn't speak English, as the first woman had, but she smiled and was congenial. She let us look at the rooms alone because she too couldn't leave the desk. This hotel was every bit as crappy as the first one, but it was $20 less and the showers worked. However, we took it mostly because the desk clerk was agreeable and smiled at us.

I had run into this Soviet type attitude in the States too. It was mostly held by people who were bored with their jobs and couldn't care less about pleasing the customer. But here the attitude was much more prevalent. Under the old Soviet system, no one had to worry about losing his job. Evidently that feeling of security was still being felt here, but no one likes being greeted by a supercilious, bored clerk. In time, even the former Soviet citizens will take offence.

This was probably the number one reason why McDonald's was so popular here. Not only was it kept very clean, but the help always smiled and made the customers feel welcome, even when they were just using the free bathrooms as we did. K-Mart, or Tesco as it was called here, was also doing a booming business. There the people were allowed to touch the merchandize and the help even smiled while they were doing it. In Soviet style stores, everything was behind a counter with the clerk. The clerk had to get each and every item for every customer. The second the item was in the customer's hands, she would ring it up on the cash register. I personally like to read labels and debate with myself over each purchase, but that was not possible in a Soviet style store. There were always ten people behind me in line, and the harried clerk had no time to dillydally. Tesco was like a whole new world to these people. It was only a matter of time before the Soviet style stores disappeared completely (in my opinion).

The Romi area is on the Danube River. As soon as we settled into the hotel rooms, we set out to explore. It was touristy, but many places had closed down for the season, so business was slow. We had lunch in a little hole in the wall, outdoor cafe. It was the kind of place where most Americans would never dream of eating, and it was absolutely delicious. I have no idea what I ate. I pointed to what some workmen were eating. Frank and Barbara pointed to something else. All the customers that were eating got into the act, helping us to order. Hungarian food was the best of the Eastern European food we had tasted so far.

SAT. SEPT. 5 ROMI, HUNGARY

I will always remember this place as Hotel Shit because Frank had a unique experience this morning. Most of the toilets here had a shelf that everything landed on. I figured this was because one could inspect his or her excrements for disease or worms. Frank was very late getting ready. Barbara and I were chatting outside the hotel for at least a half hour. He explained his adventure as follows:

"I did my usual healthy load and pulled the weighted string which flushes the toilet. You know how high up the tank is? The water came down like an explosion and everything in the toilet gushed all over me, my clothes, and the floor. I had to get into the shower and scrub all my clothes and myself."

Now you would have to know how fastidious Frank is to appreciate this story. He never changed a baby diaper in his life. He would go visit a neighbor if one of his kids needed to be changed when he was alone. If a household pet had an accident, he would vanish. He was know as Mr. Meticulous in every walk of his life. This experience in the bathroom nearly devastated him. Barbara and I roared when he told us what had happened.

We set out for the near by town of Szentendre (Saint Andrew). We were looking for a new place to live. Frank refused to spend any unnecessary time with that toilet. Szentendre is a beautiful little town on the Danube, north of Budapest. None of us wanted to stay right in Budapest, as it is unbelievably huge.

Found a parking place and the tourist office in Szentendre as soon as we arrived. The town was small so everything was easily accessible. Asked the young woman in the tourist office for an apartment where we could cook. She sent us to a house that was on a hill just up the street from the downtown area. She said she wouldn't tell us anything about it because tourist all have different opinions. She didn't want to hear, "Too dirty, or too small." She said if we didn't like it to just come back, say "No," and she would find us something else, thus absolving herself of all responsibility.

We agreed to her terms and went to look. The people were very nice. There were just two of them. The man spoke only a few words of English, but said his son would visit tomorrow and that he spoke English very well. There were two bedrooms separated by a large porch. Each room had its own small bath and one room had an alcove with a hot plate and a sink for cooking. It was definitely not elegant, but it was clean, private, and cost only $25 a night for all of us, so we took it for a week starting tomorrow.

Went back to our hotel which was only about ten miles away. Went to a fancy tourist restaurant next to the hotel for dinner. It was excellent. We were all ecstatic. Not only did we have an apartment for the next week, but we had actually found another good place to eat.

SUN. SEPT 6 SZENTENDRE, HUNGARY

Went shopping for groceries on our way to Szentendre. Then we moved into our new apartment. It poured all day and night. The landlord's son came for Sunday dinner with his parents. He told us what to be sure and see in the area and how to get to each place. It stopped raining long enough for us to walk around this quaint little tourist town in the afternoon. Came home early so Barbara could make the pasta sauce. It was Sunday after all.

The weather was depressing all of us. We all admitted today that this trip was too long, but since we haven't seen it all yet, no one wanted to quit. The first three months were great. Then Marsha came and that was a good break, but when she left and we knew we had nothing but second world accommodations ahead of us, we all got kind of down. We kept telling ourselves that we could afford better accommodations, but we never seemed to find anything better. At three or four in the afternoon, we would agree to take anything. This place we were now in was much more comfortable than we thought it would be, and for a week we would be content. But the week would be over shortly, and we all dreaded looking for new accommodations, especially when the weather was so awful.

MON. SEPT 7 SZENTENDRE, HUNGRY

It rained all morning and we just hung out at the apartment. My room was like a separate apartment from their room, and it was very comfortable. After lunch, I went into town to get a haircut. I needed to get one much more often now because I wouldn't let them cut off a lot of hair. Szentendre had a lot of tourists, and most of the shopkeepers spoke a little English, so I was able to find a beauty parlor more easily than the last time. This shop was so much nicer than the one in Lithuania, where I was sure I was going to get lice at the very least. It was clean and well set up. The young beautician was not prepared for a tourist and at first she was quite grumpy. By the time she had finished though, she had warmed up considerably. It took almost an hour, but she gave me a much better cut than the last one.

Szentendre was a shoppers paradise. There were so many beautiful things to buy, from household items to personal. I spent the rest of the afternoon looking, though lack of space kept my purchases under control. Before I went back to the apartment, I stopped at the tourist office and got tickets for a bus tour to Budapest tomorrow for all of us. It had finally stopped raining.

TUES. SEPT. 8 SZENTENDRE, HUNGRY

This morning we took the bus tour of Budapest. The mini bus came to Szentendre to pick us up, and it was worth the extra $22 round trip for the three of us. It would have cost half that on the train, but then we would have had to navigate the city alone. This was the third time we had taken a tour of a big city. Both Verona and Berlin were better tours, but only because it was hard to see out of the little mini bus in Budapest. A regular bus is much higher off the ground and affords a much better view. However we all enjoyed the tour. It had been raining for the past three days, and smoggy Budapest was clear and beautiful today. Even Barbara, who really doesn't like the big cities, enjoyed it. The driver let us off in various places of interest and picked us up an hour later. We were alone on the bus until after lunch when an American couple joined us. There seemed to be very few tourists in the city at this time of year. The last stop was at a huge indoor market, the nicest I'd seen in Eastern Europe. We were able to shop for souvenirs as well as finding a variety of fresh green vegetables. An hour later the mini bus took us back to Szentendre.

WED. SEPT 9 SZENTENDRE, HUNGARY

This morning we tried to pay for half of the week in our apartment. We never liked to carry a lot of cash around, and the amount we could get from an ATM was limited to a couple of hundred dollars with each transaction, depending on the city. Our landlord did not understand. He thought we wanted to leave. He called his son in Budapest and insisted that Frank talk to him. Frank explained why we wanted to pay half, but the son kept saying there was no need because they trusted us. Frank finally convinced him and we paid.

Went on the Danube Bend boat cruise this morning. The day was beautiful again, lifting our spirits greatly. We walked about two miles to the boat dock just outside of Szentendre. The cruise went to Visegrad, a small town about an hour and a half north. There was almost nothing in

Visegrad except the ruins of an old castle that was built in the thirteenth century. From that time on through the ages, the royalty spent millions building it up and tearing it down again because the next royal family didn't like it. Then it was abandoned for a hundred years or so until another king came along and spent a fortune of the people's money remodeling it once again. (Sounds like our congress, doesn't it?) Exploring the various additions and subtractions was enjoyable. The weather remained beautiful all day I just hoped the sun would bless us with its presence for a few more weeks. It would be nice to finally have summer, even if it was already September.

THURS. SEPT. 10 SZENTENDRE, HUNGRY

This morning we walked to the only big market we knew of in town. It was about one and a half miles from our apartment. We filled our backpacks with lots of groceries that we needed and checked out the local Chinese restaurant on the way home. There were actually Asian people running it. This was a definite plus. We would have dinner here on Saturday.

In the afternoon, Barbara and I convinced ourselves that we had room for a few more souvenirs and went shopping in town again. Frank sat in the square drinking a beer and people watching. There was a charming little Gipsy child, about seven years old, that kept him captivated. She managed to get coins from just about everyone she asked. Then she would take her booty back to Mama, who was sitting in a doorway waiting. Luckily, Mama was paying close attention because one tourist wanted hugs and kisses for his coins, and Mama had to come and disentangle him from her child. Barbara and I had joined Frank by this time, and we too saw this little scenario. I thought that Mama showed great restraint. I would have belted the guy.

We had pasta for dinner again. It was Thursday after all, and we had to take full advantage of having a kitchen.

WEEKLY BUDGET # 23 SEPTEMBER 4—SEPTEMBER 10
    LODGING

Hotels (2)	$127.00
Apartments (5)	125.00

FOOD

Restaurants:

Dinners (2)	50.00
Lunches (2)	17.00
Groceries (17 meals)	73.00

ENTERTAINMENT

Cafes & Bars	28.50
Bus Tour (Budapest)	70.00
Museum	4.50
Danube Bend Tour	11.00
Castle Entrance	1.00

CAMPER

Camper Payment	168.00
Gas	30.00
Parking	.50

INCIDENTALS

Map	1.00
Used Book	1.00
Toilet Fees	.50
	$708.50

WEEKLY BUDGET # 23

Fri.	$120.00
Sat.	148.50
Sun.	80.00
Mon.	125.00
Tues.	93.00
Wed.	66.00
Thurs.	76.00
	$708.50

$708.50 divided by 7 days = $101.21. $101.21 divided by 3 people = $33.73 per day, per person.

Week 24   Szentendre to Lake Balaton

WEEK NUMBER TWENTY FOUR SEPTEMBER 11 THROUGH SEPTEMBER 17, 1998

FRI. SEPT. 11 SZENTENDRE, HUNGARY

After walking a mile and a half to the market yesterday, we found another large market two blocks from the apartment this morning. Oh well.

Went to, in my opinion, one of the finest art museums I have ever seen. The Margit Kovacks Museum was right here in the little town of Szentendre. Kovacks was a local woman who left her home to the city to be used as a museum for her sculptures and paintings. She stipulated in her will that her work must never be taken from the Museum. These were some of the most wonderful, unusual sculptures I had ever encountered. I followed a tour guide from Spain through the museum in order to learn a little more about this unusual artist. I could tell, the tour guide really loved Kovacks' work. She was especially animated as she described the shapes of the sculpted heads. The heads were elongated and unparalleled in their configurations. Kovacks had done a sculptured bust of her mother that was extraordinary. In the paintings, the people had the same types of shapes and these too were exceptional and charming. I couldn't believe an artist of such caliber could be so anonymous to the world.

I met Barbara and Frank in the museum store trying frantically to find a book of Kovacks' work in English. They both loved her work as much as

I did. We each bought a book. One was in German, but the pictures were fabulous.

I went on a final shopping spree by myself this afternoon. I bought the cutest little Hungarian outfit for the three year old daughter of a friend of mine. I absolutely loathe grocery shopping and clothing shopping, but shopping for souvenirs was definitely one of my favorite avocations. We had another of Barbara's excellent dinners tonight. I sure was happy that she liked to cook, because I loved to eat.

SAT. SEPT. 12 SZENTENDRE, HUNGARY

Went by bus to another ethnological museum this morning. The son of the house had given us explicit instructions on how to do this. Because it was the end of the season, the museum was having a big festival. They had the usual homes from eras gone by that we had seen in other ethnological museums. There were people dressed in costumes of preceding eras as well, but they also had wonderful folk shows with singing and dancing. For $1.20 per person, we were entertained royally for an entire day. We had some surprisingly good goulash soup for lunch. It was surprising because in the States, amusement parks and Museums are famous for their high priced, infinitely boring fast foods.

On the bus going home, we met a lost young woman and her mom who were visiting from Singapore. The girl was quite fluent in English, and said it was now the first language in Singapore, however her mother only knew a few words. They were staying in Budapest and had been riding the bus all afternoon looking for Szentendre. They disembarked with us, and we walked them to town. We also showed them where they could catch a boat back to Budapest along the Danube.

This evening was our big night out on the town. Our "night to wail" as Frank proclaimed almost every Saturday night. We walked a mile and a half to the Chinese restaurant we had seen before. It was clean and tastefully decorated. The food was very good. It didn't measure up to the authentic Chinese food we'd had in Warsaw, but it was a close second.

We were feeling saturated and satisfied as we walked home. Heard music coming out of a bar that was in a small boat along the river, so we went inside. A father and son were playing various instruments and singing. The daughter was the waitress, and between waiting tables, she periodically went up front to help entertain. The only other customers were two German men at the bar. The entertainment was wonderful. They played music from all over Europe and America. The father was dressed as a sea captain and reminded me greatly of Tavia from Fiddler on the Roof. The five of us drank and sang with them until almost midnight, when a large crowd of people came in to celebrate a birthday. My favorite Aunt Sallie always summed up a party like this by saying, "And a good time was had by all." And so it was. Frank's prognostication was right for a change.

SUN. SEPT 13 BAJA, HUNGRY

Winter came back this morning. We had three glorious days of almost summer weather, and now it was pouring. We bid good-by to our Hungarian hosts, and drove south through Budapest to Baja. We had an excellent view of Buda by driving along the Danube on the Pest side. There was almost no traffic because it was Sunday. The Gothic style Parliament Building was well worth seeing from across the river.

Went to a campground within walking distance to the city of Baja. Rented a bungalow with two bedrooms, a bath and a kitchen for $39.50 a night. The catch was that the only heat was the two burner stove in the kitchen. It was far from luxurious, but at least we could cook tomorrow. Today all the stores were closed. We didn't shop this morning because we thought we might be in a hotel, so we had to go out for dinner anyway. We would have our Sunday pasta tomorrow.

Walked into town in the rain. Almost nothing was opened, but eventually we found a little restaurant with a lot of people in it. Dinner was very cheap, salad, entree and drinks for all of us was only $10. It wasn't particularly good, but it filled us up.

*There was only one camp in Baja, and it was signposted. It was on the opposite side of the river from the town.

MON. SEPT. 14 BAJA, HUNGARY

It poured all night. Then it poured all day. Walked to the market in town anyway. Got some ingredients we needed for sauce tonight, and also got lots of veggies for a stir fry tomorrow. Actually found some spinach. Again I must admit that almost always, by the time we got to the market, all the green stuff was gone. But being lazy in the morning was our prerogative. We were on vacation!

Went to a department store and shopped for ski outfits for all of us. None of us ski, but the outfits looked nice and most importantly, they were warm. These outfits were almost a uniform here in Eastern Europe. Four out of every five people wore them. I could understand why! We were all freezing. The outfits cost between $15 and $20, unless you bought one that said Adiddas or Nike. Then they cost $115 or $120. I will admit, the quality was not great on the cheap ones, but it was certainly not $100 better for expensive ones.

We did a little sight seeing. The rain was enhanced by gusts of cold wind, so we gave up and went back to the bungalow. Read and played cards all afternoon and evening. It never stopped raining. I enjoy the rain if I have a fireplace and a good book, but I hate it if I am cold. The book I was reading was not so hot either.

TUES. SEPT 15 BAJA, HUNGARY

Hooray, the sun came out! Because of the cold, getting wet yesterday, and airborne exposure, Frank came down with a cold. Thanks to Marsha, we had medicine, so he was not feeling too badly.

There was a mother cat and two kittens here in the camp. This morning I heard Barbara luring them to our bungalow. "Now I'm going to break up this pork from the sauce for you because I know you like delicate little pieces. I'm going to pour the milk right over the pork so you can have both at the same time. Oh dear, pork with milk! You're not Jewish are you?"

Drove to Kiskuhalas this morning. This is where they make Halis Lace, with the logo of the three little fishes. I must admit that none of us had ever heard of it before, but it was in one of our books and Barbara and I were interested in buying some lace for window curtains. Ha! Little did we know that four square inches cost about $50, and rightfully so. We watched the women working and they showed us exactly how they did it. The place was laid out so you could see every stage of development. At first when we saw the lace, we thought the larger pictures were appliqued onto the lace. But no, the pictures were woven by hand, with the finest of thread. Each woman, and only women were sewing, made the 4 by 4 or 6 by 6 piece by herself from beginning to end. Even Frank was fascinated. Although, I believe he enjoyed lunch a lot more. After lunch, we shopped again for ski outfits, but only Frank was able to find one.

WED. SEPT 16 PECS, HUNGARY

It was a little warmer today and still not raining. The campground in Baja was very pretty. It was located right on the river. The site was only picturesque in the river area. It was quite beautiful in fact, but the town had too many Soviet style apartments which spoiled the "Old Town" appearance. Took a long hike along the river this morning before we left Baja.

The city of Pecs was not far from Baja, and we drove there in time for lunch. We had leftover stir fry in the camper. We were trying to diet. The heaps of meat and potatoes we consumed when we ate out were beginning to show. We may not have liked it, but that didn't mean we didn't eat it anyway. Barbara's good cooking didn't help either. She was always saying, "Now there's enough here for lunch tomorrow!" And we would always eat it all. But this time we were really trying to cut down. Barbara's arm seemed to be healed. It took two weeks. However, Frank was still not up to par.

We looked at a lot of hotels before we found one with a vacancy. It was in the hills overlooking the city of Pecs. Everyone at the Hotel Mediterran spoke English with American accents instead of the usual British. The hotel was owned by an American from Tuscon, Arizona. Tuscon is the sister city of Pecs. The help was very accommodating, and the hotel was very nice, though a bit expensive for our budget, $83.50 a night for two rooms with breakfast. There was to be a convention in town the next day, which was why we had so much trouble finding a hotel. Because of this convention, we would be expected to move to more expensive rooms tomorrow if we wanted to stay here.

Went for a hike in the hills this afternoon up to a communications tower. Had to pay to go up and see the view which was quite nice. We ate dinner back at our hotel. It was one of the worst meals we had ever eaten. We were the only people in the restaurant, and it was easy to see why. The food was quite possibly poorly cooked frozen TV dinners. The salad had so much mayonnaise on it that it was sickening. We ate almost nothing. Instead we pushed it aside and drank wine, coke for me. The waiter had disappeared for a good half hour after we ordered. No one was paying attention, but afterwards we figured out that he must have gone into the kitchen to heat up our dinners.

When he saw we weren't eating anything, the waiter went and got the manager. The manager very politely asked what was wrong with our dinners. I asked if he wanted to know the truth. He said, "of course." So I was prepared to tell it all. I started by saying that a Mediterranean salad should be made with olive oil not mayonnaise. He said it was a house speciality and was not really Mediterranean, but Hotel Mediterran. Now I was embarrassed. Frank saved me by telling them it was just too much food, but we were very happy that they cared enough to inquire. They gave us a free bottle of wine and another coke. We felt badly for the young waiter who took it all very personally, so we left him a nice tip. After two full bottles of wine, Barbara and Frank were feeling no pain and no hunger either. I was starving, but I needed to diet.

*Hotel Mediterran H-7627 Pecs, Domorkapu. Tele: 36(72) 336-222

THURS. SEPT. 17 LAKE BALATON, HUNGARY

It was pouring! The wind was howling! It was winter again! Breakfast this morning was worse than dinner had been last night. (If that was possible.) The coffee tasted like chocolate mixed with mud. There was no coffee flavor at all. It was luke warm because they didn't keep it in a thermos. The tea water was the same. There was no fruit or juice. The cold cereal was covered with sugar. Luckily, the bread and cheese were edible, not great, but edible.

We decided at breakfast that we would leave this morning. The hotel was really nice but the new rooms would be even more expensive and the food was an abomination. Because it was raining and Frank was sick, we figured we would be stuck here for three meals a day. That thought alone made us want to pack-up and leave.

Frank had already gone back to the room while Barbara and I were getting ready to leave the table. At that time the manager and the young desk clerk brought the owner over to meet us. He was here from Tuscon. I had forgotten I told the clerk yesterday that I wanted to meet the owner. This was before I had tasted the food. The help at this hotel was especially good and cooperative. The owner was quite pleasant. Said he wanted to open a few more hotels in Hungary. All I could think was, "Have you ever eaten here?" Fortunately, I bit my tongue hard and told him we had decided to leave today because it was pouring and Frank was sick. I am such a coward.

I really should have told him the truth so he could do something to improve his cuisine, but discretion was still the better part of valor.

As we drove away from the hotel, we had a small argument over where to go next. I wanted to look for another hotel in Pecs. Pecs is a university city and looked to be very interesting. Barbara and Frank thought all the hotels would be full because of the convention, so we drove on to Lake Balaton. We stopped at a roadside restaurant for lunch. It was delicious. Almost every place we'd eaten in Hungry, the food had been good, except for the Hotel Mediterran. American TV dinners had never appealed to any of us.

When we got to Balatonfured at the lake side, we stopped at a place that proclaimed to have free apartment information. The woman in charge spoke English. She said everything was closed because the season was over. Then she picked up the phone and within two minutes a man with an apartment to rent was there. He lived across the street. He showed us a double room with a small fully equipped kitchen and a single room down the hall. Both had private baths. The house was almost new, very clean and quite nice. He said we could have both rooms for $37 a night if we would commit to four nights. We said it depended on the weather. It had just stopped raining again. He said he wanted $56 if we wanted to take it day by day. I told him this was the first place we had seen. Frank, who loves to haggle, said we would only commit to two nights and only for $37 a night. The man relented immediately. I also love to bargain, but afterwards I felt kind of bad. This was one of the nicest apartments we'd had in Eastern Europe, and each room had a TV with two English channels. However, we soon found out that there were empty apartments all over town.

In the afternoon, we walked down to the lake and explored the little tourist town. It was really very nice. We will probably stay more than the four days the man was bargaining for, but we were still free to go where the wind blew us, and the wind was blowing ferociously.

*Taschner Arpan, H—Balatonfured. IFJUSAG STR. 2. Bei DELTA Einkaufzentrum. 300 Metervom Pla. Hensee. Tele: 00 30 579—290.

WEEKLY BUDGET # 24 SEPTEMBER 11—SEPTEMBER 17
LODGING

Hotel (1)	$ 83.50
Apartments (3)	87.00
Camp Bungalow (3)	118.50

FOOD
Restaurants:

Dinners (3)	68.00
Lunches (3)	19.50
Groceries (15 meals)	44.50

ENTERTAINMENT

Cafes & Bars	22.50
Ethnological Museum	4.00
Other Museums	6.50
Top of Tower (Pecs)	2.50

CAMPER

Camper Payment	168.00
Gas	54.00

TRANSPORTATION

Busses	2.00

INCIDENTALS

Newsweek Magazine	1.00
	$681.50

WEEKLY BUDGET # 24

Fri.	$ 65.00
Sat.	107.00
Sun.	114.00
Mon.	70.50
Tues.	84.00
Wed.	136.50
Thurs.	104.50
	$681.50

$681.50 divided by 7 days = $97.35. $97.35 divided by 3 people = $32.45 per person, per day.

Week 25 Lake Balaton to Trencin

Week Number Twenty Five September 18 Through September 24, 1998

FRI. SEPT.18 LAKE BALATON, HUNGARY

The sun was shinning this morning. Hallelujah! Walked to the lake. It was quite nice, but this part of the lake is not as beautiful as Clearlake in California. Checked on the tour boats. We would probably go on one tomorrow. Wanted to see the whole lake. It is slightly larger than Clear Lake, about 100 miles around, to Clear Lake's 90 miles. I was anxious to see if the rest of it would be as beautiful as our books had stated. Went shopping for food, as we had decided to stay at least four days. It started raining on our way home.

Washed clothes after lunch. I sure was tired of doing my laundry by hand, but laundromats were unheard of in this part of the world. The sun came out again in the late afternoon, so we walked to the town of Balatonfured. Barbara and I were still looking for skiing outfits. They were hard to find, and when we did find them, either there were no smalls or mediums or they were badly flawed.

In the evening, I watched the news in my room. Evidently our illustrious president had submerged himself into some hot water. We got a smattering of it in Newsweek Magazine last week, but there was no substitute for watching someone do George Orwell's "Newspeak" in person.

SAT. SEPT 19 LAKE BALATON, HUNGRY

Walked to the lake for the boat ride this morning. The sun was shinning brightly, though it was bitterly cold. The boat ride turned out to be only an hour long and went just a very short distance. There was an Englishman on board who was wearing shorts and a short sleeved cotton shirt. He didn't even hug himself during the trip. We were bundled up in sweaters, coats and scarves. In spite of this, our bodies were totally numb when we got off. Even Barbara was cold.

Had really been taking it easy these past few days. Frank was still recovering from his cold and Barbara and I just seemed to be tired. We were still walking about four or five miles a day, but we were sleeping nine hours at night.

The news tonight was all about our ill-fated president. We were so excited to be able to get an American news station. We had been away from home for six months now. Our only news had been from the newspaper we bought once a week, either the international "USA Today" or the "Herald," and then only when it was available. Truthfully that was just fine with all of us. Now that we had an English channel, we were being inundated with this sordid affair. Nevertheless, no one wanted to turn it off. We all agreed that Clinton's sex life should be his own business, but lying under oath was an intolerable debasement on the part of the President of the United States, or anyone else for that matter. The message he was sending to America's children was that anyone with power and money could do whatever he or she damn pleased. I grew up under the illusion that in the United states the laws apply to everyone. Evidently, this is only true for the common people. The rules for the rich and powerful are obviously different.

To our great delight, Jay Leno came on right after the news. The show was from two days ago, but it was still very relevant. None of us had heard anything about a cigar being involved between Clinton and Lewinski, but we picked up on the innuendos right off. Actually, "innuendo" was exactly where the cigar was placed, if one were speaking with an Italian accent.

The show was hilarious, if somewhat of a denigration to the office of the presidency.

When the Jay Leno show was over, I went back to my own room and turned on the TV. Another talk show was on the screen. A young man with a very Irish sounding name was in charge. The program was still on the subject of Clinton and was extremely raunchy. I laughed out loud while saying, "How can they put this on public television?" My sides hurt from laughing so much. It was flagrantly uncouth, and I enjoyed it immensely.

SUN. SEPT. 20 LAKE BALATON, HUNGRY

It poured all morning. Drove to the north shore of the lake but could see almost nothing. Went about forty miles before we turned around. At the far end, we got out of the car and walked to the end of a pier. Not only was it freezing, but the wind was whipping our rain ponchos furiously. A German tour of older people came out on the pier too. They all had umbrellas that were instantly blown inside out. We were all laughing while wrestling with our respective encumbrances, but we were the better off of the two groups. Long rain ponchos with hoods were by far better than umbrellas under these circumstances. My advice to any traveler would be never to leave home without one. They folded up to a tiny size and were light in weight. They kept the wind out, and I frequently wore mine over my coat, even when it wasn't raining. The trick was to buy one that was not plastic. The plastic ones were hot and uncomfortable.

Stopped for some delicious spicy goulash soup on the way back to Balatonfured. The weather cleared up for the ride home. I was wrong, the lake was definitely as beautiful as Clearlake, especially the north shore, where there were lots of grape vines and beautiful green hills.

The sun stayed out all afternoon. After a rest in our rooms, we went for a walk down to the lake again, and found out that there was a harvest festival in town. We got to see a parade with marching bands and folk dancing. It was very nice, and as we sat in a sidewalk cafe, all bundled up of course, we tried to think of things our little city of Lakeport might do to enhance its image. Over our usual beer and ice cream we solved all the financial problems of the communities around Clearlake back home. This was our last day at Lake Balaton. It was very nice of the city to give us this send off.

MON. SEPT 21 GYOR, HUNGARY

Tonight will be our last night in Hungary. We had all liked Hungary. The food was so much better than the rest of Eastern Europe and the people were congenial and accommodating. Drove north most of the day to the sizable city of Gyor. The drive was pleasant and scenic, but as soon as we arrived, we had the same old problem: look for a hotel or look for a tourist office. Found both at the same time because they were practically in the same place. Went to the tourist office first. The Hotel Rana looked very expensive. The lady in the office said the entire town was full. She based this information on the fact that none of the hotels she called, answered their phones. We walked across the street to the Rana. She assured us that we were wasting our time, but to go ahead and try. We got two rooms immediately. It wasn't cheap, $168.50 for two small rooms with no amenities, such as bottled water and remote control. This was the most expensive hotel we'd had so far. (I know I have said this before, but the prices kept getting higher.)

One of the reasons we wanted this costly hotel tonight was because they had CNN, the English television channel from the states. Clinton was due to be interrogated and give his now famous double talk about oral sex not really being sex, enlightening every five year old in America about subjects heretofore considered unmentionable until at least the age of thrirty-nine. When we told the women at the desk that we wanted to see and hear our President on television, they all put their hands over their mouths and giggled. It was not exactly a proud moment for Americans.

The interrogation of Clinton went on forever. When we got good and bored, we went out for dinner. Our hotel was right downtown, so we walked all over seeing the sights. On the river, we found a boat with a 67' Chevy Monte Carlo on top of it. It was painted black and white and had printing on the side that said, "Chichago State Police." (sic) Decided we'd have to come back in the morning to get a picture of it in the daylight. Had a good dinner in a local pub, probably our last for a while. Back at the hotel, Clinton was still spinning his tangled webs. I couldn't decide who was worse, he or the righteous right that put him on international television. Nevertheless, I kept watching. I suppose my morbid curiosity was as damning as either side's portrayal.

*Hotel Rana, Gyor

TUES. SEPT 22 TRNAVA, SLOVAKIA

Stopped at Tesco (K-Mart) on our way out of town this morning. Stocked up on wine and water. Took a brand new toll road to the Slovakian border, crossing back over without any trouble. Took only about fifteen minutes, including changing our Hungarian money back into Slovakian. This was a very expensive way to get money, but usually we couldn't get to an ATM for a day or two after arriving in a country. We needed at least $20 to survive, and Hungarian money was no longer of any use to us now. We still had a little Slovakian money from when we were here before. By combining the two, we had about $60 in cash.

Drove to Bratislava to a camp with bungalows. The sun was still shining, so we thought we'd try camping again. As usual the bungalows had only beds in them and they were all taken. The camp was very run down, so we decided not to camp. Instead, we drove to Trnava, about fifty kilometers northeast of Bratislava.

Trnava is a nice little walled city. We found a small hotel outside of town in the woods near a lake. Because we were low on cash, we took just one room. For some reason they only charged us the local rate instead of the tourist rate. We decided to stay three days and go in to see Bratislava from here. Of course the hotel was full for the next two days, so that was out. We made reservations to come back to this hotel for two nights starting next Monday. We'd have to see Bratislava then.

*Hotel Koliba, Kamenny mlyn, Trnava,Slo. Tele: 0805/344 59.

WED. SEPT. 23 TRENCIN, SLOVAKIA

Drove north to Trencin. Went to every hotel and pension in our book without finding a place to stay. Even went to the campground. It was on an island surrounded by beautiful blue water. Quite lovely, but unfortunately closed and locked up for the season. Decided we would have to go on to another town. On the way out, we came across a brand new hotel called Evergreen. We took two rooms for two nights. Later we decided that since the worst part of traveling was finding a place to stay, and since everything we wanted to see was within eighty kilometers, we would make day trips and return here each night. We told the desk clerk that we would stay for five nights, and breathed a collective sigh of relief.

Walked about two miles into the city center. This town was built on a hill with a castle at the top. It was really quite interesting, but we couldn't find anything opened that served food. Finally about 7:30 P.M., we came to a cute little Italian restaurant that was opened. We were all very leery of Italian food in Slovakia since they used catsup instead of tomato sauce, but we were very hungry.

None of the help spoke English. Nor did anyone know the few German words that Barbara used in all Eastern European restaurants. Barbara and I ordered mushroom pizza. Frank, who was very hungry, ordered a first dish of Spaghetti and a second dish that the man from the next table assured him he wouldn't like because it would be too hot. Frank burned out his taste buds long ago, and was dying for something muy picante.

The man at the next table spoke a little English and told Frank that the meat dish he wanted came with potatoes. Frank said he didn't want the potatoes, just the hot meat. The waitress insisted that he must have potatoes so he could put the meat on top. We were laughing because the conversation was bizarre. The other customers were all trying to help, though only the one man spoke any English.

Finally Frank gave up and said he would have potatoes with his spaghetti if the waitress wouldn't serve the dish any other way. At this point, the waitress told the English speaking man that they didn't have any potatoes. This brought the house down. When the food came, the "very hot dish" came with rice.

A new waitress delivered the food and was visibly upset when Frank took the spaghetti and the rice dish. She gave a small pizza to Barbara and had nothing for me. The rice dish turned out to be sweet, not hot at all. Frank didn't like it, so I kept taking fork fulls across the table. Everyone was watching us and we were still laughing. Finally, when my pizza didn't come, I pulled the rice dish in front of me and ate the whole thing. I never did get a pizza. Evidently, when the waitress went back to the kitchen, she realized she had four orders for three people, so she disposed of one.

Got back to our hotel about ten P.M. Had a nightcap and decided to eat here tomorrow night. It looked pretty good. As I started to pay the bill, the waitress told us that the owner of the hotel was treating us. Frank had already gone upstairs, so Barbara and I went over to thank him. He was the same man who had asked us to have a drink when we first arrived. We had declined the drink at that time because we were leaving to go downtown. He seemed slightly annoyed with us now. I told Barbara he probably wanted Frank to drink with him.

*Evergreen Pension Restaurant. IPOR. Kubranska 8. 911 01 Trencin. Tele: 0831/441 673.

THURS. SEPT 24 TRENCIN, SLOVAKIA

Nice day. The evening was a little traumatic, but the day was fine. Climbed up to and all around the castle in town. Barbara said we walked only four miles, but the pedometer doesn't count stairs. Had lunch at the Trata Hotel where the building was built right into the rock below the castle. There was a large glass window looking out onto a carving in the rock that dated back to 179 A.D. It was pretty amazing. (Did people know back then that it was 179 A.D?)

At five o'clock we tried calling my nephew Gary back in Lakeport from our hotel. We had prearranged this call on this date when we last talked to him. The young desk clerks tried to help us, but no one could get through from the hotel. Decided to drive back downtown to the telephone office, and arrived five minutes after they closed. An English speaking woman told us the country's number had been changed when Czech and Slovakia split about five years before. MCI was really on the ball. Their listing number was the old one. Went to the Trata Hotel where the woman at the desk spoke English very well. She called information for us and got the new number. The people were so gracious to tourists in all these countries. She could have said, "You're not staying here, so you can't use our phones!" Only had a couple of minutes left on our phone card, so we quickly called Gary and told him to call us back at our hotel in a half hour.

Back at the Evergreen, we told the desk clerk that a call would be coming in and to please transfer it to the room. She did, and Barbara started taking notes on all the information from home. Barbara and Frank's other son Gene was at the house and they took turns chatting and catching up. After about forty-five minutes, the owner of the hotel came to the door, which was opened, and started literally screaming at us. He evidently wanted us to get off the phone. The desk clerk had told us there were three phone lines in the hotel, so we didn't even think about tying up one of them. Frank held up his hand to the man and said, "Five minutes." The man, who looked like he was about to have apoplexy thundered, "Nein five minutes!" Then he stormed into the room and unplugged the phone cord. He grabbed the phone out of Frank's hand and left in a frenzy.

We were all shaken up. We weren't really sure what we had done wrong. Four or five times before, we had called home and talked a long time without any problems. We came to the conclusion that we had better get away from this lunatic. At about eight o'clock, we went down to eat dinner, and discuss all the news Gary and Gene had given us. This evidently made our host even madder. He was huffing and puffing around the dining room, and at ten minutes to nine, he turned out half the lights. When we finished eating, Frank went up to the bar to tell the waitress that we would be leaving in the morning instead of three nights later. The owner was sitting on a bar stool, sipping a drink and grumbling to himself. Frank told the waitress that we didn't want to stay in a hotel where we couldn't use the phone, and where the owner was allowed to walk into our room uninvited and take our phone. As he said this, he looked right at the owner, who of course probably couldn't understand a word.

All of the help in the hotel had been kind and courteous. What the owner's problem was, we didn't know, but I think we may have unknowingly insulted him when he wanted us to stay for a drink the first day. We had never seen him before and did not know that he was the owner. We thought he was telling us to sit down and have a drink. We had no idea he was inviting us and we said, "No thank you." He said, "Why?" in English. We told him we were on our way to have dinner in town. We thought he understood, but evidently he didn't. Then we must have insulted him again when he paid for our nightcap and Frank had already left the table. If this theory was true, than the phone episode must have been his last straw. This was all speculation on my part because none of us knew what he had been yelling at us as he took our phone. Barbara had a different hypothesis. She contended that he was drunk. This was quite possible also, because he was drinking both times when he got upset with us. Whatever the reason for his ire, we were better off somewhere else.

WEEKLY BUDGET # 25 SEPT. 18 THROUGH 24
LODGING
Apartments (3) $111.00
Hotels (4)   343.00
        FOOD
Restaurants:
Dinners (4)   53.50
Lunches (3)   17.50
Breakfasts (1)   6.00
Groceries (13 meals) 50.00

ENTERTAINMENT
Cafes & Bars   28.00
Boat Ride   6.50
Trencin Castle   4.50
        CAMPER
Camper Payment   168.00
Gas   34.00
Parking   1.50
Road Tolls   6.00
TRANSPORTATION
Taxis   2.50
INCIDENTALS
Newspapers   3.00
Postage   2.00
Birthday Card   2.00
(Brother Nick) $839.00

WEEKLY BUDGET # 25

Fri.	$87.00
Sat.	75.00
Sun.	77.50
Mon.	276.00
Tues.	77.50
Wed.	120.00
Thurs.	126.00
	$839.00

$839 divided by 7 days = $119.95 per day. $119.95 divided by 3 people = $39.95 per day, per person.

HUNGARIAN GOULASH

BROWN IN LARGE SKILLET:
2 Tablespoons olive oil
1 Pound of pork (cut into 1/4 inch slices)
1 Large onion, chopped
1 Cup mushrooms, sliced

ADD:
3/4 Cup beef bouillon
1 Tablespoon paprika
Cover and let simmer 15 to 20 minutes. Remove 6 tablespoons bouillon and set aside in cool place.
BLEND:
1 Tablespoon cornstarch
1 Cup plain yogurt
6 Tablespoons cooled bouillon

ADD:
Yogurt mixture to meat, onion and mushrooms

STIR IN:
1 Cup fresh parsley

SERVE: Over noodles. Makes 3 dinners and 3 leftover lunches.

Week 26 Trencin to Telc

Week Number Twenty Six September 25 Through October 1, 1998

FRI. SEPT. 25 BANSKA BYSTRICA, SLOVAKIA

The owner of the Evergreen Hotel was no where to be seen this morning. The waitress and desk clerk were very attentive and seemed somewhat chagrined about all that had taken place. I was sure they too had caught hell for our phone call. At one point, I asked them what we had done, but no one spoke English well enough to explain it to us.

The first thing we had to do after leaving the hotel was find some place that sold propane gas for our camper. Both the stove and refrigerator ran on propane and we were almost out. We had been looking for the past month, but since we'd been staying in hotels and apartments, it wasn't so urgent. It was sold in separate tanks almost everywhere, but we needed the kind that was hosed directly into the camper. This was only the second time we'd had to buy it. A tank lasted a very long time. Luckily we found a gas station that sold it right away. It cost $5 to fill the tank. Also got gas and had the car washed.

This was the fourth time the car had been washed. The first time we did it ourselves with a hose, in a campground in Italy. The second and third times were at the Hotel Chopin in Poland. These two were a month apart, as we had gone to the Baltic Countries in between. After each washing, it rained within twenty four hours. Murphy's Law! When the car was clean, we drove to Banska Bystrica, knowing full well that we were in for a downpour. The scenery was beautiful, but the sky was either foggy or smoggy. Couldn't decide which, probably both.

Banska Bystrica was a nice little town that reminded me a lot of Gdansk, Poland. Parked the car and Barbara and I went in search of the tourist office, while Frank took a nap. There was really only one main street in this town, so we found the tourist office right away. The young woman behind the desk had long blond hair down to her butt, and was at least six feet tall, not to mention beautiful. I immediately went into my short, fat, cretin mode, so Barbara had to do all the talking. She asked for an apartment with two bedrooms, a kitchen and a bath. The woman gave us a nearby address that she said we could walk to. Didn't bother to wake up Frank. Just walked past a lovely tree filled park to a nice quiet street where we found a very large house with a fenced yard.

The landlady spoke no English, but only yesterday we found out that Slovak, Czech and Polish were all close enough linguistically as to be somewhat understandable to each other. This expanded our vocabularies by at least ten words. We were practically fluent! Having been in Poland for one and a half months, we had picked up a lot of expressions. The first apartment the landlady showed us had only one bedroom. We would have taken it because it had a real kitchen and bathroom, but Barbara took a chance and asked if she had any more apartments. I said under my breath, my voice dripping with sarcasm, "Oh sure, all these Eastern European families have an apartment on every floor." I had to eat my words when she showed us the ground floor apartment with three bedrooms, a kitchen and two baths. She didn't think we would want it because it was for four people and it cost more. The price was $16 a night for all of us. We had paid more than that to camp in our own car. The woman told us that she had a permanent boarder living in the third bedroom. He was away for a week, and we couldn't use his room. We told her we'd take it. In case anyone thinks we deduced all this information with our ten words of Polish, I must confess that the woman's ten year old daughter had joined us when we went downstairs, and she spoke passable English.

We went back to get Frank and the camper, and moved into our new home. The camper was installed safely behind a locked gate. Again, almost everywhere we'd stayed, there had been a safe place for the camper. Even most of the hotels had guarded or fenced parking lots, sometimes both. Went for a long walk in the beautiful big park nearby until it got too dark to see. It rained all night, surprise, surprise!

SAT. SEPT. 26 BANSKA BYSTRICA, SLOVAKIA

This morning we met the husband of our landlady. The whole family was very nice and willing to do most anything to make us comfortable. Everyone always thought we were Dutch because of our licence plates and the fact that we spoke English. When we told the man we were Americans, his eyes popped opened wide and he called the rest of the family out to tell them. They all seemed to be very excited about having guests from America. Evidently not too many Americans go to these small towns. After the initial introductions and excitement, the landlord, looking very woebegone, told us he had just closed the garage door on his new little car. It shattered the back window. There goes the profits from renting the apartment, all $16.

Barbara and Frank took the camper to Tesco this morning to do grocery shopping. I walked downtown, in the rain, to see what I could see.

It was an interesting little town and I scouted out all the entertainment in the area for later. We met back at the apartment for lunch, then we tried to go to the local museum. It was closed. Tried to get tickets for the opera tonight, but the box office was closed. The art museum was closed as well. All of these attractions had signs on the doors saying that they were open, but none were.

We were getting very discouraged, when we passed by a theater playing *The Jackal* in English. We went in. Very intellectual! They don't sell popcorn, candy or anything else at the movies here. People brought their own food. It cost the equivalent of $1.17 per person. The movie was entertaining, and it killed an otherwise dreary afternoon. We were going to eat out because the food in the restaurants was unbelievably cheap. The three of us could get a big two or three course meal with drinks and it would only cost between $10 and $12 for all of us. However the food was very salty and very tiresome, so we opted to go home for dinner.

On the way back Barbara was complaining about having to always wear her over the shoulder money belt. She is little and skinny, and the bag on the end of the long cord was always sliding between her legs. She said she felt like a guy adjusting his balls all the time.

SUN. SEPT. 27 BANSKA BYSTRCIA, SLOVAKIA

It was still raining. Went for a drive along the Hron River today. It was like stepping back in time about a hundred years. Because it was Sunday, we were able to see people in their native costumes coming home from church. Mostly the older people dressed this way. The women wore long dirndl knee length skirts, over black trousers and boots. They wore an interesting white conical shaped headdress or hat as well. The men wore short black jackets and hats. Every now and then, we would see young men and women wearing the same ethnic attire. The countryside was heavily forested. The scenery was wildly beautiful.

I had never really seen fall colors before. Southern California has very few trees that turn color, the odd maple here and there, but that was it. Having been a teacher, I was always back at work in September, so searching out fall colors was not an option. The colors here were amazing. They were just beginning to turn, but we could see bright reds, oranges and yellows nestled in with the different shades of browns and greens. It was definitely worth six months of washing my clothes by hand, and brushing my teeth with bottled water. On the other hand, I have been told that there are many places in the States that have both fall colors and washing machines. It was possible this cynicism meant that I might be nearly ready to go home.

We had lunch in the ancient town of Hel'pa. It looked like the village Hollywood depicted in the movie Brigadoon, small, beautiful and quaint. We were very close to the Tatra Mountains and the Polish border where we had been about a month ago. We seemed to be zig zaging our way across Eastern Europe. If one were to travel only in straight lines, many of the best places would be left unexplored.

MON. SEPT. 28 TRNAVA, SLOVAKIA

Went shopping at Tesco again before we left Banska Bystrcia this morning. Tesco carried a lot of things we couldn't seem to find in Slovak markets. Things like olive oil, drinking water without carbonation, tomato sauce and decent wine.

It poured all morning. At one point we had to drive down a dirt road and the car got completely encased in mud. The wheels were spinning and the mud went everywhere. Drove back to Trnava to the Koliba Hotel where we had stayed one night last week. This time we had reservations. They got mostly business people here and evidently had not heard that they were supposed to charge double the regular rate for tourists. We were paying $53 for two double rooms with baths. Breakfast was not included. The rooms were big, comfortable and clean. There was even a television, no English channels, but after our last experience, this was probably a plus.

Checked into the hotel about one P.M., and did laundry until about three. We have only two more weeks until we get back to Germany where, with a little luck, we'll find a laundromat. Heavy clothes do not come clean when washed by hand. Stomping on them in the shower (as described in the book, *The Accidental Tourist*), or washing them in the bathroom sink, just doesn't get the dirt out.

In the afternoon it stopped raining and we walked to the walled city of Trnava, about two miles. Walked all over town and decided it was one of the less interesting places we'd been to. Had a very good dinner, with no breaded meat, very hard to find such a meal. It was a bit pricy for here, $20 for the three of us. Barbara had a steak that was at least four inches thick and a salad. I had a mixed grill and salad, and Frank had a Slovak dish of what seemed to be eggplant, meat and cheese. We also had beer and soda. All the meals were delicious and well worth the extra cash. These meals would have cost $75 in the States, but here I had the gall to say it was expensive. Took a taxi home as it was late. Such decadence!

*Hotel Koliba, Kamenny mlyn, Trnava, Slo. Tele: 0805/344 59

TUES. SEPT. 29 TRNAVA, SLOVAKIA

It was pouring! We were hoping some of the mud from yesterday would wash off the car. Drove into Bratislava. Tranava was not a tourist town, so finding out about a bus into the big city would be more trouble than driving. Figured we could park in a guarded lot and spend the day on foot, big mistake!

It poured all the way to Bratislava. Talk about nightmares! The city was wall to wall cars. Cars were parked in every conceivable location and in many places that were completely inconceivable, on sidewalks, in driveways, and anywhere else that there was a tiny space. There were no legal parking lots to be seen. The entire city was a parking lot. The traffic was bumper to bumper, moving only inches at a time. It was Genoa, Italy all over again.

In the hour and a half that we spent driving through the city and trying to get out again, we saw a great deal of it. It was ugly. Ok, it was a wet gloomy day, but it was still ugly. In my opinion, Bratislava had almost no saving graces. Rectangular Soviet style buildings were all mixed in with timeworn Slovac buildings. It was very hard to tell where "Old Town" started and ended. In the majority of Eastern European cities, "Old Town" was an obvious separate entity, but not here. We finally found the Danube with Bratislava Castle on the hill overlooking it. That was nice, but it was too little too late. By then we had decided there was nothing we wanted to see badly enough to continue this insane drive. We decided to head for Devin Castle six kilometers away.

When we arrived, I exhaled, like a balloon slowly deflating. Devin was a lovely little village set amid green hills. There was absolutely no traffic, and very few human beings. It was still pouring and gloomy, but I felt as if a new day had dawned. The castle was high on a hill and we drove up to an almost empty parking lot. With our rain ponchos covering us from head to ankles, we climbed all around the castle.

Inside one of the courtyards we met an American missionary family, a mother and two kids. They were showing the castle to a visiting couple from home. The family had been living here for a year and loved it. They thought Bratislava was wonderful. They did not drive there, only used public transportation. I must admit my opinion of the city was somewhat biased, but I still wasn't willing to give it another chance.

The family seemed to be very nice. The kids were being home schooled. I hoped the mother was up to it, but I suppose living in a foreign country was almost education enough. None of us asked what religion they were because we were afraid they might tell us much more than we wanted to hear.

The man that was visiting the family from the states, thought he was a movie stunt man. He was climbing all over the walls of the castle. Not only was it stupidly dangerous, as there were some very sheer drops down to the rivers below, but it was a desecration of a national monument. The castle was centuries old and only about half of it was still standing. It was people like this that forced countries to fence off all their treasures, like Stonehenge in England, and Michaelangelo's Pieta in Italy. I doubt if it had ever crossed this guy's mind that he might be destroying a piece of history. He was just having a little fun. Luckily a guard came out and yelled at him, but the damage was already done. The mother and the two kids looked very embarrassed. I felt sorry for them.

Thanks to Barbara's navigational skills, Frank was able to drive around Bratislava to get back to Trnava. In the late afternoon, we went hiking around the lake near our hotel. There were plots of land where different families kept a garden to grow their own vegetables. Had a very mediocre dinner at our hotel. This was our last night in Slovakia.

WED. SEPT. 30 BRNO, CZECH REPUBLIC

The sun was out this morning and lasted all day. It was a good thing because Frank was threatening to escape to Southern France. The rain had been getting us all down. But today all was well. We drove through the last of Slovakia after a breakfast of peanut butter on stale bread. Breakfast was not included at our hotel, and no one could face another snotty egg in the hotel restaurant.

Because of total incompetence on our parts, we were forced to do another dumb money exchange at the Czech border. This one cost us $13.50.

We had $96 worth of Slovakian money. After the exchange, we got $82.90 (Changing money at the border should only be done if you absolutely have no other choice.)

When we got to Brno, we had our usual dilemma of where to stay. This would be a one night stand. Brno was another big congested city but Telc, the place for which we were heading, was too far to drive to in one day. The plan was to get another apartment for a week in Telc.

Tried three hotels in Brno before we found one that suited us. It cost us $8.50 just to park the car at the Hotel Slovan. When I commented on how expensive the parking was, the woman at the desk looked down at our U.S. passports and in a very condescending manner said, "Not for you!" She then proceeded to pick up our passports as judiciously as one would handle a diseased rat, and hand them to us with her eyes saying, "Take it or leave it. I couldn't care less." Any self respecting, red blooded

American would have turned around and walked out, but not us. We took the rooms. We were too tired and cranky to look any further.

After hot showers and cold drinks in the room, our dispositions greatly improved and we set out to explore Brno. Found a passable Chinese restaurant for dinner. It wasn't one of our best days, but at least it didn't rain.

*Hotel Slovan, Lidicka 23. 659 89 Brno, Czech. Tele: + 420/5/41 32 12 07.

THURS. OCT. 1 TELC, CZECH REPUBLIC

They had English television in the hotel, and I caught Larry King Live this morning before we left. He was interviewing Ross Perot. Perot has always struck me as an insipid little twerp, but he sure made a lot of sense. He said he never heard of oral sex until he was out of high school, but now every eight year old in the country knew about it. He thought Clinton should resign for lying under oath, and since he was reiterating everything I had said and thought, I couldn't say that I didn't agree with him.

It rained off and on throughout the drive to Telc this morning. Telc was a really quaint little town, almost completely surrounded by lakes. Went to the tourist information office first. Waited two hours to see the first place. It was a nice little house and would have been perfect, but it had no kitchen. Why anybody would build a house without a kitchen was beyond me. The second apartment was like a bed and breakfast. The landlord really wanted us to stay there, so he said we could use the kitchen whenever we wanted. However, he would be cooking the breakfasts every morning, in this same kitchen. The kitchen was one of the tiniest we'd ever seen. Nevertheless, Barbara made us spaghetti with mussel sauce for dinner. There was a third bedroom in this apartment and our landlord rented it to an Isreali couple. They spoke English fluently and were a lot of fun. Everyone came into my bedroom for some wine after dinner and we solved all the world's problems. The Israelis gave us a number to call for an apartment in Prague. They had stayed in this subleased, fully equipped apartment for a week. It had a washing machine and a dryer. Heaven!

After they left, Frank told us that he was really getting bummed out by the weather and the dreary restaurant food. He thought we should only spend one more week in Czech, and then head for Western Europe. I kind of had the feeling that he was enjoying himself less and less these days. Barbara and I agreed that another week of Eastern Europe would be sufficient. We also decided to call Delta Airlines as soon as possible to see if we could go home before November seventeenth. It was beginning to sink in that the weather wasn't going to be any better in Germany or France. We had to pick an El Nino year to make our trip of a lifetime.

*Garni Penzion Vacek, Mlynska 104, 588 56 Telc. (Jaroslav Vacek) Tele: 00420-66-721-30-99

WEEKLY BUDGET # 26 SEPT. 25—OCT. 1

LODGING

Apartments (4)	$81.00
Hotels (3)	208.00

FOOD

Restaurants:

Dinners (3)	52.50
Lunches (3)	25.50
Breakfasts (1)	6.00
Groceries (14 meals)	63.00

ENTERTAINMENT

Cafes & Bars	16.00
Movie	3.50
Devin Castle	4.50

CAMPER

Camper Payment	168.00
Gas & Oil	83.50
Propane	5.00
Car Wash	5.00

TRANSPORTATION

Taxi	4.50

INCIDENTALS

Postage	2.50
Newspaper	2.00
Dumb Money Exchange	13.50
	$744.00

WEEKLY BUDGET # 26

Fri.	$80.00
Sat.	78.00
Sun.	46.00
Mon.	162.00
Tues.	·109.50
Wed.	200.00
Thurs.	68.50
	$744.00

$744 divided by 7 days = $106.28 per day.. $106.28 divided by 3 people = $35.42 per person, per day.

Week 27 Telc to Nedvezi (Prague)

Week Number Twenty Seven October 2 Through October 8, 1998

FRI. OCT. 2 TELC, CZECH REPUBLIC

Our landlord gave us a really excellent continental breakfast this morning. He came and fixed it about 7:30 A.M. Then about 8:30 his mother came to clean up. A woman's work is never done! The Israelis left today, so the landlord was busy trying to rent their room for tonight. There will be ten people coming tomorrow to take the whole house, and we must leave in the morning. It was very cold in this little medieval town of Telc, but it didn't rain this morning, so I couldn't complain.

After lunch we went shopping for warmer clothes, without success. It was much colder than any of us ever imagined it would be. Walked all over town again and returned to our rooms for lentil stew. Since there was only one burner to cook on, Barbara made a one pot dish.

SAT. OCT. 3 CESKE BUDEJOVICE, CZECH REPUBLIC

This morning we said farewell to Telc and drove to Budejovice, the home of the original Budwiser Beer. The drive was lovely. The trees were every shade of fall colors imaginable. There were many small lakes in this area and they were surrounded by multicolored trees and shrubs. The weather was overcast and dismal for the whole trip, but even that couldn't diminish the beauty of the turning tinctures of autumn.

Around 11 A.M. we arrived, but as usual it took forever to find a place to stay. This time it was obscene. It was 4 P.M. by the time we were settled. Did have lunch in between, but we seemed to be getting worse at this rather than better. Started once again at the tourist office. Told the woman that we wanted an apartment with a kitchen.

The first place she sent us was on the fifth floor of a Soviet style building with no elevator. The "kitchen" was in a four by five foot closet, literally. It had a large fridge that took up half the space and a one burner hot plate on a small end table. There was no sink or running water of any kind and no space to even cut a vegetable. We told the elderly couple whose home it was that we wanted to look around some more. They practically begged us to stay, but Barbara was adamant, though not insensitive. The old couple, who knew a little English, started yelling as we left that we would have to pay two times as much in a hotel. Actually a hotel would have probably cost five times as much, but we didn't care.

Went to see at least five more places before we gave up on getting an apartment. Did get to see most of the town as we bounced from apartment to pension to hotel. Wound up at a pension owned by the parents of a young woman who worked in one of the unavailable hotels. The pension was in a nice quiet neighborhood about two miles from the town center, and we had two adjoining rooms.

After settling in, we walked to town for dinner. The main square of Ceske Budejovice was built around an eighteenth century fountain, a modernization that supplied the town with water from the Vltava River. The buildings had been refurbished and some were really remarkable. Chose an Indian restaurant for dinner. The food was so salty we couldn't eat most of it. All the food we ate in restaurants here seemed to have two or three times the amount of salt it needed. It was much healthier for all of us when Barbara cooked. While we were in town, we tried to call the number in Prague that the Israeli couple had given us. If we could get this apartment, we would stay for a week. None of us really cared where we were as long as we didn't have to hunt for a new place to stay every other day. No one answered the phone! The sun came out just before it got dark. Walked home about nine o'clock. None of us ever worried about getting mugged. Eastern Europe was kind of like the United States used to be in the fifties.

*Pension Nr. 36. Kalisnicka 36. 370 08 C. Budejovice. Tele. 0042/38/ 7240434. Frantisek Lahvicka

SUN. OCT. 4 CESKE BUDEJOVICE, (CESKE KARLOV) CZECH REPUBLIC

Breakfast was served in our rooms by the landlord, and was excellent. He also gave us directions to the town of Ceske Karlov, about 15 miles away.

Ceske Karlov was, in my opinion, the most beautiful little town in Eastern Europe. It was built along a serpentine river. The river was in a valley, and the buildings of the little medieval town were scattered up and down the hills surrounding the river. All the streets were cobblestone. The town by itself would have been a highlight of the trip, but in addition to its serene setting, the fall colors were phenomenal. It was definitely one of the most extraordinary places we had seen. All the roofs of the buildings were red and sometimes it was hard to tell where the roofs ended and the bright red foliage began. Near the ancient aqueduct, the water pooled and the reflection of the surrounding buildings and trees was so vivid that it was hard to tell which one was the mirror image. Stopped in a little out-door cafe beside the river for coffee. It was unbelievably picturesque. I felt like we were part of a picture postcard. It was so impressive that we even remembered to take some photographs, something we seldom did.

The weather was quite cold. I was wearing my sweat suit under my clothes. I had foolishly thought when I had packed in California that I wouldn't need long underwear. In the afternoon the sun came out, and it warmed up considerably. I even took my coat off. Had lunch in the car, hot leftover lentil stew. It was deliciously unsalted.

On the way back to Ceske Budejovice, we got lost. This was something we seldom did because Barbara was a wonderful navigator. However all over Europe the street signs were not quite the size of a postage stamp. Naturally they were very hard to read as we were passing by. They were supposed to be located on the first building of every street, but they seldom were there. Almost always, when lost, it was because we didn't know the name of the street. Eventually, we did find our way home.

Walked to town in the early evening. Had picked out a restaurant yesterday that served rotisserie chicken. This was one dish that was usually pretty good no matter where we got it, and it was generally not too salty. Naturally, the restaurant was closed, as was almost everything in town. It was Sunday. We should have been home eating pasta! Finally found a pension where they served meals. Everything was salty, but not inedible like last night. Called the woman with the apartment in Prague again. Still no luck. Had already walked four and a half miles, so we took a cab home.

MON. OCT. 5 NEDVEZI (PRAGUE), CZECH REPUBLIC

Before we left our pension this morning, the man of the house asked us to check on some tropical fish food that he needed for his aquarium. He said it was only grown in San Francisco. He wanted to be able to order it by mail. We think we told him we would do it. The conversation took place in German, a language none of us spoke, so who knows if that was what he wanted.

Started out dreading the day because we all knew that we were heading for a huge city to find an apartment. Stopped in a town close to Prague for lunch and once again phoned the English speaking woman with the apartment in Prague. Phoning from a public phone was more than difficult. First we had to find a phone that worked. Then we had to buy a phone card, totally unavailable in this little town. When plan one failed, we had to buy something small to make sure we had enough change for the whole call. When the operator came on, we had no clue as to what she was trying to tell us, so we grabbed a passing human being, shoved the phone at her and said, Prosze in a pleading voice. This word means, "please", in Polish and we hoped that it worked in Czech as well. We had done this many times on this trip. Most of the time the innocent passing stranger would do all he or she could to help. This time it was to no avail. We did not connect.

On to plan three. We gave up the idea of a beautiful apartment with a washer and dryer, and decided to look for an apartment on our own. Should we drive into Prague and look for the tourist office? An emphatic "No!" resounded from each of us. Instead, we drove to the next town, about eleven kilometers from Prague and stopped at a motel. The woman wanted $82 for two small rooms with no cooking facilities. We asked if she knew of any apartments we could rent. This verbalization was accomplished in a variety of languages including Italian, but mostly in German. The woman shrugged her shoulders and we left. I went back inside to tell her we might return.

At this point she remembered a motel that had bungalows. She wrote down the name for me, pointed in the direction of Prague, and said, *Funf kilometers, links*. We went five kilometers down the road and turned left. We had to stop and asked directions at a restaurant full of men. The stench of urine was so overpowering, I nearly lost my lunch. Nevertheless, someone pointed in the direction we needed to go, and we actually found it! There were bungalows much like the camp bungalows in Italy, two bedrooms, a kitchen and a bath. For $58 a night, it even had a T.V. and was reasonably clean. We took it for seven nights. Had linguini with fish sauce for dinner. After all, it was Monday and we had missed it on Sunday!

TUES. OCT. 6 NEDVEZI (PRAGUE), CZECH REPUBLIC

Today we did laundry and caught up on personal needs. Walked into town about eleven A.M. to find out how to get a bus to Prague tomorrow. It took awhile, but we eventually got both information and a few groceries.

Our little house was in the woods with autumn all around us. It was quite lovely though freezing cold. I was wearing layers of clothing at all times, nearly everything in my suitcase. On top of my turtle neck undershirt, I wore a T-shirt and a sweat suit, top and bottom. On top of that, a jogging suit and on top of that, I wore a heavy coat, a hat, a scarf and gloves. People kept stopping me in the streets to ask directions. My little round body must have looked very familiar to them.

Drove to a larger town this afternoon to do some serious grocery shopping. A woman stopped me to ask something. When she saw I didn't understand, she switched to English and asked where I was from. "California," I answered. She looked at me like I must be out of my mind for choosing to be here, freezing my buns off, instead of home in the sun. I was wondering the same thing.

After dinner we had another discussion about what was good and bad about this trip. Again Italy and Poland were our favorite most fun parts. Ceske Karlov, won hands down for picturesque autumn beauty. Barbara felt we didn't stay long enough in each place and that too many of the places we had stayed were tacky and uncomfortable. The bungalow we were in now was clean and comfortable, but there was no living room. Amazing how important a living room could be for just sitting around and doing nothing.

Barbara and Frank wanted their next trip to be a month or six weeks long, in a nice house, and all in the same place. I was not sure that would happen because there were always places too far away that you would want to see. If you could afford to keep your house and go away for weekend trips, that would be ideal. On a middle class budget, that might be a concept too extravagant for contemplation.

WED. OCT. 7 NEDVEZI, CZECH REPUBLIC

Didn't go to Prague this morning because we all overslept. Decided to drive to Kunta Hora instead. Barbara was interested in this town because it was the home of Saint Barbara, her patron saint. The town also had a silver mine that we wanted to see. The car wouldn't start. It had been needing a quart of oil every few days lately and was generally deteriorating. We were once again thinking we should head back to Amsterdam before it fell apart completely. By the time we got it started and set out, it was nearly noon.

We arrived in Kunta Hora just in time for lunch. I had Czech chicken, good but salty.

Went to the silver mine museum next. Donned white coats, helmets and lights and went down into the mine. As mines go, it was rather uninteresting, but it did demonstrate how little space those miners had to work in and the ominous conditions under which they did their excavations. An American man behind me was explaining to his young son how the miners used live canaries to test the mine tunnels for noxious gas. Just before I left California, I had read Emile Zola's horrendous book *Germinal*. It was about early mining conditions in France. It told how child labor was the norm, with many of the children dying stunted and deformed with lung disease. Once people, men, women and children descended into the mines they worked long relentless hours, with death being their only reprieve. Most of them died in their prime or before. The conditions in this mine looked to be about the same as those described by Emile Zola.

Saint Barbara, the patron saint of miners, was next on our agenda. The cathedral was very ornate with wonderful flying buttresses. It was well worth seeing. Frank, who had been having mucho flatulence lately and was practically self propelled, implored St. Barbara for a little relief. His wife and I were compelled to pray for his success. Frank claimed he had a roommate in college that could ignite his farts with a match and activate his own thrust. He evidently desired to emulate this hero. Doubtful as well as dangerous, to say the least!

It started raining after dinner while we were busy singing "El Paso" in our little bungalow. Luckily there was no one else living near us because this song can not be sung quietly. By the time the cowboy received his "one little kiss" from Felina and died, it was pouring. The conversation returned to getting out of this weather for good. Since we couldn't leave Europe until the seventeenth of November, we started talking about flying to someplace warm for the last few weeks, after returning the camper to Amsterdam.

Frank, who was usually pretty quiet, except when he sang, began lamenting about our living conditions.

"I'm tired of being cold and wet! I'm tired of eating lousy, salty food, and I'm tired of sitting on toilets that are not connected to the floor. I'm also tired of the smell of pee permeating every bathroom I've ever entered!"

We all agreed we had been in Eastern Europe long enough, almost four months. Had the weather been good, the other negative parts would have been endurable, but enough was enough. We were ready for western luxury. As one of my Peace Corps roommates said near the end of our service, "Yeah, I've proved I can be happy being poor. Now I want to prove I can be happy being filthy rich!" Like him, we were ready to be rich again too, so we will skip Karlov Very and head for Nurnberg on Monday. A flight to Spain may have been out of our reach financially, but a second class hotel in a first class country was not.

THURS. OCT. 8 NEDVEZI (PRAGUE), CZECH REPUBLIC

I loved Prague. It was really ugly on the outskirts riding in on the bus, worse than most big cities. Then we rode the underground train, and when we came up, Alacazam, a beautiful city! It was all very magical. We saw only half of the inner city today, so we will come back on Saturday.

After walking around until we were ready to drop, we took a tour that included a boat ride on the Danube, and a lot more walking. Our guide, a young Czech woman, sat and chatted with us on the boat as we were drinking coffee. Martina Vakocova said she loved the new freedom she was now able to enjoy. She had been camping in France last summer with her husband and two little boys. She said they never could have done that before the fall of the Soviet Union. I told her about the teenager we had met in Latvia who spoke so openly about her dissatisfaction with the new system. Martina said that for people in small towns it was much more difficult to make a living because there was not enough work, but here in Prague, there was no unemployment. I don't know how accurate her observations were, but she was delightfully enthralled with her new way of life. We gave her our address and invited her to come and visit us in the states. It would be fun to show sunny California to some freezing Czechs.

WEEKLY BUDGET # 27 OCT.2—OCT.8
LODGING

Apartments (1)	$33.00
Pensions (2)	72.00
Bungalow in Motel (4)	228.00

FOOD
Restaurants:

Dinners (2)	43.50
Lunches (2)	30.00
Groceries (17 Meals)	45.00

ENTERTAINMENT

Cafes & Bars	18.00
Palace Museum	2.00
Art Gallery	1.00
Castle Tower Entrance	2.50
Silver Mine	10.00
St. Barbara's Cath.	3.00
Boat Tour, Prague	39.50

CAMPER

Camper Payment	168.00
Gas	61.00
Oil	3.00

TRANSPORTATION

Taxi	3.50
Busses	3.00

INCIDENTALS

Spending Money	
(500 KC each)	50.00
	$816.00

WEEKLY BUDGET # 27
Fri. $114.00
Sat.   115.50
Sun.   102.00
Mon.   90.00
Tues.   99.00
Wed.   152.00
Thurs.   143.50
                $816.00

$816 divided by 7 days = $116.57. $116.57 divided by 3 people = $38.85 per day, per person.

Week 28 Nedvezi to Wetzlar

Week Number Twenty Eight October 9 Through October 15, 1998

FRI. OCT. 9 NEDVEZI (PRAGUE), CZECH REPUBLIC

It was still raining this morning, but not too hard. Set out for Melnik in the north of Czech. Had to drive the freeway circle around Prague. The freeways were every bit as ugly and congested as the ones around Los Angeles, but they sure beat driving through cities. Like millions of others, we bitched a lot, but we didn't hesitate to use them. The sky got more and more foggy as we went. By the time we left the freeway, the visibility was about twenty feet in all directions, shades of Lake Balaton.

The town of Melnik was quite ordinary until we climbed up the hill to the church. Then there was a fantastic panoramic view of the river and two bridges. One of the bridges was very old and unusual. It was quite a sight down into the valley. The fog was still very thick, but didn't diminish the beauty of the view. Had a good lunch that wasn't salty, amazingly enough. Walked all over town. Then headed back to our bungalow. It rained all the way and the Friday night traffic was horrible. Tomorrow we'll return to Prague.

SAT. OCT. 10 NEDVEZI (PRAGUE), CZECH REPUBLIC

Once again took the bus, about two blocks from our bungalow, to the city. The motel people had given us a schedule and it was really very easy to do. The underground train seemed to be waiting for us as we got off the bus. Plowed about two miles through the bowels of the earth, and emerged once again in this fairy tale city. Today we explored the city on the opposite side of the Danube. One of the features that made Prague so accessible was its size. If you didn't do museums and entertainments, you could see the whole city and be well acquainted with both halves in two days. For those not enamored with big cities, this was a plus.

First we walked over the bridge to the castle. The castle was quite a climb, but the view of Prague in full fall colors was worth it. We then walked all over what was called "Lesser Town" in English and Mala Mesto in Czech. The architecture was varied and fascinating. Stopped to have Greek gyros for lunch. They had very few vegetables here, but tomatoes, cucumbers and onions were among the few. They also had yogurt, so they could easily have made an authentic gyro. However, our gyros were full of cabbage, turnips and mayonnaise. Barbara and I liked them because they were a little different and both of us are little piggies anyway, but Frank thought their rendition of Greek cuisine was absurd.

Spent the afternoon shopping for souvenirs. There were many unusual things to buy here, and shopping in the stores below the castle was a pleasant experience. The shopkeepers here were friendly and accommodating. The entire day was very enjoyable.

Made great connections going home on the underground and the bus even though we had forgotten to bring the schedule with us. The trouble with staying outside the city was that you couldn't easily go to the theater. Prague was famous for its wonderful entertainment. We had taken a schedule of performances home with us the last time. We had planned to see a show and take a taxi home this time. However, the season was almost over and there was very little of interest to any of us, so we didn't bother.

SUN. OCT. 11 NEDVEZI (PRAGUE), CZECH REPUBLIC

This was the last day that I would have to brush my teeth with bottled water. We were very exuberant today. It was kind of like the memories we all had of leaving the Peace Corps. It was great fun. We wouldn't have traded it for anything. The memories would live with us forever. Nevertheless, it was time to get on with our lives.

Spent the day packing and repacking. All those new souvenirs had to go someplace. Why had I bought so much? Took a break from fretting and walked into the next little town just for exercise, about three miles round trip. After lunch, Barbara and I compared our journals of this trip to make sure that I didn't leave out anything important for the book I was planning to write. Frank came in to listen and we spent a very enjoyable rainy afternoon reliving Italy and Poland. That was as far as we got because we reminisced about each wonderful day when the trip was comfortable and pleasant. Ended a warm and cozy day with a delicious pasta dinner. It was Sunday after all.

MON. OCT. 12 NURNBERG, GERMANY

It rained most of the night. Then it poured all day. Drove from 10 A.M. to 4 P.M. Stopped for lunch at a roadside rest and spent most of our Czech money before we crossed the border into Germany. Sometimes it was raining so hard we could hardly see out the windows. It was also very cold, but every time Frank put the heat on, all the windows fogged up. It was not a very good day! However, in spite of the limited visibility, the fall colors were still unbelievably beautiful.

When we arrived in Nurnberg, we took the second place we looked at. It was a Gausthaus and cost $150 for two rooms, almost three times the cost of our little house in Prague. Nevertheless, we could brush our teeth and swallow the water from the tap. Dinner in a local pub was also three times as much as we had been paying. Welcome to the real world.

Called Delta Airlines and they could change our frequent flyer reservations to Oct. 20 or Nov. 3. Strange that they couldn't have given us those dates before we left home! Because of the change, Barbara and Frank would lose their business class status. Delta would make out like a bandit, but we all would get to go home to sunny California before it snowed!

*Jagerheim Hotel, Valznerweiher str. 75, 90480 Nurnberg, Ger. Tele: 09 11/9 40 85-0.

TUES. OCT. 13 NURNBERG, GERMANY

It was pouring. Had to wait until eleven o'clock for Delta to call. We decided at dinner last night to take the early date of Oct. 20. The weather was just too miserable for touring. At eleven, Delta called. Frank made the arrangements with a very pleasant Italian woman who was extremely happy that we had toured her country.

None of us had ever been to Nurnberg before, so we were anxious to be off exploring. Had to stop at the camper to get our rain gear. We all had to jump inside because it started hailing hard enough to hurt. Soon the hail stopped and once again it poured. Decided if we wanted to see Nurnberg, the weather must be endured. Did six miles round trip. Saw old town which had some really beautiful old churches. Had lunch and later stopped again for hot coffee. Both repasts were a shock. After being able to get three course meals with drinks for $10 or $12 dollars for all of us, it was traumatizing to pay $16 for two coffees and one beer. We were really having trouble adjusting to this. It was a good thing we were going home early. Of course the United States wasn't any cheaper, but we wouldn't have to eat in restaurants there.

Had dinner at the same pub tonight. The conversation got around to why we were in these cold countries in October. I reminded Frank and Barbara that we were originally supposed to return to Italy for the last month of the trip, but we had changed the itinerary because it was such a long tedious ride down to Italy. None of us had wanted to be in the car for that amount of time again. We had stayed less time in each place in Italy and had seen it all in two and a half months. We all agreed that that decision had been a mistake. Had we stuck with plan one, we wouldn't have frozen our butts off.

Used the last few minutes on the phone card tonight to call Gary. He will pick us up at the San Francisco airport and drive us three hours back to Lakeport. What a delight!

WED. OCT. 14 BERGHOUSEN (WETZLAR), GERMANY

Drove northwest of Frankfort to the Wetzlar area. After about an hour, the rain let up. The "Romantic Road" in Germany was very picturesque.

There were quaint little towns nestled between the hills with church steeples reaching toward the horizon. That alone was certainly worth seeing, but to take this road in the fall was like stepping out of a drab little house in Kansas into the beautiful land of Oz. The colors went way beyond spectacular. Everywhere we looked there were light and dark, bright and dull shades of every hue known to the human eye. The most surprising adjuncts to all this were the bright fields of yellow mustard scattered throughout the hills. We had seen a lot of mustard in the spring. I did not expect to see it again in the fall.

We were in the Wetzlar area because this was the home of Euler Beer. Barbara thought there was probably no connection between her grandfather Euler and the beer, but she wanted to take a few bottles home to her sons and her Euler cousins, if the beer was still in existence.

Took two rooms in a pension in Berghausen, a tiny town close to Wetzlar. It was very nice, but far from reasonable. By the time we got settled in, it was time for dinner. A very nice couple owned the pension and the woman walked in the rain with us to show us the way to a local pub. We sat down, and on the table were coasters that said, Euler Landpils Bier. The Greek proprietor said that Euler had merged with another company, and these coasters were old and no longer used. When he saw how excited Barbara was at seeing the coasters, he gave her a whole carton of them. She literally squealed with delight.

*Pension Arnau, I.N.H. Renate U. Rudolf Kurdat, Bei der Arnau 10, 35614 0 Asslar—Berghausen. Tele: 064 43/ 9904.

THURS. OCT. 15 BERGHAUSEN (WETZLAR), GERMANY

Had the usual cold buffet breakfast, but it was better than most. There was an English news channel from England on the tube here. However, I couldn't get the television to work last night. We hadn't had any news for over a week. The proprietor showed me how to work the television so I could catch the news tonight.

Off to the beer factory in Wetzlar this morning. The rain ceased momentarily. The sky was beautiful and blue. Wetzlar is a very nice little town with many crooked old Tudor buildings. The beer factory is just outside of old town. The people at the factory were very friendly and accommodating. A woman in charge of the store spoke a little English. She said she was sure Barbara's name was Euler. When we asked why, she said no one else would want an empty bottle from the old stock that said "Euler" on it.

Walked around at a street fair after lunch. Everything here seemed to cost more than we would pay in the States. Common household items were about thirty percent higher in price. I had been looking for bed pillows because they were shaped differently than ours and I found them more comfortable on my shoulders, long ago injured at work. Everywhere we had stayed in Germany and Eastern Europe, these pillows had been on the beds. In Slovakia, I could have bought a pair for $22, but I didn't want to carry them. They were very large and would have taken up too much space in the camper. Here the same pillow cost almost $90 for one.

Took some pictures in the park in town. We posed in front of some multicolored trees by the river. I don't think any photo could capture fall here, but I wanted to try. Hard to believe that fall in New England could be better than this. I guess I'll just have to go and check it out for myself. Retired people can do this!

The disposition of each of us had improved greatly since we decided to call it quits. We were all acting giddy, Everything was fun again. Nevertheless we were all glad that we had seen the autumn here, cold and wet as it was, it was still spectacularly beautiful.

WEEKLY BUDGET # 28 OCTOBER 9—OCTOBER 15

LODGING

Bungalow in Motel (3)	$171.00
Guesthaus (2)	307.00
Pension (2)	218.00

FOOD

Restaurants:

Dinners (4)	134.00
Lunches (4)	56.00
Groceries (13 meals)	33.00

ENTERTAINMENT

Cafes & Bars	35.50

CAMPER

Camper payment	168.00
Gas	74.00
Parking	3.00

TRANSPORTATION

Busses	3.00

INCIDENTALS

Money Exchange	1.00
Phone Call	1.50
Postage	1.00
Gifts	6.00
Sneaky ATM fee	6.00
	$1218.00

WEEKLY BUDGET # 28

Fri.	$101.50
Sat.	98.50
Sun.	81.50
Mon.	273.00
Tues.	254.50
Wed.	209.00
Thurs.	200.00
	$1218.00

$1218 divided by 7 days = $174. $174 divided by 3 people = $58 per person, per day.

(Can you tell what day we got back to Western Europe?)

STIR FRY

BROWN LIGHTLY ON LOW FLAME:
1 tablespoon olive oil
2 cloves finely chopped garlic
1/2 inch piece fresh ginger (or press ginger and garlic in garlic press)

CHOP INTO 1/2 TO 1 INCH PIECES OR STRIPS:
1/2 cup chicken, pork or beef (any combination can be used)
And/ Or
1/2 pound firm tofu
STIR FRY LIGHTLY IN OIL AND GARLIC.

CHOP INTO 1/2 INCH PIECES:
About 4 cups of any combination of following green vegetables:

Broccoli	String beans	Bok choy
Spinach	Cabbage	Zucchini
Chard		

COOK AND STIR FRY WITH MEAT ABOUT 10 MINUTES.

ADD ANY OR ALL OF FOLLOWING: (About 1 to 2 cups)

Bean sprouts	Onions
Chopped celery	Bamboo shoots
Water chestnuts	

STIR FRY AND COOK ABOUT 10 MINUTES.

ADD IN LAST ONE MINUTE:
1/4 to 1/2 Cup chopped green onions
1/4 to 1/2 Cup chopped cilantro

2 Tablespoons toasted sesame seeds

COOKING SAUCE:

BRING MIXTURE TO BOIL WHILE STIRRING:
1/2 Cup chicken bouillon
3 Tablespoons soy sauce
1 Tablespoon sherry

ADD A DASH OF:
Hot oil (Dried red pepper seeds soaked in olive oil)
Sesame oil

SERVE OVER BOILED OR STEAMED RICE

Week 29 Wetzlar to Amsterdam

PARTIAL WEEK NUMBER TWENTY NINE
OCTOBER 16 THROUGH OCTOBER 20, 1998

FRI. OCT. 16 KALKAR (KLEVE), GERMANY

Gave our table and chairs from the camper to our landlords this morning and invited them to visit us in California. We couldn't take the patio furniture home with us, and it would be much easier to pack without the furniture in the car. Our German landlords were really very nice. The man tried to call the camp where we would stay tonight to make reservations for us, and he printed out a map of all the roads we needed to take today on his computer.

For the first forty five minutes that we drove northwest towards the border of the Netherlands, the morning fog enveloped us like a thick blanket. Visibility was no more than a few feet in every direction. Then the fog lifted, the sky was bright blue, and the fall colors dressed up the dense forest with a dazzling array of splendor.

Later in the morning, we went past some big cities, Essen, Oberhausen, and Duisburg. There the smog blanketed the entire horizon, causing the trees and landscape to look dismal. Even the beautiful fall colors could not penetrate the muck. There were large piles of coal everywhere and many huge factories vomiting their billows of gray foulness into the already bellicose air. In short, it was ugly! Looked worse than Los Angeles in the summer time. This was one of the reasons why we had found the countryside and small towns so much more inviting.

When we stopped for gas, I called Rene in Amsterdam to make sure he would be there on Monday to take the camper. He pretended he didn't know who I was or what I was talking about, trying to panic me. He was just sore because of the postcard we had sent saying that Italian campgrounds were far superior to Dutch ones.

After lunch in the camper, we arrived at the campground our landlord had tried to call for us. He had not been able to get through, and as we had suspected there were no vacancies. This camp did not have cabins, we had wanted to rent another motor home so we could clean our camper thoroughly without being in it. It would have cost us more than $30 just to camp here in our own car. Quoting our favorite Uncle Mickie from Brooklyn we said, "Da hell wit poverty!", and spent an extra $100 on a hotel. We had only four days left and camping was no longer appealing. It was bound to rain again during the night.

We stayed in a quaint old hotel in the little town of Kalkar, near Kleve. As soon as we had settled in we took a walk around town. It didn't take long, and we wound up at a local bar. The bartender was from Corfu, Greece and spoke English as well as German. We asked him why all the bartenders and hotel staffs in Germany were from other countries. He said this was where the jobs were. I thought all of Europe had tourists, but evidently Germany has more, or maybe they just pay better. Had pizza for dinner.

*Hotel Siekmann, Kesselstrasse 32, 47546 Kalkar, Ger. Tele: 0 28 24/23 05 + 45 77

SAT. OCT. 17 KALKAR (KLEVE), GERMANY

Spent the morning repacking and cleaning out the camper which was parked on the street. I couldn't really pack my stuff because I had left my suitcase in Amsterdam with Rene. After everything was clean and in order, we went shopping for Bierkenstock shoes and the pillow I still wanted.

Last night while we were strolling around this cute little town, we saw a really nice pillow in one of the shops, and some Bierkenstock shoes in a shoe store. Bierkenstocks were probably the only items in Germany that were less expensive than in the States. The pillow cost $44. With the pillow case and tax, it came to $60.31, and it was on sale. Now I understand why my friends from England had wanted to shop when they visited me in the States. They had told me everything was cheaper there. However, we didn't have pillows like these, so I splurged and bought one. Next we headed to the shoe store. Frank got some Bierkenstock sandals on sale for $37. Barbara and I couldn't find any to fit.

Had lunch in the camper because we were trying to use up all the food. Barbara couldn't stand to waste anything. Took the car to be washed in the rain. It will get dirty again before we get to Amsterdam, but it was really disgraceful. Oh, yes, it was raining again. We'd had a two day break and it was wonderful. Naturally, since we had to wash the car, it had to rain.

While walking to dinner tonight, we heard some interesting music coming out of an old hotel. Went in and there was the bartender from Corfu that served us last night. This was a different hotel, across the square from the other, but evidently owned by the same people. A rowdy group from the Netherlands was having a party. They welcomed us right in and Barbara started clog dancing with them. We sang a few songs, watched a few really good magic tricks performed by a drunken Dutchman, and drank a few beers. Then we had to eat or fall down. We said our farewells and headed for yet another Italian restaurant. Italian and German were the only choices we could find in this town. This one was run by a Greek family. The food wasn't very good, but the people were very pleasant. The teenage boy translated for us.

Wanted to call Wolfgang and his family tonight, while we were still in Germany. We owed them a dinner, and since we were not returning to Stuttgart, we wouldn't be able to repay them until they visited us in the States. Frank told them the weather was just too awful for touring. They would be coming to California in another year or two, and we would see them there.

SUN. OCT. 18 AMSTERDAM, NETHERLANDS

Drove to Amsterdam this morning and completed the very irregular, amoeba shaped circle we had been making on our journey. The scenery was flat and rather uninteresting. It was just as cold here as in Germany, but the fall colors had noticeably lessened in both brilliance and abundance. There were plenty of trees, but the majority of them were still green, and of the ones that were changing, only the odd maple was spectacular. We stopped by a river surrounded by condominiums for lunch. Barbara made pasta with all the leftover macaroni put together, Sacrilege! To use up all the food before we left was impossible, however we came very close. The Rotini (curly macaroni) didn't cook as well as the linguini and spaghetti, but all was delicious.

Got a hotel near the airport. Took a long time to unload everything from the camper to the hotel. My room looked like a rummage sale because I didn't have my big suitcase yet. I had been using two little ones that folded up into their own pockets, very handy. Barbara and I went for a walk in the neighborhood around the hotel. The hotel seemed to be the only commercial establishment for two or three miles, so we decided we would have to eat there tonight. The area, which looked like any middle class neighborhood in the States, was full of people working in their gardens and talking outside. It wasn't warm, but it wasn't freezing either. We spoke with many of the people and were surprised that they all spoke English fluently, even the little kids. We had soup for dinner in the hotel restaurant. None of us was very hungry after our big pasta lunch.

MON. OCT. 19 AMSTERDAM, NETHERLANDS]

Had peanut butter sandwiches and coffee for breakfast in the room. Tomorrow we would not be able to make coffee because we would be selling the camper back to Rene today. The camper was completely covered with frost when Barbara went out to make the coffee this morning, Burr!

Drove into the city and Frank faced all those skinny little streets for the last time. Once again, it was hair raising. The one way street to Braiteman and Woudenberg, where we had to leave the camper, was blocked off by construction workers. Barbara and I ran into the office and Rene said to tell Frank to go around and come down the street the wrong way. He did this, double parking in front of the B & W garage. He came into the office and said, "When I got out of the camper, a weight was lifted from my chest. I suddenly realized I was no longer responsible for anything. If the cops came and put a boot on the wheel, like they did to a lot of cars on the street already, it was not my problem. I am a free man!"

We had traveled a total of 13,359 miles round trip without a serious accident. We had made some small repairs on the car and two more costly ones totaling about $300. We all congratulated each other as we walked away from the B & W office. We had originally paid $8,191 for the camper. That included $2,250 for the insurance and $1,050 for the taxes, neither of which were refundable. This morning Rene credited our account at home with $3551. We had been told that we wouldn't get our refund for six months, but we got it immediately. Rene gave us about $90 extra because the car had broken down. We had no complaints about Braiteman and Woudenberg. Rene was another story of course. I liked nothing better than to bitch about him, but in truth, he was very honest and fair, and he even listened to us rave about the Italian campgrounds. He was a little annoyed by the big black and white "I" (for Italy) on the front of the camper, but he didn't deduct any money as Frank had thought he would.

Walked around town and looked for good Indonesian food for lunch. Rene gave us the name of a restaurant, but it was closed and so was almost everything else. By asking around, we found that restaurants didn't generally open until after six P.M., and sometimes not at all on Mondays. We went to a fast food place that advertised Bambi Goring, an Indonesian noodle dish. It came from a little frozen box and was not very good, but it was a lot better than some of the salty meals we had eaten in Eastern Europe. Before we went back to the hotel, we bought a box of cigars for Gary and went back to Braiteman and Woudenberg to say good-by and to pick up my big suitcase.

Decided to take the train to the airport station and then take a cab to the hotel. Looked upstairs and downstairs in the train station trying to find out where to buy the particular tickets we needed. Asked a number of people, but no one seemed to know. Finally we just found the direction chart, looked up which train we needed to take and got on. A woman told us this was perfectly acceptable as long as we waved at the conductor to alert him as to where we were. We had done this before with no problems. (Unfortunately, as we remembered later, we had done this in Berlin not in Amsterdam. Our book specifically said to never get on a train in Holland without a ticket.) The conductor told us there were twenty six places in the station that sold tickets for this train. He was very annoyed with us and said there was no excuse for getting on a train without a ticket. He then proceeded to charge us $12 each for a $3.50 ride. When we got to the station, we still had to take a cab to the hotel. That was another $12. It cost us $48 when a taxi from door to door would have cost only $30. I knew the Dutch had a lot of problems with freeloading young people, but they were certainly not going to gain favor with tourists by ripping them off with impunity.

All in all, it was a fabulous trip. I even forgave the Dutch conductor because the people of the Netherlands were wonderful everywhere we met them. Had it not been for the weather, the trip would have been perfect. Even the food wouldn't have seemed so bad, if we could have camped and cooked more. We met many interesting, congenial people, and visited some of the most fascinating places in the world. It was really a dream come true, except the part about finding a lover, Latin or otherwise. Oh well, there are still a lot of countries that I haven't been to yet. I'll to have to hurry though. I'm going to be a senior citizen soon!

TUES. OCT. 20 LAKEPORT, CALIFORNIA

Took the airport shuttle and flew home.

PARTIAL
WEEKLY BUDGET # 29 OCT.16—OCTOBER 20
LODGING   (FIVE DAYS)
Hotels (4) $512.00
Airplane (1)   0.00
FOOD
Restaurants:
Dinners (4)   95.00
Lunches (1)   20.00
Groceries (7 meals)   12.00
ENTERTAINMENT
Cafes & Bars   37.50
CAMPER
Camper Payment
(3 days)   72.00
Gas   94.50
Car Wash   4.00
TRANSPORTATION
Trains   36.00
Taxi   12.00
Tip for Airport Bus   3.00
INCIDENTALS
Phone Card   3.50
Toilet   .50
Postage   1.00
Gift   19.00
                    $922.50

WEEKLY BUDGET # 29

Fri.	$247.50
Sat.	189.50
Sun.	223.00
Mon.	257.50
Tues.	5.00
	$922.50

$922.50 divided by 5 days = $184.50 per day. $184.50 divided by 3 people = $61.50 per person, per day.

Epilogue

The following is a breakdown of the actual money we spent during our six and one half months in Europe.

ACTUAL COSTS FOR EUROPE:

(Time Spent: 200 days)

Car:

1. Camper (inc. ins. & tax) $4,658.50
2. Gas $2,345.50
3. Maintenance (inc. oil) $307.00
4. Parking and tolls $254.00

Food:

1. Restaurants (137 meals) $2,964.00 ($21.63 per meal—for all)
2. Groceries (441 meals) $2,064.50 ($4.68 per meal—for all)

(These figures do not include breakfasts that were part of the hotel price nor meals that we had at our relatives' homes. They also do not include the two days we spent at an all inclusive hotel in Austria.)

Entertainment: $1,970.50

Lodging:

1. Hotels: $5,676.00
A. Regular (65 nights)
B. Pensions (4 nights)
C. Airplane (2 nights)

2. Apartments (93 nights) $4,357.50
A. Private apartments & houses
(43 nights)
B. Bungalows or camp Apt.
(50 nights)
3. Camp sights (36 nights) $ 968.00
Transportation:
(Inc. trains, busses, ferries
& taxis) $ 651.00
Incidentals:
(Inc. everything else) $455.00
                              $26,671.50

As you can see, we did not spend anywhere near the amount of money
we had thought we would, mostly because we paid so little for the camper.
We spent less than $27,000 for all of us. That is a little less than $45 a day
per person. Three of these weeks we had four people, which made it even
cheaper. This of course did not include the air fair. But let's round this off
a little and say we spent $30,000 to allow for air fair, which in the spring
is five or six hundred dollars a person, and also to allow for errors, not that
I ever make any! That's still only $10,000 per person. This would include
everything that is in the actual budget, plus the air fair. With a basis of
$10,000 per person for the entire trip, it comes to about $50 a day, per
person. Arthur Frommer's famous book, Europe on $50 a Day, (an
upgrade from his original Europe on $5 a Day) includes only room and
board for that $50, and that was a few years ago. It does not account for
any type of transportation, or entertainment. Those two items were a considerable part of our expenses, and we included them, along with room,
board and air fair, for essentially the same amount of money.

In reality this budget can only be achieved if you travel through
Western Europe out of the high season, or summer. Of course, it is more
economical to travel with three people. If you have four people, you
would need a slightly bigger camper. During the three weeks that we had

four people, we stayed in apartments or hotels only, and used the camper as a car. Another person could camp in the VW, but it would be very tight and uncomfortable, even if it was two couples. However, it would probably be about $1,500 less per person. I based this on the fact that housing and groceries would probably cost just a little more, but you would divide everything four ways. On the other hand, if you were to do it with just two people, it would probably cost about $2,500 more per person. Though most things would cost less, you would be dividing car costs only two ways. Nevertheless, with just two people, you probably wouldn't mind camping more often, and that would bring the costs way down.

The vehicle you choose can also make or break a trip. A large camper would mean not having to use camp bathrooms. In Eastern Europe that would be a definite plus. However, it would also mean you would have to avoid almost all big cities because a large camper would not fit on many of the streets. We avoided driving in most big cities anyway, but that is all personal choice. Choosing an older vehicle, as we did, can also cause many problems. The synchromesh gears in the VW made a lot of noise and caused us a great deal of concern. Had the gear box failed completely, we would have had it replaced. Had that happened, Braiteman and Woudenberg most likely would have picked up some of the cost. Even if they didn't, it would have added only $800 to our costs, not an insurmountable amount. The moderate expense of choosing an older vehicle was the most important factor in keeping our costs down.

The second most important factor was not eating in restaurants most of the time. We paid for 137 meals in restaurants. Barbara cooked 441 meals. As you can see in the budget, it cost about $900 less for the 441 meals we cooked for ourselves than for the 137 meals we had in restaurants. We ate out only about 25% of the time. These two areas, buying a vehicle and meals, can make your trip as extravagant or economical as you choose it to be.

The weather was a major factor in our dissatisfaction with camping. The campgrounds in Eastern Europe were not very good generally speaking, except in Poland. Nevertheless, had the weather been better, we definitely would have camped more. The most advantageous plus we discovered on the trip was that apartments were available in almost every country, if we looked for them. They were always set up for cooking, and cooking can save a lot of money.

For the three of us that took this trip of a lifetime, there were no regrets. Our future trips, together or separately, will definitely be shorter, but all of us agree that one long trip in a lifetime is a must for the serious traveler. It really doesn't matter how you take the trip. Just take one. I truly believe that nothing broadens your overall knowledge more than travel. You can read thousands of books, but not one of them will take the place of actually going to foreign lands and seeing everything for yourself. The best advice I can give to anyone is to try traveling, and to do it before you get too old to really enjoy yourself!

BIBLIOGRAPHY

Birnbaum's *Eastern Europe*. New York, NY: Harper Perennial. 1st ed. 1992
A Steven Birnbaum travel guide.

Europa Camping & Caravanning. Europe Camping 1998 ed. (Purchase at
REI.)

Let's Go: Europe, 1998. By Let's Go Publications ; Caroline R. Sherman,
editor; Rachel A. Farbiarz, associate editor; Catherine M. Hornby, associate editor. New York: St. Martin's Press, c1998.

Let's Go 1999: Italy. By Krysztof Dydynski...[et al.] 2nd ed.1998. New
York: St. Martin's Press.

Lonely Planet Eastern Europe. By Krzysztof Dydynski, Steve Fallon, Kate
Galbraith, Paul Hellander. 5th ed. 1999.